MASTERPIECES OF BRITISH MODERNISM

MASTERPIECES
OF BRITISH
MODERNISM

Marlowe A. Miller

Greenwood Introduces Literary Masterpieces

GREENWOOD PRESS
Westport, Connecticut • London

Library of Congress Cataloging-in-Publication Data

Miller, Marlowe A.
   Masterpieces of British modernism / Marlowe A. Miller.
      p. cm.—(Greenwood introduces literary masterpieces, ISSN 1545–6285)
   Includes bibliographical references and index.
   ISBN 0–313–33263–0 (alk. paper)
   1. English literature—20th century—History and criticism. 2. Modernism (Literature)—
Great Britain. I. Title.
PR478.M6M55 2006
820.9'112—dc22   2006020369

British Library Cataloguing in Publication Data is available.

Library of Congress Catalog Card Number: 2006020369
ISBN: 0–313–33263–0
ISSN: 1545–6285

First published in 2006

Greenwood Press, 88 Post Road West, Westport, CT 06881
An imprint of Greenwood Publishing Group, Inc.
www.greenwood.com

Printed in the United States of America

The paper used in this book complies with the
Permanent Paper Standard issued by the National
Information Standards Organization (Z39.48–1984).

10 9 8 7 6 5 4 3 2 1

Contents

Preface   vii

Introduction   1

1   Joseph Conrad, *Heart of Darkness* (1899)   9

2   E. M. Forster, *Howards End* (1910)   35

3   James Joyce, *A Portrait of the Artist as a Young Man* (1916)   61

4   D. H. Lawrence, *Women in Love* (1919)   87

5   T. S. Eliot, *The Love Song of J. Alfred Prufrock* (1917)
and *The Waste Land* (1922)   113

6   Virginia Woolf, *Mrs. Dalloway* (1925)   151

Bibliography   177

Index   187

Preface

This book is a critical introduction to seven central texts by six authors of the Modernist period in British literature. Each text is a classic of the period, reflecting the immense change and upheaval of the first half of the twentieth century. And each work is a widely read masterpiece, addressing universal themes that cross the boundaries of time and place.

The authors and texts examined here have been the subjects of a great deal of critical writing. However, this criticism has often been addressed to an audience of specialists: professional scholars and graduate students who will make their careers as scholars and teachers of literature. This volume is for the general reader. It offers a critical understanding of each work and the period in which it was written by including a summary of the work; an analysis of important characters, themes, and symbols; a discussion of style; and historical context. The biographical sections on each author aid the reader in situating the work in the life of the author, and the bibliographical sections at the end of the text lead readers to further essential reading. Ultimately, those who peruse this volume will become more knowledgeable readers of British Modernist literature.

The texts studied in this volume are primarily novels that are widely read in and out of an academic setting. However, one cannot adequately address the Modernist period without considering T. S. Eliot's seminal poems, *The Love Song of J. Alfred Prufrock* and *The Waste Land*. These poems helped to create the lexicon of British Modernism and have often been cited as the first poems of the modern period. Although other novels, plays, poems, and essays could also be selected as masterpieces of this period in Britain, the five novels and the two poems discussed give readers ready access to the central concerns and styles of the Modernist period in Britain.

Examined in chronological order of publication, these works cover a 25-year period following the turn of the century and represent Modernism in theme, style, and content. Although this may seem like a short period of time, these 25 years are in fact generally agreed to mark the height of Modernist literature. The remarkable social, cultural, and political transformations of this short time were reflected in the outpouring of innovative art and literature that these works so brilliantly represent. Students of Modernism will find that a deeper knowledge of this period will give them the information and background they need to consider the complicated territory of late Modernism and Postmodernism.

I wish to thank the University of Massachusetts-Lowell for a reduced course load during the writing of this book. I also wish to thank Melissa Pennell for her friendship and guidance. Finally, I wish to thank Art Miller, Juanita Miller, Mary Kramer, and David Keevil; their careful readings of each chapter of this volume provided essential focus and direction.

Introduction

On or about December 1910 human nature changed.... All human relations shifted—those between masters and servants, husbands and wives,
parents and children. And when human relations change there is at the
same time a change in religion, conduct, politics, and literature.

—Virginia Woolf, "Mr. Bennett and Mrs. Brown"

There are many arguments about when Modernism began. But let us take
Woolf at her word and look at December 1910. In 1910, London, England, was
the center of the world's largest empire, an empire that dominated world trade
and politics. Yet, as Woolf's comment suggests, change was in the air for all
aspects of British society. This was the year that King Edward VII died, the year
that Roger Fry's revolutionary exhibit of Post-Impressionist art shook the staid
London art scene, and the year that women's efforts to procure the vote gained
momentum and met violent police retaliation. 1910 was also the final year of
the dominance of the Liberal Party in English politics. It was superseded by the
Labour Party, with its base of working class support and union interests.

Whether we accept the date Woolf offers or one of the many others
proposed by her contemporaries or by scholars of the period, we know that,
broadly speaking, the Modernists occupied the first 40 years of the twentieth
century. But we also know that social and political change had been pro-
gressing for some time, especially at the end of the Victorian period, which
preceded the Modernist period. Both industrial advancement and capitalist
expansion in Victorian England set the pace for this change. Over the course
of Queen Victoria's long rule, from 1837 until her death in 1901, England

reached the height of the Industrial Revolution, and experienced social, economic, and technological transformations as the British Empire expanded. By the time of Victoria's death in 1901, the labor class and middle-class workers were primarily engaged in manufacturing and production that matched the rapid urbanization of the country. Victoria's son, Edward VII, ruled from 1901 until his death in 1910. Under his rule, the growth and expansion of England continued, and the writers identified with his name, the Edwardians, produced prose that reflected the decadent and self-assured tone of the times.

Although each generation tends to reject the previous one, the generation that came of age in what we have come to call the Modernist period may have had more cause than any other generation to reject the values and traditions of its predecessors. Virginia Woolf, for one, links this to the radical shift in the modern world caused in large part by World War I. In "How It Strikes a Contemporary," written in 1923, Woolf states, "We are sharply cut off from our predecessors. A shift in the scale—the war, the sudden slip of masses held in position for ages—has shaken the fabric from top to bottom, alienated us from the past" (*The Essays*, Vol. 4, 238). Writers like Virginia Woolf felt that the Victorians and Edwardians had a far too complacent and self-assured view of the world, which made their work pompous, wordy, and preachy. Certainly, both the Victorians and the Edwardians shared stable, rooted beliefs in God, truth, and the justice of law. This can be seen in a masterful poem by the eminent Victorian poet Alfred, Lord Tennyson. Tennyson confidently concludes his poem "In Memoriam" with the assertion that civilization will progress toward a future ruled by the following "truths": "One God, one law, one element / And one far-off divine event, / To which the whole creation moves" (292). What made this confidence and optimism all the more difficult for the Moderns was that it stood beside the intense poverty that had spread inexorably with industrialization in England.

In many of the texts examined in this volume, most notably in *Howards End*, *Mrs. Dalloway*, and *The Waste Land*, the authors note the speed of life in modern cities, where individuals have less and less time for each other as they hustle through the crowded streets, ride in fast automobiles, or observe the commercial saturation of their cities. Indeed, "78 percent of the inhabitants of Great Britain lived in cities and towns" by the beginning of 1900 (Kershner 34). In the cities, life was increasingly influenced by technological advancement: mass transit, alarm clocks, rush hour, and traffic jams became features of life in the city for the first time. The telegraph, telephone, and the mass media introduced an ease of communication that only accelerated the pace of industrial and capitalist expansion. The critique of modern life, with the city at the heart, is a unique feature of the work of many Modernist writers: Whereas they vociferously denounce the past for its self-deception and pious propriety, they appreciate its pace; most do not wholly embrace the speed of industrial and commercial progress that is a hallmark of their time.

There are, of course, exceptions to this. Wyndham Lewis celebrated progress in much the same way as the Italian Modernist Fillipo Marinetti. But there is, in all the writing examined in this text, a certain degree of aversion to the explosive growth of the modern world. Responding to industrialization culminating in advanced capitalism, these artists found themselves in opposition to not only their confident Victorian and Edwardian predecessors but also to their bourgeois contemporaries

This discomfort with capitalist expansion and city life was not new to the Modernists. It was experienced dramatically by their spiritual predecessors, the French Symbolists: Mallarmé, Laforgue, Rimbaud, and others. By pursuing the poets' emotional response to experience, the symbolists sought to transcend the tainted quotidian world marked by repetition and greed. For the symbolists, the individual emotional experience is rightfully the subject of art. Because they believed that feelings and perceptions are idiosyncratic and fleeting, the symbolists maintained that the only way this experience could be conveyed in writing was through the use of symbols. Like the symbolists before them, the Modernists turned to interiority and a world of private symbolization as the focus of art. Also like the symbolists, Modernists took both the squalor and vibrancy of the city as the material for their writing. We see this in Eliot's poetry, in Woolf's Mrs. Dalloway, in Forster's Howards End, and in Joyce's A Portrait of the Artist as a Young Man.

Modernism cannot be separated from an understanding of other broad movements of the time and the cultural forces that created them. Sigmund Freud was important to Modernism, as he attempted to articulate the influences of the subconscious on the conscious life. Indeed, his language for subconscious drives began to infiltrate both literature and popular lingo very soon after it was published. But Freud's psychology was just one of a number of disciplines that served to disrupt Victorian assumptions about what governs human behavior. Marx's political theories, like Freud's theories of psychology, suggested that there are powerful subterranean forces, both within the individual and within society, that govern human behavior much more than reason and logic. Newtonian physics, Darwinian evolutionary theory, Einstein's Relativity Theory, and Max Planck's quantum theory were all part of the shifting worldview, for each provided growing evidence that the world was not the predictable, stable place once assumed. Each also added evidence to challenge the accepted order of God, father, and country; it began to appear that the world was not governed by these pillars of Victorian stability. With the loss of these pillars, there was an increasing loss of confidence in the stability of identity—individual and collective. In the Modern milieu of rapid change and capitalist progression, artists struggled to evoke the new, the "authentic." These new writers, the Modernists, attempted to write texts that did not overtly preach or teach, but rather reflected in style and form the instability of modern existence.

Although Modernism was a global movement, reflecting a worldwide shift in values and artistic expression, British Modernism had its own issues that were determined by the interests and concerns of British writers and artists. The nature of British society meant that Britain was comparatively slow to accept the radical changes in form and content that the Modernist artists introduced. So, whereas Picasso and Gauguin were accepted and appreciated in France, their work was considered childish at best and vile at worst by the majority of the British public. The staid world of British tradition was precisely the world that Woolf saw shifting. But it is important to remember that this shift was not overnight, as her comment might lead us to believe.

Although we can speak of Modernism and Modernists, British Modernists were not a monolithic group with a single artistic philosophy. Wyndham Lewis and Ezra Pound shared an affinity for a rhetorically violent rejection of the past (and much of the present, for that matter), whereas writers allied with the Bloomsbury Group, like Woolf and Forster, were influenced by Walter Pater and shared an investment in friendship as it was articulated by the Cambridge philosopher G. E. Moore. D. H. Lawrence, in contrast, who rarely shared the company of any group for long, vociferously rejected the Bloomsbury writers as elitist and overintellectualized. There were so many efforts to define the Modernist perspective that the breadth of Modernism can be conveyed by a list of just a few of the many movements within it: Vorticism, Imagism, Dadaism, Futurism, Cubism, and Surrealism. Although many of these were continental movements, some had adherents in England, and most were known by British artists. Perhaps most important to understanding the landscape of British Modernism is a knowledge of the central influences on shaping that landscape: the Bloomsbury Group, Wyndham Lewis's "men of 1914," and the perspectives of immigrants like Conrad, Joyce, Eliot, Katherine Mansfield, and Hilda Doolittle.

To this day, the Bloomsbury Group is still dismissed by some as composed of elitist snobs who contributed little to the British literary tradition, even though this "set" included Virginia Woolf, one of the greatest Modernist authors. More commonly, people dispute whether this was ever an organized movement with a shared philosophy about art or life. Setting aside questions of philosophical consensus, one can identify a group of artists and intellectuals who came together as friends and influenced one another over the long course of those friendships. Among others, the friends who composed the Bloomsbury Group included Desmond McCarthy, Clive Bell, Vanessa Bell, Virginia and Leonard Woolf, Roger Fry, Lytton Strachey, Maynard Keynes, and Duncan Grant. What many have acknowledged as the central importance of this group of friends was the avenue it provided for sharing advances in European art with the English public. For example, the critic Peter Stansky argues that Bloomsbury was the "dominant English conduit" for European Modernism, the force of which "would dominate the cultural world until well after the Second World War" (229).

Of course, one could argue that the works of Virginia Woolf and E. M. Forster were also central contributions that Bloomsbury made to British Modernism; in other words, these works were not conduits for European thought per se, but were quintessentially British yet irrevocably new. In this writing, which Woolf so vehemently defended as distinct from the work of Edwardians like Bennett and Galsworthy, we see the effort to create the novel anew. Woolf's argument with the Edwardians is apropos here. Noting their materialism and bourgeois complacency, Woolf criticizes the Edwardians for their formalism, their heavy reliance on plot, and their rejection of the nuances of a character's interior life. Stansky reminds us that, although Bloomsbury was an elite group whose lives as artists were supported by the very same bourgeois world that they criticized in the Edwardians, "yet [Bloomsbury's] ideas emphasized, at least in theory, the 'democracy' of art, of sensibility, the equality of the aesthetic reaction" (250). The writers of the Bloomsbury group, then, began to articulate the values of a British Modernism that was anti-materialist, featuring work centered on the inner life of the character, and that was resistant to plot and closure in the novel.

Bloomsbury was not the only source of British Modernism. In coining the term "the men of 1914," the Canadian writer Wyndham Lewis had in mind Ezra Pound, T. S. Eliot, and James Joyce. Notably, the men of 1914 were not born in England, and this fact shapes the focus of their art. They were distinctly aware of their status as outsiders. For a time, these three men shared a mutual rejection of direct representation of character that was so apparent in Victorian and Edwardian literature. Each was attempting to find a form to reflect the individual's fractured experience of the Modern world; early in their careers as artists, these men were particularly interested in finding a structure that would make the novel, poem, or painting new. They all emphasized the importance of the object that externalizes emotion. From this, Eliot, for example, develops his "objective correlative," the object that stands in for the emotion and carries that emotional weight in his poetry.

Moving away from Eliot and Joyce, the art of Lewis and Pound from this period is strident in its insistence upon differences between the sexes, directness in poetry and writing, and a paternalistic sanctioning of Modernism. Influenced by the Italian Futurist Filippo Marinetti, Lewis and Pound launched the quarterly magazine *Blast*. Intended as a venue for the Modernism that Lewis and Pound espoused, the only two issues of *Blast* that were published did include the writing of very important Modernist figures like Eliot, Ford Madox Ford, Henri Gaudier-Brzeska, and Rebecca West. But its content reflected a strain of Modernism that sought to embrace the mechanism and energy of the modern world, rather than work in opposition to it. It was also a Modernism that was on the radical edge of experimentalism and freely critical of all others as part of a dead culture. This led Pound and Lewis to write their Vorticist manifesto, in which they articulated the theory of Vorticist art—art that moved away from mimetic representation and reflected a kind of abstract, angular directness that is evident in Lewis's paintings of this period. Vorticism, as it turned out, with its resistance to mimesis and its abstraction, was more suited to visual than literary art.

Like the "men of 1914," a number of the Modernist figures in literary England were either immigrants, colonists, or individuals who were steeped in other cultural contexts: Immigrants to England, Conrad and Eliot both became British citizens late in life; James Joyce, like Yeats, was Irish and sharply criticized the British for their imperialist tyranny over his homeland; and D. H. Lawrence was the son of a coal miner and always felt ostracized by writers like Woolf and Forster, who, however they critiqued it, were securely upper-middle class.

Reflecting the Modernist rejection of the communal focus of Victorian society, themes commonly found in Modernist literature feature an exploration of the consciousness of the individual. The Modernists believed that truth could no longer be found in the organization of family and society based on the authority of the father or a select male few. As a result, these writers explored the psychological interior of characters struggling to make sense of the disrupted world around them. From interiority, one moves logically to the theme of the alienated individual so commonly found in Modernist literature. Again, one can find the source of this theme in the fracturing experience of life in the modern world, where all sense of a stable center has been annihilated. Thus, most of the central characters discussed in this volume feel profoundly alienated.

This new and transformative attention to interiority and alienation in Modern literature demanded a new style; writers of the period were acutely conscious of the need to find a new language to convey the reality of experience in the modern world. In her critical work, Woolf turns repeatedly to Joyce and Katherine Mansfield as examples of artists who are forging new styles and lexicons to reflect the Modern times. Woolf herself creates a prose that relies heavily on breaks, fragments, and ellipses that disrupt the linear flow of narrative and convey the fractured sense of modern time and the indirect course and allusive quality of subconscious thought. The American poet Ezra Pound, who was so instrumental to the success of writers like T. S. Eliot, James Joyce, and the poet Hilda Doolittle, provided the catch phrase for his generation of artists: "Make it new," he said. What this came to mean was, of course, highly idiosyncratic and varied from writer to writer. With *A Portrait of the Artist as a Young Man*, Joyce began to forge an entirely new style that resisted conventions of plot, character development, and lexical reason. His final work, *Finnegan's Wake*, is often cited as the logical end of the line of Joyce's radical experiment with language and style. Yet, as Woolf notes after reading *Ulysses*, Joyce found a way to capture in style and language the shattering experience of Modernity. In a similar manner, T. S. Eliot developed a lexicon suited to the condition of being modern through allusion and layering. Blending references to ancient texts, popular song lyrics, and mythology into a potent mix that resisted absolute and singular truths, Eliot's poetry reflects the openness of the modern world.

Eliot is not alone in his references to antiquity. Throughout much of Modernist literature one can find an interest in ancient literature and mythology. Distrusting the texts of the recent past, Modernists began to "make it new" with the shards and fragments of ancient times. Pound, Eliot, and Joyce each turned to quest legends, the epic form, Greek myths, and the works of other ancient cultures as they sought a hero for the modern world. Interestingly, female Modernists were less likely to attempt a recreation of the epic form. Woolf, Mansfield, Stein, and others were all radically experimental but not as interested in the epic nature of their experiment.

The subtle difference in focus between male and female Modernists is consistent with the interrogation of gender roles that occurred in the modern period. With everything fair game for redefinition, with all authority and established order under question, women across society challenged the status quo. The suffrage movement is a prime example of this. Many women in England were willing to be ostracized as they fought for the right to vote, a right they ultimately won in 1918. Women who served the war effort in World War I by working in traditional male professions found themselves reluctant to return to domesticity or more menial jobs. This added to their frustration with gender roles. In the early decades of the twentieth century, women in England experienced advances in education as well.

Along with the challenge to gender roles came the exploration of the boundaries of sexuality. The Modernist period was witness to a great deal of sexual experimentation, specifically, homosexual and bisexual experimentation. Many of the artists of this period not only publicly expressed their preference for their own sex, but attempted to articulate this experience in their writing. Thus we see the intimation of lesbian love in Mrs. Dalloway and the proud defense of love between two men in D. H. Lawrence's Women in Love. Although he did not publish it in his lifetime, E. M. Forster wrote his novel about homosexual love, Maurice, during this time. Indeed, many of the members of the Bloomsbury Group were openly homosexual; and for a time Virginia Woolf was a lover of Vita Sackville West, who inspired her most gender-bending novel, Orlando. Not all experimentation in this area went without backlash from the establishment, however. It was during this time that Radcliff Hall was censored for her lesbian novel The Well of Loneliness, a novel that never explicitly described sex between women but which defended the right of women to love each other.

"Make it new," wrote Ezra Pound. And indeed, the Modernists worked to do just that. They made it new as a revolutionary reaction to centuries of stolid, British calm. They made it new in an attempt to respond to and reflect the radically, catastrophically altered world pre–, during, and post–World War I. They evoked new, interior, idiosyncratically personal voices, within new narrative structures. And in so doing, they destabilized established structures of class, gender, and politics.

1

Joseph Conrad
Heart of Darkness
(1899)

BIOGRAPHICAL CONTEXT

Joseph Conrad became a British citizen and a writer relatively late in his life. Born in Russian occupied Ukraine in 1857, he was christened Josef Konrad Nalecz Korzeniowski and descended from the landed gentry of Poland, who had been dispossessed of their titles and country by Russia, Prussia, and Austria since 1772. Conrad's father, Apollo, a poet and translator of French and English literature, was a militant nationalist who was outspoken about his belief in the need for Polish independence from Russia. In 1863, this militant nationalism landed Apollo, his wife, Ewa, and son Konrad in exile in the village of Vologda north of Moscow. Conrad's parents died in exile and he was orphaned at the age of 12 years. He was adopted by his mother's uncle, Tadeusz Bobrowski, who by all accounts was firm and generous toward young Josef. Bobrowski sent Conrad to school in Krakow and Geneva, providing him with a personal tutor.

However, Conrad struggled with his tutor and education. In 1874 he convinced his uncle to allow him to join the French merchant navy. Conrad spent four adventurous years with the French navy, sailing to the West Indies and South America. In 1878, new French laws forbade immigrant employment and ended his days as a sailor for the French merchant navy, a change which led Conrad to sail on British ships for the next 16 years. He became a British subject in 1887 and began writing fiction, in English, in 1889 with his first novel, *Almayer's Folly*.

Perhaps the most relevant biographical material for the purposes of discussing *The Heart of Darkness,* however, comes from Conrad's experience sailing for Belgian interests on the Congo River in 1890. Already a British subject, but in search of an opportunity to serve as captain of a sailing vessel, Conrad used the connections of his aunt by marriage, Marguerite Poradowska, to secure a position with the Societé Anonyme Belge pour le Commerce du Haut-Congo, replacing a captain who had died at his post as captain of a ship, *The Florida,* in the Belgian Congo. Conrad set out on this adventure with a sense that he was on an important and heroic expedition. Little did he know of the horrors existing in the cruel world of King Leopold's Belgian Congo. In his letters to his aunt and in his journal entries, it becomes clear that Conrad discovered that the basest of aims were at the root of the Belgian "exploration" of the Congo: It was an opportunity for the European explorers to loot and plunder. The cruel and inhumane treatment of the native Congolese at the hands of the Belgians and Europeans in their "colonization effort" appalled Conrad and haunted him for years after the brief experience he had in the Congo.

Conrad arrived at Matadi in spring 1890. He then traveled overland to Kinshasa, where the Congo River becomes navigable, and took up his command as captain of *The Florida.* Conrad's diary records this difficult journey, which took more than a month of foot travel, without mules and short of fresh water. In his diary, one detects Conrad's growing discomfort with the Belgian agents he encounters and their treatment of the Congolese. One particularly low character is a man named Camille Delcommune, who was the agent at the station in Kinshasa. When Conrad discovered that *The Florida* had sunk to the bottom of the river and that he would merely serve as a sailor on the *Roi des Belges,* he was deeply disillusioned. To add to this disillusionment, Conrad discovered that Camille Delcommune intended to travel with him on the *Roi des Belges* as far as the Inner Station at Stanley Falls (now Boyoma) in order to recover a Belgian agent named Klein, who was ill. The month-long trip to the Inner Station to retrieve the body of Klien, who had died in the meantime, left Conrad disgusted with the Belgian projects in the Congo. He left Africa as quickly as he could, getting out of his contract with the Societé Anonyme Belge pour le Commerce du Haut-Congo.

Conrad did not write *The Heart of Darkness* until 10 years after his experiences on the Congo, but readers can easily see the degree to which this work of fiction pulls from Conrad's personal experiences there. Nonetheless, *The Heart of Darkness* is a work of fiction, not an autobiographical memoir. It is a cautionary tale that, in true Modernist fashion, leaves the reader wondering about the narrator's reliability. It is also consistent with the themes of

Conrad's earlier fiction, reflecting his contention that the world is a place of conflict between the forces of darkness and the forces of goodness. Conrad constructs a deceptively dualistic world in this and other fiction he has written, tempting us to fall into a binary worldview, only to throw us off guard with his unique structural and narrative techniques that lead us to question ourselves and the dichotomies we embrace. This becomes clear in *Heart of Darkness* with the shifting implications of the concept of darkness, for example.

PLOT SUMMARY

The primary narrator of this novella is never named. He tells us that he is repeating the tale that he and some other friends were told by Charles Marlow one night on a boat that was anchored in the Thames. The narrator then proceeds to tell the tale in its entirety—apparently from his memory. The first section of the novella begins with the narrator's description of the gloomy scene in a cruising yawl on the Thames at sunset with four other men: the Director of Companies ("our captain and our host"), The Lawyer, The Accountant, and Marlow. The men are gathered on the deck, meditative and placid. With a tone belying pride in his empire, the narrator remarks on the Thames: "What greatness had not floated on the ebb of that river into an unknown earth! … The dreams of men, the seed of commonwealths, the germs of empires" he states (4). With the sun fully set and the "lurid glare" of the city of London visible upon the water, Marlow takes up his tale with the ambiguous comment, "'And this also … has been one of the dark places of the earth'" (5).

Before we hear Marlow's tale, the unnamed narrator interrupts to tell the reader a little more about Marlow. We learn that he is the only one of the five men who is a seaman. But he is not typical of that group either, we are told, for he is a wanderer whose tales are not typically straightforward and simple like a seaman's yarns. We are warned that in Marlow's tales, "the meaning of an episode was not inside like a kernel but outside, enveloping the tale which brought it out only as a glow brings out a haze" (6). This caveat offered, the narrator tells us that the company received Marlow's comment without surprise and awaited his tale. The rest of the first section is Marlow's tale as the narrator remembers he told it to the men on the *Nellie* that night on the Thames.

Marlowe begins his tale with a tone that contrasts with the narrator's praise of the "tamed" quality of the river Thames: "I was thinking of the very old times, when the Romans first came here" (6). Marlow conjures the image of the Roman captain of a trireme sent to "conquer" the north and asks us to imagine him on the Thames, surrounded by "marshes, forests, savages— precious little to eat fit for a civilized man" (7). His intention appears to be to draw the connection between the Thames and its environs a thousand years before and present times in European colonies in Africa. Marlow goes on to describe the Romans who came up the Thames: "They were no colonists.... They were conquerors, and for that you want only brute force" (8). This force, he says, is necessary "for those who tackle a darkness" (8). The only thing that redeems this brute force, Marlow maintains, is the idea: "An idea at the back of it; not a sentimental pretence but an idea; and an unselfish belief in the idea" (8). This reflection on conquest justified by some "idea" is what leads Marlow to the point of his tale: his own journey up a river that thereafter shed a "kind of light" on everything he saw (9).

Taking his listeners back to what led to his experience on another mighty river, Marlow reminds his listeners that he had returned from six years of sailing in the East, and, unable to find himself a new ship, he remembered his youthful passion for maps and uncharted territories. He sought command of a steamboat on a mighty river in the dark center of the African continent, working for a "Continental concern," a trading company. With the help of his aunt, he tells us, he got an appointment "very quick." He relates how he had to rush to Brussels to meet his employers, a Company that was "going to run an overseas empire, and make no end of coin by trade" (14).

Marlow is shown into the offices of the Company located on a "deserted street" in "deep shadow." (This company is never named but always capital-ized in the text.) He is greeted by two women, one fat and one thin, who sit and knit. His attention is drawn to a "large shining map, marked with all the colours of the rainbow," which, the reader quickly realizes, are the colors of the flags of European nations that have colonized the different parts of Africa (14). Marlow observes that he is going into the yellow (Belgian) territory, "dead in the centre" (14). Marlow is called in to meet the "great man him-self," apparently found acceptable, and dismissed. Back in the waiting room, he tells us, he grows anxious, feeling as though there is some conspiracy afoot, with the two women "guarding the door of Darkness, knitting black wool as for a warm pall" (16). In a tone of detachment, he concludes that not many of the men who passed through that waiting room ever saw those women again. The final "formality" of a doctor's examination must then be seen to before Marlow can leave the building.

A shabby, ink-stained clerk leads Marlow to his appointment with the doctor. As they are early, Marlow proposes a drink, and they sit to discuss the company's prospects over a glass of vermouth. Curious that the clerk does not choose to go "out there," Marlow is surprised to hear his response: "I am not such a fool as I look" (17). On this ominous note, they part and the doctor examines Marlow. The doctor takes his pulse and performs other actions that one might expect and "then with a certain eagerness" asked if he might measure Marlow's head (17). The doctor tells Marlow that he always asks to measure the head of those "going out there" (17). When Marlow asks if he measures them when they return, he replies lightly, "Oh, I never see them" (17). He asks if there is a history of madness in Marlow's family and then dismisses him with the caution to stay calm in the tropics.

With an odd sense that he is setting out for the center of the earth rather than the center of a continent, Marlow tells us that he left on a French steamer that stopped in every port. "I watched the coast," Marlow tells us. "Watching a coast as it slips by the ship is like thinking about an enigma. There it is before you—smiling, frowning, inviting, grand, mean, insipid, or savage, and always mute with an air of whispering, Come and find out" (20). The monotony of the coastline leaves Marlow feeling that he was slipping away from the "truth of things" (21). Finally, late in his 30-day journey to the mouth of the Congo River, from where he will have to find his way 200 miles up river, Marlow tells us, "It was like a weary pilgrimage amongst hints of nightmares" (23).

From the mouth of the Congo River, Marlow takes passage on a steamer captained by a morose and lanky Swede, who tells him of a fellow Swede who hung himself once he got into the wilderness. At the Outer Station, the first of the company's three stations that Marlow will visit on his journey up the river, Marlow's first observations are of decaying commerce and industry: "I came upon a boiler wallowing in the grass, then found a path leading up the hill. It turned aside for the boulders, and also for an undersized railway truck lying there on its back with its wheels in the air" (24). As he makes his way up the steep path to the buildings, he is passed by a group of black men chained together, gaunt and sweating, and followed by another black man carrying a rifle. Marlow notes that the natives in the chains are in a state of decline, decay, and abuse equal to the surroundings. He links their state with the conquering whites: "They were called criminals, and the outraged law, like the bursting shells, had come to them, an insoluble mystery from the sea" (25). All the while, there is a pointless blasting of dynamite that shakes the earth beneath them all. The man carrying the rifle behind the chained men smiles at Marlow in "partnership." The state of things at the Outer Station grows even more sinister when Marlow turns down the path and descends into what he calls the "Grove of Death." Here he encounters black people dying in the shady grove: "They were … nothing but shadows of disease and starvation…. Brought from the recesses of the coast in all the legality of contracts" (27–28). With this language of contracts, Marlow again links this human suffering and misery to the colonizers.

Marlow leaves the horrors of the grove and heads toward the station, where he encounters a white man "in such an unexpected elegance of get-up" (29). This turns out to be the Company's chief accountant. Marlow first hears of Kurtz, the agent who will become central to Marlow's journey, from this "hairdresser's dummy" (30). As Marlow waits 10 days at this station, the chief accountant tells him that he will no doubt meet Mr. Kurtz in the interior. He describes Kurtz as a "first-class" agent, a "remarkable" person, who is chief of the Inner Station, a trading post that "sends in as much ivory as all the others put together" (31). The accountant asks Marlow to tell Kurtz that all is quite correct with the bookkeeping and concedes that he would not send this by message because he does not trust all the Company's agents. Building Marlow's curiosity, he concludes by stating his belief that Kurtz has a great future in the "Administration."

The next day, Marlow leaves with a crew of 60 black men on a 200-mile trek to the Central Station. The journey is relatively uneventful, except that Marlow encounters the body of a black man, shot in the head. He also must struggle to help the other white man who travels with him, an overweight man who has the "nasty habit" of fainting in the least shady portions of the scenery. Marlow's efforts to get the natives to carry this man are singularly unsuccessful. Ultimately, the natives abandon Marlow altogether, leaving him with this human burden.

Arriving at the Central Station two weeks later, Marlow learns that his steamer is at the bottom of the river as a result of the Central Station Manager's botched attempt to head up river with a volunteer captain, who tore the bottom off on some rocks. Marlow's first encounter with the Manager of the Central Station reveals that man to be a common trader who had managed to secure and maintain his position because he was never made ill by the tropical climate and because he inspired "uneasiness." Marlow observes from the state of the station that the Manager had no genius for organization, "no learning and no intelligence" (37). Marlow must spend three months at the Central Station, repairing his steamer and awaiting parts that seem never to arrive. In that time, he observes the numerous conniving young men, whom he compares to pilgrims, hanging around the station, carrying "absurd long staves in their hands," and waiting for a chance at a trading post where they can get their hands on some ivory (39). On the occasion of a storage house fire, Marlow falls into conversation with a "first-class agent" with an aristocratic manner. The man invites Marlow to his room and it becomes clear that he is pumping Marlow for information. Finally, frustrated that he can get nothing out of Marlow, he pronounces him one of the "new gang—the gang of virtue," of which he considers Kurtz a member as well. It becomes clear to Marlow that this man has been reading the company mail. In a curious turn, Marlow finds himself in sympathy with the mysterious Kurtz and vows that when "Mr. Kurtz is General Manager" the agent will not have the opportunity to read such correspondence. This draws Marlow out of his narrative briefly to remind his listeners that he detests lies and to reflect on the marvel that at this point Kurtz was no more than a "word" to him, and yet he came close to lying for him. He has done so by acting as an initiated member of the "new gang" and positing a day when Kurtz would be General Manager. The narrator relates that Marlow pauses in his story at this point and struggles with the realization that he seems to be "trying to tell you a dream" (47).

Before Marlow's narrative is taken up again by the narrator, he pauses to reflect that, sitting apart from the other four men on the yacht in the middle of the Thames, Marlow seemed as though he was "no more to us than a voice" (48). He observes that all the while he, for one, was listening carefully for the "sentence, for the word, that would give me the clue to the faint uneasiness inspired by this narrative" (48). And then he continues relating Marlow's narrative, apparently verbatim.

The second section of the novella begins with Marlow overhearing the voice of the Station Manager and his uncle, a pompous fellow who has recently arrived with a large group of men and an enormous amount of equipment and calling himself the head of the Eldorado Exploring Expedition. The Station Manager and his uncle are talking about Kurtz, who has remained at the Inner Station and is sending his ivory down river with an "English half-caste clerk." Both men are mystified that Kurtz, who had started to make the journey himself, had suddenly turned back after 300 miles. But Marlow notes that "I seemed to see Kurtz for the first time. It was a distinct glimpse: the dug-out, four paddling savages, and the lone white man turning his back suddenly on the head-quarters, on relief, on thoughts of home" (57). For the reader, Kurtz is emerging as a man who clearly lives by his own rules.

At last, without fanfare, Marlow is on the river, steaming toward Kurtz and the Inner Station with the Station Manager, several pilgrims, and some "cannibals" aboard. In one long paragraph, the length of which works to convey the interminable quality of the journey up the Congo, Marlow describes their journey. He notes the otherworldly, dreamlike quality of the place. "Going up that river was like traveling back to the earliest beginnings of the world," he tells his listeners (60). "We were wanderers on a prehistoric earth," he says (63). With increasing regularity, Marlow's narrative refers to the jungle that surrounds the stations and the rivers as a pure and patient force, though whether it is evil or good he does not know. He remarks on the sounds of the native peoples in the evenings, their drumming and music leading him to speculate on their common humanity, which "civilization" has all but erased from consciousness. The narrative conveys the sense that Marlow is being drawn into the wildness of the jungle around him. He suggests that the task of navigating the river is all that keeps him from setting out into the wilderness.

The boat comes to a station about 50 miles below Kurtz's Inner Station, where the crew finds a rude shelter and a stack of logs with a faded note scribbled on a piece of wood. The note reads, "Wood for you. Hurry up. Approach cautiously" (67). In the empty dwelling at this place, Marlow discovers a tattered book, titled *An Inquiry into Some Points of Seamanship* (68). Marveling at his find, Marlow feels that this relic of a different time and place restores some reality to his surroundings. Taking the book with him, Marlow reboards the boat, and they head on toward Kurtz. Near the end of the next day, the steamer is only about eight miles from Kurtz's camp, and the company decides to stop and travel that most treacherous part of the journey in the daylight. Because of the warning scribbled on the wood at the last station, they anchor the steamer midriver and spend a fitful night only to wake up in a thick fog. When the fog lifts and they begin to lift anchor, the crew hears a "very loud cry, as of infinite desolation" followed by more cries that seem to come from the very fog that descends around them once again (71). Tense and uncertain, they wait to see what might happen next.

Two hours later, when the crew of the steamer is navigating a narrow passage just a mile below Kurtz's station, they are attacked by a group of Congolese natives. In the melee, the helmsman is killed by a spear. It is finally Marlow's sounding of the steam horn that disperses that crowd into the jungle that surrounds the boat. As Marlow tells of throwing his blood-soaked shoes into the river, he becomes suddenly caught up in the telling of the desperate and mournful fear he experienced at that moment when he thought that Kurtz must be dead and realized that he had been "looking forward to—a talk with Kurtz" (86). The narrator relates that Marlow tells his listeners on the yacht in the Thames that he could not have felt more "desolation" if he had missed some "destiny in life" (87). There is the suggestion that one of the listeners on the yacht doubts this, for Marlow abruptly asks, "Why do you sigh in this beastly way, somebody?" (87). The narrator interrupts the retelling of Marlow's narrative, relating Marlow's actions on the *Nellie*. Marlow lit his pipe and took "vigorous draws" before he took up the tale again, still protesting, "Here you all are, each moored with two good addresses, like a hulk with two anchors, a butcher round one corner, a policeman round another.... And you say, Absurd!" (87). Briefly trying to explain his state of mind in the context of the river, Marlow continues his narrative. Kurtz is not dead and Marlow does have the "privilege" of hearing him speak, but he is "very little more than a voice" by the time they arrived to take him away (88).

Interrupting the narrative flow, Marlow suspends his telling of the events immediately following the helmsman's death and his disposal of his bloody shoes and relates various reflections on Kurtz. He tells us that the wilderness had taken Kurtz, had "loved him, embraced him, got into his veins, consumed his flesh, and sealed his soul to its own by the inconceivable ceremonies of some devilish initiation" (89). Marlow seems both enraptured with and in horror of Kurtz. Marlow wonders at Kurtz's originality and is shocked by his arrogance and hubris. He seems to want to explain or excuse Kurtz for what appears to be his loss of civilization and apparent return to something more "primitive." Telling of Kurtz's pamphlet, written for the International Society for the Suppression of Savage Customs that Kurtz had entrusted to Marlow, he concludes that "all Europe contributed to the making of Kurtz" (91). Finally, Marlow finds his narrative way back to the helmsman, who lost his life for the sake of retrieving Kurtz from the Inner Station, and takes up the thread of his tale again.

As they approach Kurtz's station, Marlow looks through his binoculars and sees a house surrounded by a "half-a-dozen slim posts ... with their upper ends ornamented with round carved balls" (96). On the shore is a white man, waving and signaling for the crew to come ashore. When the Manager shouts that they have been attacked, the man on the shore says, "Come along. It's all right. I am glad" (97). Marlow describes this man as looking like a harlequin with his patched clothes and cheerful demeanor. As the Manager and the pilgrims head up to the house to take charge of Kurtz, Marlow shares a pipe with the harlequin, and learns that he is a Russian who was outfitted to find ivory two years ago by a Dutch man. He had met Kurtz in the Congo and asserted that Kurtz had "enlarged my mind" (100).

The third and final section of the novella takes up Marlow's effort to solve the puzzle of Kurtz. As the Russian tells Marlow of how he met Kurtz and how they had talked all night, his devotion to Kurtz becomes apparent. He had nursed Kurtz through two illnesses. We learn that Kurtz mostly wandered alone through the country. We also learn that Kurtz was seen by the tribes of the region as a god, a deity. Making use of this role, Kurtz took the natives' ivory in massive quantities. As the Russian talks on,

Marlow surveys the woods around them with his binoculars, nervous that they might be attacked by the natives who surround them. In his survey, he turns again to the house and realizes that the "round knobs were not ornamental but symbolic" (107). They were heads on stakes and all but one were facing inward toward the house. Marlow claims that the heads "showed that Mr. Kurtz lacked restraint in the gratification of his various lusts, that something was wanting in him" (108). Seeing the direction of his gaze, the Russian attempts to persuade Marlow that Kurtz was not to be misunderstood; the heads belonged to "rebels." Finally, he resorts to the same argument that Marlow uses with his listeners on the yacht: "'You don't know how such a life tries a man like Kurtz,' cried Kurtz's last disciple" (109). The young man at last breaks down and bemoans that fact that Kurtz has been "shamefully abandoned" by the Company. "A man like this, with such ideas. Shamefully! Shamefully!" (109).

The Russian's voice trails off and the evening is pierced with the cries of the natives who emerge from the trees, carrying spears and bows. They surround an improvised stretcher bearing Kurtz. The Russian murmurs that if Kurtz does not say the right thing, they are all dead. Kurtz lifts his arms and from the distance Marlow can tell that he must be shouting to be heard. Most of the crowd falls away and the rest proceed to the steamer with Kurtz. On the shore, a woman appears walking with "measured steps" and "treading" proudly. Marlow relates that "she was savage and superb, wild-eyed and magnificent" (113). She walked on and stood beside the steamer, and after a full minute of wavering resolve, "suddenly she opened her bared arms and threw them up rigid above her head, as though in an uncontrollable desire to touch the sky" (114). Then, she turned and walked away, slowly. This woman is paralleled with Kurtz's "Intended," who is back in Belgium awaiting his return. Kurtz has clearly taken on a new life in the Congo.

With Kurtz safely aboard the boat and evidence of his "unsound method," which is what the Station Manager calls Kurtz's fraternizing with the native people, written in a report to the administration by the Station Manager, the steamer leaves the Inner Station, abandoning Kurtz's young Russian disciple. That first night with Kurtz aboard, Marlow awakens to a sense of danger. Seeing that Kurtz's cabin is empty, he realizes that he has left the ship to join the crowd of natives "keeping vigil" in the forest. As he finds his trail, Marlow discerns that Kurtz is unable to walk and is crawling. He circles and comes between Kurtz and the crowd by the fire in the woods. Kurtz pulls himself to his feet and commands Marlow to leave. Appealing to Kurtz's soul, Marlow tells him he will be lost, "utterly lost" (123). Wavering, Kurtz protests that he has "immense plans," that he is on the "threshold of great things" (123). Marlow assures him that his success in Europe is secure and carries him back to the steamer. When they depart the next day, the natives fill the shore and the woman joins the crowd once more as they chant the words she cries. Marlow blasts the steamer whistle when he sees the pilgrims take up their rifles. All the natives scatter except the woman, who stands resolutely on the shore while the pilgrims begin firing. Marlow tells us that he "could see nothing more for smoke" (127).

As the steamboat makes its way rapidly down the river, Kurtz's life ebbs away. He is consigned to Marlow, who feels his choice to be loyal to Kurtz is like a choice between nightmares. Kurtz talks incessantly of "my Intended, my station, my career, my ideas" (128). He entrusts Marlow with some papers that he fears the Manager may get, further weaving Marlow into the web of his nightmare. When Kurtz dies, Marlow is by the bedside. He is fascinated by his face, which seems to express all the passions of his lifetime, only to settle in a look of "intense and hopeless despair" (130). Then Marlow hears his final words, "'The horror! The horror!'" (130). The pilgrims bury Kurtz in the mud by the river.

Returning to the "sepulchral city" of Brussels, Marlow shares all of Kurtz's papers with the appropriate people, refusing to divulge anything to the Company, though in the name of "Commerce" and "Science" they press him for information. With nothing left to dispense with except a few letters and the picture of Kurtz's Intended, Marlow goes to see her. Their interview is shrouded with the darkness of evening that comes to represent the darkness of Marlow's deceit. In the face of her purity and devotion, he cannot bring himself to tell her Kurtz's final words when she presses him. Rather, he tells her that Kurtz's last words were her name. Marlow has finally lied for Kurtz, directly and irrevocably. He concludes by saying that he "could not tell her. It would have been too dark—too dark altogether." (146). The narrator tells us that Marlow ceased talking at the conclusion of his narrative. He "sat apart"—"in the pose of a meditating Buddha." The narrator reflects upon the river Thames, stating that it "seemed to lead into the heart of an immense darkness." Thus, the narrator invites the readers to reflect on the meaning of Marlow's tale for England.

CHARACTER DEVELOPMENT

The tale that unfolds in this novella is obviously Marlow's. However, one must frame any discussion of Marlow's character and his role as narrator with a reminder that there is a shadowy figure whose voice frames and retells Marlow's tale as it was told to him and the men on the *Nellie* that evening

on the Thames. It is the voice of this man, the primary narrator, who introduces us to the setting that provokes Marlow to begin his story. He is one
of the five men aboard the *Nellie*, including the Director of Companies, the
Accountant, the Lawyer, and Marlow. Except for Marlow and the unnamed
narrator, all are identified by their profession. The reader is told by this narrator that they are all very good men who share a love for the sea. We do
not know anything more about them and their relationships to each other
save that their "bond of the sea" makes them tolerant of each other's stories
and convictions. Without a name or profession to define him, the primary
narrator is an unknown element. He apparently tells Marlow's tale verbatim,
as it was told to him that evening on the *Nellie*. From his description of the
old memories of Empire and glory that the Thames evokes, we can discern
that this man may take exception to the implicit critique of imperialism that
emerges in Marlow's tale. It may be for this reason that he listens carefully
for a clue to the "faint uneasiness that Marlow's tale inspired." Finally, the
primary narrator's role remains ambiguous, and this helps to create the mood
of confusion, disruption, and isolation that infuses this tale.

Charles Marlow, we are told repeatedly by the narrator, sits apart from
the others on the yacht, in a position akin to a Buddha. He is described as
having "sunken cheeks, a yellow complexion" and an "ascetic aspect" (2).
Finally, the narrator tells us that Marlow's only fault is that he is a seaman
who is not typical of that group; that is, he is not straightforward and simple
in his storytelling. Marlow thus appears to us as a curiously isolated and
complicated figure. He is obviously a man of action, for his abilities are aptly
demonstrated in his tale of the journey up the Congo River. But he is also
meditative, gloomy, and susceptible to a mystical turn of thought. In this way,
Marlow transcends the one-dimensional Victorian or Edwardian protagonists
and becomes more like the complicated modern hero we see in the works of
Joyce, Lawrence, and Eliot. Marlow is, ultimately, alone, apart from his fellows and struggling with existential questions about his own complicity in
imperialist atrocities and deceit. Indeed, the narrator's description of Marlow
as having "sunken cheeks" and a "yellow complexion" suggest a malaise
or sickness that might well be due to the experience Marlow relates in his
"yarn" and to his fundamental loss of faith in the system he set out to serve.

Marlow tells us that he began his journey to the Congo with heroic and
altruistic visions. He reminds his audience that he had a boyhood "passion
for maps" and evokes visions of adventure stories (10). Marlow tells us that
he has already visited many of the spots he had vowed to visit one day, hinting at his active nature and his ability to pursue a goal to its end. But, he
tells us, there is one spot he had not visited, a vast country with a "mighty

big river" (11). And, although this country was no longer the unexplored blank spot it was on the maps of his childhood books, he is still curious to explore it.

The more altruistic vision of his journey Marlow attributes to his aunt, conveying both his sexism and his skepticism. His aunt sees him as one of the "Workers," an "emissary of light, something like a lower sort of apostle" (19). Marlow filters this rhetoric by reminding his audience that this was the talk of the times (the promise that civilization could be brought to the ignorant people of Africa) and by reminding his aunt that the "Company" was "run for profit" (19). Yet the reader suspects that Marlow did not know what he was getting into. This suspicion, established in the reader by the hints of the doctor and the clerk who work for the Company, among others, leads us to bond with Marlow as a sort of duped hero who is doomed to fail. We begin to look to Marlow as a captain who will steer us through the snags and shallows of the tale that unfolds, even though Marlow is repeatedly protesting that words cannot make one understand the story he is trying to tell. Thus, in this way most emphatically, Marlow is a Modernist figure like Eliot's Prufrock or Joyce's Dedalus, struggling to find his way in a world of decay and deceit, and intent upon having his story be understood, incomprehensible though it may sometimes be even to himself. He is a voice in the dark on a boat in the middle of an ancient river, desperately trying to use his words to connect, to shed light in the dark yet always aware that he is doomed to fail.

Marlow tells us that in the course of his experience in the Congo, what had begun as a "job" commanding a river boat had become nothing less than a quest. The ostensible goal of that quest is Kurtz, who remains more of a symbol than a flesh and blood character. As a symbol, he evokes other literary figures like Faustus, to whom many critics have compared him. Like Faustus, Kurtz is an eloquent pawn of the devil. His voice and words are the outstanding features of his power over others, and he seems to be able to render one "possessed." But ultimately he is revealed as "hollow at the core" (108).

Kurtz is as much a construction of the stories others tell about him as he is a real character, which does not diminish his evil or the atrocities he commits. The Station Manager at the Central Station believes that Kurtz is arrogant and self-aggrandizing. The Station Manager's lackey, the Brick-maker, believes that Kurtz is a sign of the new "gang of virtue" that he imagines the Company has begun to send into the Congo (44). Thus, Kurtz becomes, at least for a time, a figure of virtue and benevolence who will change the practices of the Belgian agents in the Congo. To the Russian, Kurtz is a deity, who is unlike ordinary men and not to be held by their laws. For a time, Kurtz is this as well: He is a man who appears to have made himself godlike to the tribes of people he encountered in the Congo.

Marlow reminds us that Kurtz speaks often in terms of what belongs to him: "My Intended, my ivory" (89). But Marlow also intimates that what is more interesting than what belonged to Kurtz is what possesses Kurtz: "The thing was to know what he belonged to, how many powers of darkness claimed him for their own" (89). Again, he alludes to Kurtz as a Faustian figure, a victim of the devil. Throughout the tale, Marlow uses language that suggests that Kurtz, wasted and eloquent, was possessed by the "wilderness" and "this alone" had "beguiled his unlawful soul" and allowed him to "kick himself loose of the earth" (123–24). But this wilderness is not just the wilderness of the African jungle that seems to take on a life of its own in Marlow's tale; it is also the potential every human being has for breaking free of social constraints. Marlow reminds us that the jungle is by no means alone responsible for Kurtz's fate. He tells his listeners, "All Europe contributed to the making of Kurtz" (91). This multivalent sentence not only suggests that Europe is responsible for the devil in the heart of Africa and that imperialism is that devil, but it also reminds us that Kurtz is a fictional construction, a composite.

The Manager of the Central Station and his lackey, the Brick-maker, like the Pilgrims milling about the Central Station, quarreling and bickering, and the Chief Accountant at the Outer Station, are representatives of the lies that can embed themselves in the Imperialist mission. Each of these characters practices a kind of self-deception that Marlow sees through and abhors (though, oddly, he does appreciate the Chief Accountant's efforts to keep up appearances in the face of decay). Still, in each of these minor characters we see either the deception of the imperialist mission or its futility as a force for individual good. Marlow notes that the sartorially impressive Chief Accountant is busily making "perfectly correct transactions" while just "fifty feet below the doorstep" of his meager little office rests the "Grove of Death" (32). The juxtaposition of these two contradictions suggests the lie at the heart of the entire enterprise. Similarly, the General Manager rules with no other talent or authority than his strong constitution and the fact that he inspires "uneasiness" in his subordinates. He is a sham who has managed to gain power and will hold onto it through a selfish and mock devotion to the mission of the Company. These small lives and the lies they represent appall and anger Marlow, driving him to the lesser of two nightmares: Kurtz. In contrast to the petty deceits of these minions who serve to perpetuate the grand deception of the entire imperialist and "civilizing" mission in the Congo, Kurtz's honest devilry is refreshing to Marlow.

The Russian, or Harlequin, as Marlow calls him, also chooses Kurtz as his ideal. For the Russian, a young man of 25 who managed to convince a Dutch trading company to outfit him for his exploration of the Congo, Kurtz's ideas are a revelation. Perhaps a representative of the next generation of Europeans coming into the Congo, this young man is sustained by the romance and optimism of youth and has none of the restraint or sense of impropriety that Marlow has. He is a colorful and somewhat endearing fellow whose role in the narrative serves to remind the reader that Kurtz could have an enthrall-ing power over Europeans as well as Africans. He is swept up in the ideas that Kurtz so eloquently expounds upon, apparently unable or unwilling to see how they might not reconcile with Kurtz's own methods and actions. It is conceivable that this figure is a warning, offered by the mature Conrad, that the next generation of explorers might have even less wisdom or restraint than those who have gone into Africa before them. They might be drawn, as youth often is, to the appeal of living freely, outside conventions.

The relatively minor characters, Kurtz's African Mistress, Kurtz's Intended, and Marlow's Aunt in Brussels, are all central figures in this tale insofar as they represent two of the key tenets upon which imperialism was based at the time. With the rise of what has been called "The New Imperialism," begin-ning in the 1870s and reaching a fever pitch in the 1890s, came a renewed scramble by the various European imperialist powers, large and small, to pro-cure the last remaining colonies. This scramble took place mostly in Africa and was clearly articulated and sanctioned in the Berlin Treaty of 1885. The "rot let loose in print and talk just about that time"—to which Marlow refers when he tells of his Aunt's rapturous rhetoric about his role as a "Worker" and an "emissary of light"—indicate the way this scramble for colonies was being explained to the citizens of at least Belgium, if not the other European countries involved in the race (19). Marlow tells his listeners that his Aunt spoke of "weaning those ignorant millions from their horrid ways," and this reveals the common perception of the native people of Africa held by most Europeans (19). Thus, Marlow's presentation of the cannibals who served on the steamship for a few meager pieces of copper wire each week reflects his inherited understanding of them. We have no concrete evidence that they were indeed cannibals; Marlow only offers that one of them would have made a meal of those who attacked the steamboat, given a chance. Rather, they represent the ignorant misperception of the African people that the Europeans used to justify their imperialist actions in the Congo.

This stereotype of the African is perpetuated in Marlow's depiction of Kurtz's presumed mistress in the Congo as a "wild and gorgeous apparition of a woman," "savage and superb, wild-eyed and magnificent" (113). His description here, along with his stereotypical conflation of this woman with the "immense wilderness, the colossal body of the fecund and mysterious life," reveals his inherited understanding of the primitive and sexual nature of the African people, and women in particular, which is part of the misunderstanding that drove the "civilizing" mission of the imperialist expansion in Africa (113). But Marlow's description of the African mistress also merges with his perceptions of women in general; to him, they represent beauty, fecundity, and purity. And for these ideals, Marlow says, women must be kept entirely out of the business afoot in Africa. He tells his listeners on the yacht, "We must help them to stay in that beautiful world of their own, lest ours gets worse" (88). In the rhetoric of the time, it was for this civilized world, mostly inhabited by women, that explorers and missionaries did their "work" in Africa. Marlow's sexism here is indicative of the larger context in which the imperialist mission took place.

THEMES

Although there has been much appropriate debate by critics about whether Conrad was participating in a larger imperialist enterprise with his implicit acceptance of the superiority of the Europeans over the countries they colonized, it is certain that one of the central themes of *Heart of Darkness* is the evil and hypocrisy at the heart of the Belgian imperial enterprise in the Congo. This theme emerges emphatically through the juxtaposition of absurd and grotesque scenes awaiting Marlow in the Congo. For though even Marlow knows that the Company is in the business of trading ivory to make money, he does not know, until he witnesses the scene, just how far its actions are from its policies. The Belgian enterprise appears to be more of a disorganized and inhumane grab for goods with the mere illusion of propriety offered in the midst of chaos. Thus, for example, we find the finicky Chief Accountant who, by implied force, has trained a "native woman" to wash and press his clothes so that he looks the part of a proper accountant as he accurately adds up sums all day and bemoans the intrusions of the "savages" in his work. His work of adding sums seems to take precedence over all the humanity surrounding him, even the sick men and women in the "Grove of Death," which Marlow so dramatically juxtaposes to his little office. Marlow observes the futile blasting in the wilderness and the wanton wreckage of machinery taking place in the midst of obviously starving and abused native Congolese. All these scenes mock the "civilizing" enterprise of progress that the Belgians claim to be pursuing. Every stop Marlow makes along the river reveals this abuse of the native people.

This is not to say that Marlow himself is able to transcend his indoctrination in European superiority so far that he can see the natives around him as fully human. He cannot. He speaks of them as he might an instrument or a valued piece of machinery. He tells us that he had come to love his steamer as he labored to make her serviceable again: "I had expended enough hard work on her to make me love her" he says (51). In the same tone of loyalty to a good piece of machinery, Marlow speaks of his African Helmsman, explaining his mourning over the death of "a savage" as the result of a bond they had forged by working together. Marlow even offers a sort of grudging respect for the restraint the "cannibals" showed on the river trip in not eating the crew, revealing his low estimation of their character in general. But Marlow's racist sense of superiority does not blur his vision of the evil wrought at the imperialist hands of the Belgians in the Congo. Although we modern readers might take him to task for this racism, most critics have defended his larger purpose of challenging Belgian imperialist practices.

Conrad's criticism of the Belgian imperialist effort in the Congo is also revealed through the characters of the agents at the three stations on the Congo River, who make every effort to appear to be serving the ostensible altruistic goals of the Company but are revealed to be ivory-grubbing and dishonest. His belief also emerges through the rhetoric of the agents for the Company in the city of Brussels who use words like "noble cause" or the company doctor who speaks of his part in helping his country reap advantages from "the possession of such a magnificent dependency" (18). At the Central Station, Marlow wonders at the pilgrims waiting for months on end for their chance to get a trading post. He says their plotting among themselves was as unreal as everything that surrounded him there, "as the philanthropic pretense of the whole concern" (42). Thus, both in deed and word, all the affiliates of the Company appear to Marlow to be concealing the truth of the enterprise.

Another central theme that emerges in Conrad's tale is the loss of a moral center in a modern world of political and economic expansion. Kurtz has "kicked himself free of the earth," and Marlow is lost in the face of Kurtz's untethered existence: "He was alone, and I before him did not know whether I stood on the ground or floated in the air" (124). Marlow is trying to convey to his listeners on the yacht that in the context of all the grotesque injustice and absurdity of the Belgian endeavors in the Congo to which he was witness, Marlow is left grasping for a moral center, a truth, an idea. He speaks directly to his listeners at one point, trying to make them understand why Kurtz might take a "high seat amongst the devils of the land" (90). Sensing that they do not understand, he says, and he might as well be speaking directly to us, "You can't understand. How could you?—with solid pavement under your feet, surrounded by kind neighbours" (90).

One senses in Conrad's novella a nostalgia for a time when there was an "unselfish belief in the idea" behind the enterprise of exploration, or perhaps even colonization (8). The hazy, ambiguous world that Marlow depicts in the Congo is a world without a moral center, without an "idea at the back of it" (8). It is a world of absurdities, where a man carries a bucket with a hole in the bottom to put out a towering fire, where native men blast into the hillsides for no reason at all, and where one stumbles upon drainage pipes tumbled in a ravine next to a grove of silent, dying men. In this world, Marlow cannot make words convey meaning, and he cannot get a firm grasp on truth. Nor can he do so as he sits on a yacht in the river Thames, telling of his experience in the Congo. So, we might read Marlow as the modern "anti-hero" who, like Prufrock, is broken by his encounters with the emptiness at the center of it all; who cannot redeem the "idea" now that it has been shattered along with his illusions.

The novella challenges us to consider a man cut free from the social constraints of his "civilized" life and the madness that results. From the very beginning, when Marlow imagines the commander of a trireme ordered to conquer the north, we have a foreshadowing of the madness that can occur in isolated places. He intimates the difficulty of proceeding so far into the "incomprehensible" and the "longing to escape" that the commander must have felt (8). We sense that Marlow speaks of his own command of a boat proceeding up a river into an incomprehensible place, cut free from social constraints, rules, and laws. The profound irony is that it is in the name of social constraints and civilized life that the imperial enterprise is promoted and embraced; by civilizing the natives, by bringing them rules, Christianity, and government, the Belgians claimed that they were "taming" the mad wilderness. Instead, they were producing carnage and creating a madness in themselves; they were robbing the land of ivory and killing the native people and their cultures.

SYMBOLS AND MOTIFS

Conrad's themes are conveyed by various symbols and motifs. One of the most prevalent motifs is that of an obscuring haze or fog that carries with it a certain brooding malevolence. As the yacht is brought to anchor in the Thames and the company of friends take meditative positions on the deck, the primary narrator observes the encroaching gloom that was "brooding motionless" over London. He describes this gloom becoming "more sombre" when Marlow begins his tale. It is a tale that seems to take place almost exclusively in a dim and hazy light. This motif contributes to the obscuring of reality and truth that is so central to the novella. Other critical scenes take place in this hazy half-light of evening. Marlow's discussion with the Brick-maker, when he is just beginning to make out the misperceptions the Brick-maker and the Station Manager have of him, takes place as night falls. They part in darkness, seeing each other less clearly, metaphorically and literally. Marlow's encounter with Kurtz as he tries to rejoin the native people occurs in the night with the eerie background light of a campfire and the beating of a drum. In this light, Kurtz rises up before Marlow as a "vapour exhaled by the earth," becoming the very mist that obscures truth and light. Indeed, Marlow leads us to understand that the struggle he had to get Kurtz back to the boat that night was as much spiritual as physical; he tells us that Kurtz is under a spell, and he seems ready to fall under Kurtz's spell himself at any moment. These encounters in twilight, moonlight, and haze add to a dreamlike and ambiguous quality of all that Marlow encounters. They are endowed with an eerie, magical, and sinister import by the very way that Conrad describes the atmospheric light. In fact, at no time or place in the novel are we within a clear and straightforward light.

A related motif is that of not seeing or of the incomprehensible. Early in his journey, the French boat in which Marlow finds passage comes upon a man-of-war firing into the dense forest. No one can see an enemy, but apparently the enemy is there. Throughout his journey up the Congo River, Marlow feels there are unseen faces in the forests observing him. This feeling becomes an actuality when his steamer is caught in a fog and they hear the screams of natives in the forests around them, but they can see nothing. For two hours they wait for the fog to lift and wonder if they will be attacked. And as he waits on the boat for Kurtz to be brought down in the stretcher, Marlow is all the time aware of the presence of native people whom he cannot see, even as he is exposed to view himself. This motif, repeated in so many ways throughout the novella, leads the reader to wonder about the possibility of really seeing another human being. As one learns from the scene with the man-of-war shooting into the forest, the fear of the unknown is entwined with the inability to see. Clearly, the Europeans in the Congo either did not see the native people as human or did not understand them, but they obviously feared them. Fear and failure to understand led to the brutality of Europeans toward the native people. Furthermore, it led Europeans at home to condone that brutality in their blindness to the real reasons behind the "civilizing" of the natives.

In a similar vein, the numerous references to darkness and the color black coalesce as a motif that usually signifies evil but can, on occasion, play the opposite role. When Marlow tells of his childhood love of maps, he tells his comrades that he preferred the blank spots on maps, the unexplored. One of the largest of these blank spots was the Congo. True, he concedes, it is no longer "a white patch for a boy to dream gloriously over. It had become a place of darkness" (10). This early mention of the once "white" place as one of "darkness" now is a foreshadowing of the evil Marlow encounters in the Congo, but it is not the evil of black men. It is the evil of white men. Thus, in this case, white is evil and black is not. Marlow says he thought of the two women knitting black yarn that he encountered in the Company offices in Brussels as "guarding the door of Darkness" (25). He observes that it is as if they are knitting a pall, or the blanket for a dead body, and he greets them in Latin, "We who are about to die salute you" (16). These women, with their symbolic color of death, are portrayed as the guards to some dark underworld. Conrad uses his references to these colors to build up the mystery surrounding Marlow's journey into the Congo. Darkness is everywhere in this world and usually it masks some human evil or, at the very least, danger.

Relevant to this motif of darkness and the color black are Marlow's repeated references to Brussels, the city where the Company is located and where Leopold II reigns, as the "whited sepulchre." A sepulchre is a grave or burial vault. The phrase "whited sepulchre" is used in the Bible, in the book of Matthew, to describe something that is beautiful on the outside and containing death or horrors. Conrad's attack on the sham of Belgium's supposed "civilizing" mission in the Congo is clear in his use of this term. The city may look pretty, but it contains the source of the horrors and death that are carried out in name of Empire. Inside the city, as inside the offices of the Company, all appear corpse-like.

Throughout the novella, beginning with the primary narrator's warning that the meaning of Marlow's stories was not "inside like a kernel but outside," we encounter the motif of interiors and exteriors. Conrad's repetition of the phrase "whited sepulchre" contributes to the motif, indicating the radical differences between surfaces and interiors. Elsewhere in the novella, the motif emerges: There are the Stations surrounded by the forest; Conrad writes of the "unreal" quality of the purposeless pilgrims chattering about ivory and wandering around inside the Station and observes that "outside, the silent wilderness surrounding this cleared speck on the earth struck me as great and invincible, like evil or truth" (39–41). Not only does Conrad reiterate the motif of interiority and exteriority here, but he emphasizes that there is an outside that hides what lies within: the "whited sepulchre," the forest that hides "enemies," the story that hides its meaning. Similarly, when seen from the coast, all of the African continent looks quiet, green, and benign to Marlow. It is only inland that the real death and horror lie.

Both the river and the wilderness function as quotidian realities that are endowed with symbolic meaning in this tale. Rivers, whether the Thames or the Congo, are portrayed in the novella as the points of entry into a country, a place. In the case of the Thames, the primary narrator also imagines it as the point of exit and return for great heroes of the nation, a body of water that has proudly served its country. He tells us that it had "borne" the famous ships (and famous men), "returning with ... round flanks full of treasure" (4). It is greatness that the primary narrator imagines floating on that river. Marlow is not so rosy in his view of either the Thames or the Congo, though he does appear to prefer British Imperialism to Belgian. Marlow imagines a Roman commanding a trireme up the Thames. "They were conquerors," he tells his listeners, a job for which you need only brute force (8). From this, he segues to his tale of his own command of a steamer up the Congo River. What he witnesses there, and what some say he helps to perpetuate, is a similar "conquering" brute force. He does not speak of the Congo in heroic terms, but in terms of horror and brutality, equating the Belgian "mission" to a Roman conquest. The text returns to the Thames at the very end of Marlow's tale when, once again, the primary narrator intercedes and states, "the tranquil waterway leading to the uttermost ends of the earth flowed sombre under an overcast sky—seemed to lead into the heart of an immense darkness" (146). In these lines we have both outside and inside, and here, as elsewhere, the darkness is on the inside. It is possible that for all Marlow's allusions to the good done by British imperialism, Conrad is warning that there is evil in that enterprise as well.

NARRATIVE STYLE

Like Forster, Conrad is an early Modernist and has been placed with the Edwardians by some critics. His early fiction is particularly appropriate for classification as Edwardian. As is true in his earlier fiction, in *Heart of Darkness* Conrad also creates a context in which his characters are tested by conditions of extreme danger and difficulty. Marlow vociferously attests to this. But Marlow faces more existential difficulties in this tale than perhaps any Conradian character before him. He is up against the Modernist dilemma of a meaningless world—a world without a moral center. With *Heart of Darkness*, Conrad not only introduced a Modernist hero, alienated in a world devoid of meaningful values and beliefs, but he has also achieved a new narrative style that one can only read as early Modernist. In this narrative style, the narrator is distanced from his audience and their perspectives. He does not take the tone of an authoritative Edwardian or a chatty Victorian; he is always present, often invisible, but present like the faces in the forest that Marlow cannot see. He makes us uneasy. Yet, even with this lack of clarity, the author's struggle to present his tale accurately and in a way he is sure the audience can grasp is everywhere apparent in the style of his prose.

Conrad's use of a primary narrator who frames Marlow's tale provides yet a further layer between the reader and the narrative. Although the primary is not an omniscient narrator who intrudes on the flow of events to steer our eyes occasionally in a new direction, he makes his authority clear. This primary narrator has no credentials. We do not know his name, background, or opinions. He is unseen, not unheard. What he introduces into the text does not shed light on his reliability. We cannot be sure what he thinks of Marlow, Marlow's "yarn," or its possible meaning. This would not be a problem if we did not have to rely on this primary narrator to accurately repeat Marlow's tale, apparently from memory. So, we are forced to step back, to wonder at Conrad's intentions and to always remain slightly suspicious of the story as it unfolds. This narrative distancing is Modernist in style. Conrad is not interested in putting his readers at their ease; he wants them to remain alert.

There are features of Marlow's tale that further distance him from his audience, calling attention to his struggle to convey his meaning and disorienting us when we feel we have discovered his meaning. For example, although we might find ourselves settling into what looks as if it could be a typical nineteenth-century gothic romance, with its clear elements of plot and character, we find that Marlow's journey is not grounded within a solid reality. Marlow sets out to command a steamboat on the Congo for a Belgian company. One might have supposed that he would be expected to travel up and down the river, ferrying people and supplies to their various destinations. Instead, Marlow's journey loses this purpose, or never had it, and picks up another along the way (the quest for Kurtz, an enigmatic figure who might already be dead). As Marlow is sucked into the darkly absurd world that surrounds him, he appears to have forgotten why he is there. He waits three months for rivets, all the while growing intoxicated with the idea of holding a conversation with an ailing genius madman who is living in the jungle hundreds of miles up river. Clearly we are not to trust Marlow's sanity. And we are not to trust that this is a traditional gothic romance.

Marlow appears to sense his audience's disbelief, and he grows more agitated when he relays the less believable elements of his tale. He breaks off, protests that he cannot find the words to make his audience see what he means to convey, berates the listeners on board the yacht for their comfortable lives, and ultimately resorts to the same argument that the Russian resorts to in his defense of Kurtz: No one knows how a life in the wilderness tries the soul. All of these narrative gestures separate the narrator from his audience, calling his isolation to our attention and reminding us that he is a Modernist figure. Marlow's narrative technique and his apparent existential struggle situate him as a figure somehow still lost in the wilderness, even as he tells the tale of Kurtz getting lost. Marlow sits apart from the other men on the deck; he holds no title, as they do; and he is not typical of the other men of his trade. His sallow cheeks give further evidence to some inner torment.

Finally, it is the intense focus on the subjective experience of Marlow that moves this novella into the canon of Modernism. Joseph Conrad embraced the idea of literary impressionism, practiced by Ford Madox Ford, with whom Conrad coauthored a short story about the Belgian Congo. This concept of literary impressionism is articulated by Henry James in "The Art of Fiction," in which he describes the novel as a personal impression of life. This emphasis is reflected in a prose style that will forgo sustained description and contextualization for the sake of the character's immediate impressions. Because of this emphasis on perception, much impressionist writing, like Conrad's, is more vague and diffuse in its meaning. Ultimately, this is why Conrad's novella cannot be lumped with nineteenth-century literature, though he may borrow from its genres and styles. He is far more interested in the interiority of his character, in his metaphysical struggles, than he is in the apt objective description of a setting or scene. Conrad's character is a modern hero, often called an antihero, insofar as he is an ordinary man who struggles with alienation and the chaos of the modern world, in which he finds no moral center. He does not transform the world, but ends his tale on an inconclusive note, leaving his readers to wonder about final meanings and possible endings.

HISTORICAL CONTEXT

Heart of Darkness is unique to its historical moment of late European Imperialism. Even as it forges new ground by interrogating the imperial project and the assumed superiority of Europeans over the native people of the countries they colonized, the novel appears to accept many racist and imperialist assumptions that we not only question today but generally find repellent. It was a commonly held belief in late nineteenth-century Europe that the peoples of the colonies "belonging to" great nations needed to be civilized, educated, and enlightened. Rarely did anyone think to challenge the concept of empire and the possession of colonies upon which it was predicated.

The Congo that Conrad visited in 1890 was the personal property of King Leopold II of Belgium. It was officially made Leopold's property in 1884, when the first chancellor of the German Empire, Otto von Bismarck, saw that other European nations could secure more by granting possession to Leopold in return for Leopold's agreement that all nations would be free to trade in the Congo without monopolies or taxes. Bismarck worked with Jules Ferry of France to organize a conference in 1884, which was attended by 14 of the states of Europe. From this conference came not only Leopold's possession of the Congo, but, in 1885, the Treaty of Berlin, which effectively began a new period of colonialism, in which the major European empires partitioned Africa.

A notoriously corrupt and tyrannical ruler, Leopold readily agreed to fair trade but never upheld his end of the deal in the Congo. Leopold promised to bring civilization and Christianity to the Congo. What he did instead was barely disguise his army as "managers" and "agents" who secured a Belgian monopoly in ivory, the most precious and plentiful commodity in the region. The methods by which these managers and agents secured the ivory were brutal: The natives were enslaved and any non-Belgian found in possession of ivory could be shot on sight. In 1885, King Leopold established the Congo Free State and made himself its absolute sovereign. This move granted Belgium a virtual monopoly on the exploitation of the Congo. Rather than cry foul, many other imperialist nations followed suit and established similar charter companies to develop other parts of Africa, granting their countries monopoly rights to the areas. Because Africa was so far away and there had been a general reemergence of imperialist fervor across Europe, it took a long time before there was any public outcry at the atrocities committed by imperialist agents in Africa in general, and Leopold's agents in the Congo in particular.

When Conrad began writing his novella 10 years after his experience in the Congo, there was a growing rumble of protest against the abuses of power practiced by Leopold's agents. Perhaps the protests closest to Conrad's experience in the Congo were registered by two men. One of these men, Roger Casement, was an antislavery advocate. Conrad had met and shared a room with Casement in Matadi before he began his journey to Stanley Pool (now Malebo) in 1889. Casement was in the Congo to abolish the slave trade carried on by Arabs and to establish a railway to facilitate trade. Like Conrad, he was ignorant of the slavery and brutality being practiced by Leopold's government. Casement went on to establish "The Congo Reform Association" in 1903, for which Conrad wrote a letter of support.

The other protest closely related to Conrad's experience in the Congo was registered by an American, George Washington Williams, in his 1890 piece, "An Open Letter to His Serene Majesty Leopold II." Williams had been a soldier in the U.S. Civil War as a member of the U.S. Colored Troops. He traveled to Brussels in 1889 for an antislavery conference, where he had the occasion to meet King Leopold, whose ostensible purposes for claiming the Congo Williams applauded. (Leopold had claimed that his government in the Congo would bring Christianity, foster care, and secure the welfare of the native people.) In 1890, Williams was commissioned by U.S. President Benjamin Harrison to report on conditions in the Congo. Williams's report, President Harrison felt, would inform his own decision on whether or not to recommend ratification of the Berlin Act of 1885, which would divide Africa among the competing European imperialist powers. Williams traveled to the Congo in 1890, the same year that Conrad was there. His report to President Harrison unveiled the lie of Leopold's supposedly benevolent efforts in the Congo. Williams's "Open Letter to His Serene Majesty Leopold II" is an indictment of the atrocities in the Congo for which Leopold is responsible. It levels 12 charges against Leopold's government, each revealing another layer of the inhumanity and deceit of the Belgian Government in the Congo. This letter was published as a pamphlet in England and the United States and was, no doubt, familiar to Conrad.

Further evidence that all was not right in the Congo came with the reports on the war between the Belgian agents in the Congo and the Arab slave-traders there; the brutality of this war and the Belgians' involvement were described in the British papers. In 1897, Captain Sidney Hinde published his account of this war in *The Fall of the Congo Arabs*. In addition, reports of the Belgians' brutality and forced labor written by Edmund Morel and others continued to make their way to England from Africa and were duly made public in the press. Thus, by the time that Conrad began to write *Heart of Darkness*, there was a growing consciousness of and discomfort with Leopold's practices in the Congo, if not with the new imperialism in general.

2

E. M. Forster
Howards End
(1910)

BIOGRAPHICAL CONTEXT

Edward Morgan Forster was born January 1, 1879. He was the only child of Alice Clara "Lily" Whichelo and Edward Morgan Llewellyn Forster, who died in 1880, when his son was just a year old. Young Morgan was raised almost exclusively by women—specifically, his mother and his influential paternal aunt Marianne Thornton. Both of these women shaped Morgan's sense of morality and justice, ideals with which he would engage throughout his life. His aunt Marianne Thornton had very strong ideas about one's obligation to do social good and uphold the national character, which grew out of her experience as the daughter of a leading member of the Clapham Sect. The Clapham Sect was a group of evangelical, philanthropic families who were given their name because they lived on the Clapham Common in London at the end of the eighteenth century. Members of this group fought to abolish the slave trade and used philanthropy to fight social injustice. They also sought to convert others to Christianity. The descendants of the Clapham families tended to distrust institutions. We see this distrust of institutions combined with a strong sense of the social injustice of the English class system in Forster's novel *Howards End*.

Forster has observed that his happiest childhood years were spent at a house called Rooksnest in Stevenage, Hertfordshire, from 1883 to 1893. This house is widely accepted as the model for the house in *Howards End*. He loved the quiet pattern of life there. His mother chose not to associate with many families in Stevenage, and Morgan was therefore isolated from other children.

However, he did not come to know his loneliness dramatically until he left Rooksnest for Tonbridge in Kent. There Forster attended Tonbridge School, where he was unhappy and lonely. In fact, while at Tonbridge in 1894, he wrote a memoir of Rooksnest that captures all he had lost with the end of his quiet country life and highlights all he despised about Tonbridge School. Like the young Stephen Dedalus in Joyce's *Portrait of the Artist,* Forster seems to have loathed the rivalrous noise, jostling, and banter of schoolboys.

Forster attended King's College, Cambridge. There he found a community of like-minded young men and was inspired by G. E. Moore. Moore emphasized the importance of relationships and intellectual inquiry. In *Principia Ethica* (1903), Moore advanced the moral philosophy that was to have such a formative impact on Forster's generation of students attending King's College. G. E. Moore was a member of The Apostles, an exclusive undergraduate society at Cambridge that included as members Leonard Woolf, Lytton Strachey, and other central figures of what would come to be known as the Bloomsbury Group, a collection of artists, writers, and intellectuals who shared a common perspective very much informed by Moore's philosophy. In 1901, Forster was elected to The Apostles and, through them, came into the fold of the Bloomsbury Group, though he always remained somewhat peripheral to their lives and work because he was more conservative and private.

In the years 1901–1905, Forster traveled extensively in Italy and Greece. He also lectured on the Republic of Florence at schools in Harpenden and Lowestoft during these years. In 1904, he settled with his mother in Weybridge, which would remain his home until 1924. As he became accustomed to life in Weybridge, Forster's passion for the English countryside grew and deepened. *Howards End,* which reflects this passion, was published in 1910. It was Forster's fourth novel and assured his literary stature. Like Forster's first three novels (*Where Angels Fear to Tread, The Longest Journey,* and *A Room with a View*), *Howard's End* engages questions of injustice by inviting readers to examine the very structure of the British class system, industrialism, and upper-class liberalism. *Howards End* comes at a critical moment in history. It deals with the impact of gross inequity and social imbalance, impending war, and rapidly expanding industrialism upon individuals and families, criticizing the complacency found within industrialism and ineffectual upper-middle-class liberalism. Following his earlier novels, with their consistent focus on themes dear to Forster (the English abroad, the value of friendship, the conflict between liberalism and imperialism), *Howards End* engages the liberal imagination through the characters of Margaret and Helen Schlegel. But, written as it is in 1910, it takes on a wider perspective, asking its readers to consider larger questions.

Forster only wrote one more novel, *A Passage to India* (1922–24). After he gave up novel writing, Forster did publish two biographies, his Clark lectures from Cambridge (published as *Aspects of the Novel*), and various political essays. From writing novels, Forster moved on to other personally satisfying engagements. Nicola Beauman writes of his political work that resulted from his liberal values: "He broadcast on the BBC, attracting vast audiences. He wrote articles, sat on committees, attended congresses and signed letters on a whole range of subjects of concern to the liberal conscience—individual liberty, censorship, penal reform and, above all, the rise of fascism" (355). Forster was the first president of the National Council for Civil Liberties and held the post again in 1942. He consistently defended liberal causes.

In his personal life, Forster's long struggle to find love and domestic peace was realized in the early 1930s with the unique "family" that he created with his lover Bob Buckingham and Buckingham's wife, May. Together, they managed a life of friendship, love, parenting (of May and Bob's boy, whom they named Robert Morgan), and grandparenting that endured until Forster's death in 1970. Forster has noted that these were the happiest times of his long life.

PLOT SUMMARY

The first of the 44 chapters that make up the novel *Howards End* is composed of three letters written by Helen Schlegel to her sister Margaret. The central protagonists of this novel, Helen and Margaret, are the daughters of a German father and an English mother. Orphaned more than 10 years before this scene, they have grown into a philosophy of life that embraces the primacy of personal relations above all else. They are idealist, liberal, and essentially innocent. As the elder sister, Margaret is far more clear-headed and pragmatic than her impulsive younger sister Helen. Helen's letters arrive at her sister's breakfast table at Wickham Place in London from Howards End, a country house belonging to the Wilcoxes, an upper-class mercantilist family with whom the sisters became acquainted while traveling in Europe. Accepting an invitation to visit them at their country house, Helen has gone to Howards End, while Margaret has agreed to stay home with their brother, Tibby, who is ill.

Helen's first letter describes the beautiful house and the love that Mrs. Wilcox appears to have for it. The letter also captures the pragmatic and brusque manners of Mr. Wilcox, his son Charles, and his daughter Evie. The second letter, composed three days later, still conveys Helen's great pleasure at visiting the Wilcoxes, but it also reveals more about the patriarch of that family, Mr. Wilcox. Through the letter, it becomes clear that Mr. Wilcox is a conventional and conservative member of the upper class who believes firmly in the division of the sexes and gently mocks Helen's liberal views. Helen is not at all offended; in fact, she praises him as a "really strong" person, observing that he has put her off her liberal theories without hurting her feelings, a point that is revealing of Helen's youthful inconstancy.

It is the third and briefest letter that sets the plot of this novel into action, announcing, as it does, that Helen and the youngest Wilcox son, Paul, are "in love." Read at the breakfast table in the Schlegel's London home, where Margaret sits with her aunt Juley (her deceased mother's sister) and her brother Tibby, Helen's letter creates a sudden crisis as Aunt Juley insists that an engagement is entirely too sudden and that someone must go down to Howards End immediately. After much discussion, Margaret allows her Aunt Juley to make the trip, urging her to speak only to Helen about the engagement, not to members of the Wilcox family. When Margaret returns from taking her aunt to the station, she finds a telegram from Helen stating, "All over. Wish I had never written. Tell no one" (13). Of course, Aunt Juley is already on her way to Howards End, and there is no way to inform her of the broken engagement and the futility of her visit.

Chapter 3 begins with Aunt Juley using the hour's northward journey to reflect on her nieces' lives. She conveys her own conservative (though humanist and nonmercantilist) values, observing that the sisters entertain far too many "unshaven" artists at their home in London. She considers them flighty and prone to "throw themselves away." Encountering Charles Wilcox at the train station, Aunt Juley mistakenly takes him for the younger son, Paul. She attempts to control her agitation, but as they drive through the countryside they fall into an ugly and heated argument, "stating in so many words that Schlegels were better than Wilcoxes, Wilcoxes better than Schlegels" (21). They arrive at Howards End in a confusion of rage and frustration, only to have Helen rush to her aunt saying that it is all over. Charles begins to berate his younger brother, Paul, and Mrs. Wilcox descends on the scene to separate the parties and make time for the tensions to dissipate, telling Charles, "They do not love any longer" (23).

Chapter 4 has aunt and niece returning to the Schlegel home at Wickham Place, each shaken by the experience. Helen *had* fallen in love, though not with Paul—she had fallen in love with the Wilcox family. The critical point is that "new ideas had burst upon her like a thunder clap," and they had left her "stunned" (24). The nature of these "new ideas" will be explored, and rejected, by Helen in the course of the novel. But on her first visit to Howards End, as she relates the whole story to her sister Margaret once she is home, the energy of the Wilcox family and the comfort of their home and life in the country had tempted her to accept their conservative views over her own philosophies of social justice and reform. We are told that she had rather enjoyed "giving in" to them when they asserted that "her notions of life were sheltered or academic, that Equality was nonsense, Votes for Women nonsense, Socialism nonsense" (24). All of these convictions are typified as "Schlegel fetiches," and Helen is temporarily bewitched into accession to the Wilcox's conservative and mercantilist notions. This, she tells Margaret, is what left her poised to fall in love with Paul when she first met him at the near-end of her week-long visit with the Wilcoxes.

Yet, once the splendor of their kisses had worn off the next morning, and Helen observed the near terror in Paul's face lest she tell his family of their engagement, she knew it was over. Presciently, she was appalled at seeing "that kind of man" frightened; it made the self-satisfied Wilcox clan appear to be a fraud: "just a wall of newspapers and motor-cars and golf clubs," behind which there was nothing but "panic and emptiness" (26). Helen's description of the hollowness she glimpsed behind the tidy, athletic, and successful lives of the Wilcoxes leads Margaret to reflect on her and her sister's approaches to life, with their emphasis on personal relations. After her "episode" with the Wilcoxes, observing how they apparently have their "hands on all the ropes" of life, Helen concludes with conviction that "personal relations are the real life, for ever and ever" (28). With this, the stage has been set for one of the central dichotomies of the story: those who value duties and the outer look of things versus those who value personal relations above all—Wilcox versus Schlegel.

Chapter 5 begins with the three Schlegels attending a concert at "the dreariest music-room in London," the Queen's Hall. A performance of Beethoven's Fifth Symphony moves Helen to imagine she sees the heroes and the goblins of emptiness vying for dominance on the stage and in the world. When the goblins dominate, all is "Panic and emptiness, Panic and emptiness!" for Helen. They abolish the heroes and the "flaming ramparts of the world" (35). Once Beethoven had chased them away and returned the "splendour, gods and demi-gods" to victory, Helen is swept up with hopefulness, attempting to convince herself that the goblins were merely the "phantoms of cowardice and unbelief" that could be dispelled by one "healthy human impulse" (34). But, as Helen observes, even though Beethoven chooses to make it all right in the end of the symphony, the goblins were still there. This awareness drives Helen from the music hall, inadvertently taking with her the umbrella of a man seated next to her sister Margaret.

Helen's mistake makes the man suspicious of the Schlegels. He is convinced that they have played a confidence game. At the close of the concert, Margaret invites the man to come home with them to retrieve his umbrella. As they walk back to Wickham place, Margaret chatters on about the music and arts in general, and the subtle but definite differences in class between her and the man emerge more distinctly. He reflects, "If only he could talk like this, he would have caught the world" (41). When they arrive at Wickham Place, Margaret succeeds in alienating the gentleman further by rifling through their umbrellas and rejecting one as his because it is torn and "appalling" and therefore obviously her own. But the shabby umbrella does in fact belong to the young man, and he leaves abruptly, refusing to stay for tea. As the Schlegels reflect on the incident with the man and his umbrella, they all feel that it remains a "goblin footfall": a reminder that "beneath these superstructures of wealth and art there wanders an ill-fed boy, who has recovered his umbrella indeed, but who has left no address behind him, and no name" (46). This reminder leaves the sisters eager to effect some change in the world, to improve one man's position.

In chapter 6, the reader's attention is shifted to Leonard Bast, the young man whose umbrella was "stolen" by Helen. The narrator tells us that because he has had the misfortune of being born into modern times, when the "angel of Democracy had arisen," Leonard is obliged to assert his gentility, and is therefore always anxious to "improve" himself (47). For this reason, he attends concerts that cost him too much of his meager income and reads Ruskin and tries to imitate his style. All of this he does with the hope that "he would one day push his head out of the grey waters and see the universe" (52). As Leonard returns home, we follow him into the squalor of Camelia Road, where he lives. Leonard enters a block of flats, "constructed with extreme cheapness," where he inhabits a basement flat that is "dark" and "stuffy." Compared to the Schlegels', Leonard's life is precarious, as he owns nothing in the flat but some books, a photograph, and some decorative cupids. The cupids, in fact, belong to Jacky, Leonard's companion. She is described as an "apparition," a woman who is "not respectable" and who is "past her prime" (53). It becomes clear that out of his very English sense of duty and obligation, Leonard has agreed to marry Jacky when he comes of age. If he tried to marry her before that, he tells her, his brother would stop it. Jacky, whose eyes alone reveal her anxiety, repeatedly seeks reassurance from Leonard that he will "make it all right" (54). She obviously does not care that he wants to improve himself "by means of Literature and Art" (46); she merely wants reassurance that he will see her through. Their domestic scene is bleak and anxious.

The next three chapters return to the comforts of Wickham Place, beginning when Margaret learns from Aunt Juley that the Wilcoxes have taken the flat just opposite their own. Thus, the Wilcox balcony is in plain view from the Schlegel's home and, according to Aunt Juley, will be an obvious irritant to the inhabitants. Margaret argues that Helen is entirely over Paul Wilcox. But when Helen enters and overhears their discussion, she blushes at Paul's name. Margaret rather blithely maintains that there is no great risk, "as long as you have money" (62). She explains this philosophy to Aunt Juley, asking her to imagine what would have happened if the families had not had the means to whisk Helen and Paul away from each other when first they made their misalliance. This question leads the reader to think of poor Leonard Bast and his obvious mismatch with Jacky. But the Schlegels do have the means to manage such problems, and Helen chooses to go traveling with her cousin (just as the Wilcoxes see Paul off to Africa).

The families' proximity reinitiates contact between Margaret and Mrs. Wilcox. Margaret visits Mrs. Wilcox to apologize for the rudeness she has shown her in an earlier letter that rejected all contact. The two patch up the misunderstanding and go on to speak of the Wilcox family, their move up to London for Charles's wedding, and Howards End, the only subject about which Mrs. Wilcox appears to show genuine interest and joy. Margaret then gives a luncheon in Mrs. Wilcox's honor, an affair that does not come off well. Mrs. Wilcox baffles the other guests whom Margaret has invited: She does not know culture, art, or politics, and they can find no "common topic." The conversation at the table moves rapidly from one social topic to another with many differing opinions offered unabashedly. When pressed for her opinion on a topic, Mrs. Wilcox offers an apparent snub by asserting, "I think Miss Schlegel puts everything splendidly" (79). When Margaret protests, Mrs. Wilcox asserts that she did not intend the comment as a snub. When Mrs. Wilcox leaves the lunch early, Margaret reflects that Mrs. Wilcox has wisdom beyond all the sophisticated intellectual talk that went on at lunch.

After a period of some time, Margaret and Mrs. Wilcox meet again to do some Christmas shopping. Margaret mentions that they will have to begin house-hunting, as Wickham Place will be torn down to make room for bigger flats like the one that the Wilcoxes occupy. This news strikes Mrs. Wilcox as tragic and she launches into protestations of injustice and the crimes of progress that would put the Schlegels out of their father's home. She tells Margaret, "Howards End was nearly pulled down once. It would have killed me" (86). Mrs. Wilcox impetuously urges Margaret to go with her to Howards End immediately. Margaret gently declines her offer and, annoyed, Mrs. Wilcox directs the carriage driver to return them to Wickham Place. At lunch with her brother, Margaret broods over the interaction and realizes that Mrs. Wilcox "had only one passion in life—her house—and that the moment was solemn when she invited a friend to share this passion with her" (89). Decisively, Margaret sets out to join Mrs. Wilcox. She takes a cab to King's Cross station where she finds Mrs. Wilcox and asks if she still might join her. As they walk to the platform to catch their train, they encounter Mr. Wilcox and Evie Wilcox, who are just returning from their travels. Margaret is reintroduced to Mr. Wilcox and introduced to Evie; the plans to travel to Howards End are dropped.

Chapter 11 begins by letting the reader know that Mrs. Wilcox has died. The funeral is held in Hilton, near her beloved Howards End. As is the custom, it is attended by the local people of the district as well as the family. We are not privy to the moods and conversations of the family; we regard the funeral from the perspectives of the poor village people: the wood-cutter (who is pollarding the elm just over the grave), his mother and her friends (who mourn the passing of the "old sort"), and the grave-diggers (who dislike Charles Wilcox, though they know this is not the time to speak of it). The wood-cutter fells the branch, and as he leaves the graveyard, he steals a flower from the grave to give to his girlfriend. As he passes the grave in the morning, "after a night of joy," he regrets that he had not taken all the lilies and chrysanthemums the night before.

The morning at Howards End is taken up with silent diners at the breakfast table. Mr. Wilcox has chosen to dine in his room and is only drawn out of his funk by the morning mail, which brings an astonishing letter from Mrs. Wilcox with a cover letter from the head of the nursing home where she spent her last days. Her penciled and unsigned letter wills all of Howards End to Margaret Schlegel. Faced with a problem of this magnitude, Mr. Wilcox and Charles are in their element. They consider legality, the state of mind of Ruth Wilcox when she composed the letter, and they conclude that the house should not go to Margaret Schlegel. Charles and Evie are suspicious of Margaret, believing that she somehow influenced their mother to give away the house. Mr. Wilcox is more generous and concludes that Margaret has no doubt been as duped as they in this whole matter. Margaret Schlegel's innocence in the whole affair is confirmed at the beginning of the next chapter when we are told that she had never heard of Ruth Wilcox's "strange request." Indeed, we learn that she will only hear of it years later, when it will become central to her life. At the time that the Wilcoxes receive the letter, Margaret is concerned with whether or not she and her siblings will be able to find a suitable new home when the lease expires on Wickham Place.

Leonard Bast, the young man who lost his umbrella to Helen, reenters the Schlegel's lives and stays with them throughout the rest of the novel. Jacky, who is now his wife, suddenly arrives at Wickham Place in search of her husband, who has not been home for two days. Helen finds the whole scene quite humorous, but it depresses Margaret; she reflects that Jacky "had risen out of the abyss, like a faint smell, a goblin footfall, telling of a life where love and hatred had both decayed" (119). In the next chapter we learn from Mr. Bast, who arrives to apologize for his wife's visit, that he had set out walking into the country and had walked all night, attempting to follow the polar star. The sisters are charmed, and applaud Mr. Bast's adventurousness. They find a great potential in him when he does not rely on books to interpret his experience but simply tells of his adventure.

Following Leonard's visit, the sisters attend a dinner party with a debate society that they belong to. The subject of debate that evening is a question of where an imaginary wealthy person should leave her considerable fortune. The case of Leonard Bast is much discussed. The members of the party debate how one might best help a man of Mr. Bast's limited means in order to nurture his potential: Should he be given money? No money but opportunity? Food? Books? Return tickets to Venice? The evening does not resolve the question, and the sisters leave still debating the subject. As they head home, the sisters encounter Mr. Henry Wilcox, who has grown quite rich and well-established since his wife's death. They put their question to him. He asks what work Mr. Bast does and where he works. When they tell him that Mr. Bast is a clerk for Porphyrion Fire Insurance, Mr. Wilcox says that he cannot say what to do with the imagined inheritance, but that Mr. Bast should clear out of Porphyrion, for he knows that it is about to go bust.

In Chapter 16, the sisters invite Mr. Bast to tea. He eagerly joins, thinking that they will discuss books and ideas. As they have Leonard's financial well-being in mind, they grill him instead about the company that he works for and warn him of its instability. Just as Leonard Bast is reaching the peak of frustration with their interfering, Mr. Henry Wilcox and his daughter Evie are shown into the room. Leonard Bast storms out, insulting the sisters as he goes. Helen rebukes him for his rudeness, and all three engage in an argument. Leonard Bast accuses the sisters of trying to obtain secrets about his company so that they might benefit financially; they retort that they were trying to help them. Leonard tells them that he does not need their charity, and Margaret tries to clarify their position by reminding him that they have wanted to be his friend. Helen follows Mr. Bast out as he leaves the room, and Margaret is left with the Wilcoxes. Assuming a fatherly and businesslike manner, Mr. Wilcox warns Margaret against befriending men of Mr. Bast's "type." While she insists that he is not a "type," Mr. Wilcox asserts that she is too kind to people and does not treat them properly when she invites them to "forget themselves" and their stations in life. Margaret counters that she recognizes something special in Mr. Bast and wants to encourage that, rather than leave him in his "grey" life. Mr. Wilcox asks, "What right have you to conclude it is an unsuccessful life, or, as you call it, 'grey'?" (152). While Margaret attempts to defend her interest in Leonard Bast, she detects jealousy in Mr. Wilcox and recognizes for the first time that he is interested in her romantically. Still, neither is able to persuade the other to embrace the opposite position on Leonard Bast. The sisters affect a cheerful offhandedness about the whole event to appease their guests.

In the next four chapters, the relationship of Henry Wilcox and Margaret Schlegel grows in intimacy and purpose, concluding with their engagement. Their first "date" is arranged by Evie, who invites Margaret to have lunch with her and her fiancée. Margaret takes time from her house-hunting to join the couple and discovers Mr. Wilcox there as well. In the course of this and other such arranged meetings, Mr. Wilcox manages to ascertain that Margaret, for all her "intellectual" ideas, is not opposed to comfort or having money. For her part, Margaret finds much to like in Henry Wilcox. Not so her sister. Helen is appalled by the engagement and insists that it will mean "panic and emptiness" (180), a phrase she used when describing her reaction to the "goblin footfall" in Beethoven's Fifth symphony, signifying the erasure of "splendour and heroism" in the world (34). Margaret maintains that although Henry Wilcox lacks sympathy, is afraid of emotion, and "cares too much about success," she does not "intend him … to be all my life" (182). Margaret enters her engagement and eventual marriage pragmatically, keeping in proportion all the aspects of her life.

The next several chapters reveal the nature of Margaret's and Henry's developing relationship as they travel to Hertfordshire to see Charles and visit Howards End. In these chapters, Margaret is revealed as the advocate of connection. She sees Henry Wilcox completely and is not frightened or frustrated by his fear of passion. In fact, she is convinced that she can help him see the "salvation that was latent in his own soul…. Only connect! That was the whole of her sermon" (195). But the going is not easy for her. Henry Wilcox proves particularly obtuse to the subtleties of life. He does not see shades of color or meaning—only black and white.

When Helen receives a letter from Leonard Bast indicating that he has changed jobs on their advice and has been forced to take a much lower salary, she is outraged to hear Henry Wilcox praise Porphyrion, the very business Bast has left on Wilcox's advice. When Helen confronts him, he shakes it off. He tells Helen: "I'm grieved for your clerk. But it is all in the day's work. It's part of the battle of life" (199). Mr. Wilcox advises Helen not to take up a "sentimental attitude over the poor" and to avoid "absurd schemes of Social Reform" (199–200). Helen dismisses Henry Wilcox as the type of man she despises, one of the type of men who have "reconciled science with religion" and therefore believe that good can come of their ruthless and inhumane business practices. Helen promises Margaret that she will do her best to be polite to Henry, and she assures Margaret that she will always love her sister but intends to go her "own way" (203).

Even after this exchange with Helen, Margaret is undaunted by the challenge of bridging the gap between Henry's extreme callousness and her compassion for others. She even holds out hope that she might help Helen and Henry to appreciate each other one day. Margaret observes that Helen, too, is following an extreme path, though hers is quite in the opposite direction of Henry's. Margaret pursues balance and proportion. She feels that both Henry and Helen fail to make the effort to know both "metaphysics" and "the absolute" respectively. According to Margaret, truth was only to be found "by continuous excursions into either realm" (203). Proportion, to her mind is the "final secret." The emerging balance that Margaret struggles to find is available in the country, specifically Howards End. Upon her first visit there, Margaret experiences a calm that she feels London lacks, with all its speed and emphasis on "bigness," which is not the same thing as "space." Space, she realizes is the basis for "all earthly beauty" (213). Recapturing this sense of space, Margaret discovers an "unexpected love" of England, "connecting" reality with the "inconceivable" (214). This is the beginning of Margaret's powerful connection with Howards End.

The next few chapters focus on Evie's marriage and, specifically, Margaret's role in the preparations and ceremony. Margaret discovers that she is to figure prominently in the event as the fiancée of Evie's father. Margaret and Henry are walking about after the wedding and reflecting upon its success when they notice the arrival of what appear to be some townspeople come too late to the event. Margaret tells Henry that she will deal with them and rushes forward only to discover her sister and the Basts. Helen shouts that the Basts are starving because Leonard Bast has lost his position at the bank as they have had to downsize. She says, "We upper classes have ruined him" (234). Hell-bent to make Henry Wilcox own his responsibility for the predicament of the Basts, Helen says that she will "show up the wretchedness that lies under this luxury" (234). Observing the "perverted" nature of her philanthropy, bringing the Basts all the way from London to Shropshire, Margaret urges Helen to take the Basts to the Inn in Oniton, suggesting that this downturn will pass and he will find new work. But Leonard Bast was "near the abyss, and at such moments men see clearly" (237). He speaks up:

"I shall never get work now. If rich people fail at one profession, they can try another. Not I" (237). Margaret manages to send the Basts and Helen off to the hotel in town and persuades Henry to see Leonard Bast and consider him for a position with his firm. She negotiates this settlement with Henry using the most traditional of feminine techniques, entirely aware that she gains her victory "by the methods of the harem" (240). Yet, Margaret recognizes that she hovers in the gulf between Henry, or, "men as they are," and her sister Helen, who yearns for truth (241). Margaret seeks to bridge this gulf, even though, "on the whole, she sided with the men as they are" because they will save the Basts while "Helen and her friends were discussing the ethics of salvation" (241).

Yet "men as they are" have other aspects of their character as well. When Henry and Margaret discover that Mrs. Bast has been left to dine on the left-over wedding food and drink while Helen and Mr. Bast go to town to engage rooms, Henry's past is revealed. As Henry attempts to remove the drunken Mrs. Bast, she recognizes him and calls him "Hen." Enraged that Margaret and Helen have trapped him, and assuming that they have long known of his past with Jacky, Henry releases Margaret from their engagement. Though troubled by the news of an affair he had with Jacky ten years before while he was in Cyprus, Margaret calculates that it is not between them but between Henry and his first wife. Assessing the situation with the Basts as impossibly complicated, she sends two letters to the Georges hotel in Oniton; one informs Leonard Bast that Mr. Wilcox has no position available for him at this time, and the other asks Helen to leave the Basts at once and return to Mr. Wilcox's home to sleep. The next morning, Margaret assures Henry of her forgiveness and desire to put the past behind them. He tells her the story of his liaison with Jacky, protesting that he is no good. Margaret, for her part "played the girl, until he could rebuild his fortress and hide his soul from the world" (258). Thus, they collaborate to restore the equilibrium of their relationship, each playing a familiar role. As Margaret and Henry restore their balance, Helen and Leonard succumb to a moment of passion at the Inn while Jacky sleeps off her drink.

Chapter 30 finds Tibby in his rooms at Oxford, studying Chinese and awaiting his lunch. He is greeted by a "pathetic yet dignified" Helen who has appeared to ask favors of him. As they dine, she tells him of the events that led her to Oniton with the Basts and of her discovery of Mr. Wilcox's affair with Jacky. She indicates that she is leaving England and would have him do her two favors: the first is to decide whether or not to tell Margaret of Henry's liaison with Jacky (Helen assumes Margaret does not know about this) and the second is to facilitate the delivery of 5,000 pounds from her estate to the Basts. When Tibby protests at the enormous amount, Helen echoes the position she took when the idea of giving money to the poor was merely a topic of discussion for her debate group: "What is the good of driblets?" (266). Tibby agrees to her requests and sends 100 pounds to the Basts, indicating that much more is to follow. The Basts, for their part, refuse the money. At Helen's request, Tibby goes to redeliver the money in person, only to find that the Basts are nowhere to be found, having been thrown out of their lodgings because they did not pay the rent.

Meanwhile, Margaret's Aunt Juley has contracted pneumonia and looks as if she may not live. Tibby and Margaret head to Swanage to be with their aunt, and they write to Helen of her illness. Helen arrives in London, but she cannot stay, and she will not allow herself to be seen by her sister and brother. Hearing that her aunt is recovering, she says that she will not see her but asks where she can find the family furniture (which is being stored at Howards End for the time being) so that she might procure a few of her belongings before she leaves England again. Tibby and Margaret attempt to arrange a face-to-face visit with Helen and fail. In desperation, they seek Henry's advice, and he hatches a plan to "entrap" her at Howards End, where she will be directed to go to collect her belongings. On the appointed day, as Margaret drives to Howards End with Henry and a doctor, she grows quite nervous. She slips ahead of them when they arrive and has time to discern that Helen is pregnant. Quickly, she unlocks the house and scoots Helen inside before Henry and the doctor arrive at the door. She asks them to let her handle Helen. With news of Helen's state from the driver of her cab, Henry and the doctor leave reluctantly. At first, Margaret and Helen are awkward with each other; but slowly the house and all their belongings begin to work on them and they decide that they should spend one night together in Howards End before Helen leaves England for good. Margaret asks Henry if she and Helen might spend this one night at Howards End. Henry refuses and will not bend to Margaret's pleading. Fed up with the superior stand he takes, Margaret reminds him that he has sinned like Helen: "You shall see the connection if it kills you, Henry! You have had a mistress—I forgave you. My sister has a lover—you drive her from the house. Do you see the connection?" (322). But Henry does not see and counters that Margaret is attempting to blackmail him. Margaret leaves him and returns to her sister at Howards End, fully convinced that her marriage has ended.

The next several chapters track the paths of Charles Wilcox and Leonard Bast until they collide at Howards End. Charles meets with Tibby at Ducie Street and seeks to uncover the name of Helen's "seducer." Entirely unwittingly, Tibby casts suspicion on Leonard Bast. Charles leaves in a fury. Later that night, his father shares with him Margaret's decision to spend the night at Howards End with her sister. Charles agrees to go up early the next morning and demand that they should leave at once. Leonard Bast is also headed for Howards End that morning. Since Helen left him at the Inn in Oniton, he and Jacky have been able to live on handouts from his family. Tortured by his sexual liaison with Helen, he lives in a state of remorse. As chance might have it, he had spotted Margaret recently in London. This chance sighting inspires him to confess his sin to her. Thus, he sets out to find her and ends up at Howards End at the same time that Charles, already suspicious of Leonard Bast, has arrived to remove the Schlegel sisters. In a scene of confusion, Helen spies Leonard and cries out his name; Charles turns, grabs a sword that hangs on the wall, and strikes Leonard twice. Leonard reaches out to steady himself on a bookshelf and manages to pull it down upon himself. He dies under a pile of books. At the inquest, Charles is pronounced guilty of manslaughter. Henry Wilcox is broken and "ended" by this. He turns to Margaret for comfort and succor. Following her instincts, she takes Henry and Helen to Howards End where they might recover from their "illnesses."

The final chapter begins with the cutting of the big meadow at Howards End, an event that would have pleased the first Mrs. Wilcox (whose spirit permeates the house and the "family" there). It is 14 months since Leonard Bast's death, and his son plays in the grass with Tom, a farmer's son. Margaret and Helen are nearby. Helen praises Margaret for settling things so well. She imagines what her life and Henry's life would have been like if Margaret had not rescued them. "You picked up the pieces and made us a home," she tells Margaret (354). For her part, Margaret knows that there have been other forces at work in "settling" them all. As they chat, Henry is inside with Paul and Evie and Dolly, arranging to leave Howards End to Margaret exclusively. When she enters and they all agree to this arrangement, Dolly blurts, "It does seem curious that Mrs. Wilcox should have left Margaret Howards End, and yet she gets it, after all" (358). When Henry later explains this remark to Margaret she is not angry, but "something shook her life in its inmost recesses" (358). Throughout her years with the Wilcoxes she has felt Ruth Wilcox's presence. She articulated this feeling to Helen on the night they stayed at Howards End: "I feel that you and I and Henry are only fragments of that woman's mind. She knows everything. She is everything. She is the house, and the tree that leans over it.... She knew about realities" (328). Margaret's feelings about Ruth Wilcox are confirmed on the day that Henry tells her of Ruth's intention to leave her Howards End.

CHARACTER DEVELOPMENT

The epigraph to this novel is "Only connect." Margaret Schlegel emerges as the symbol of connection between the two worlds in this novel—two worlds that are broadly represented by the Wilcoxes and the Schlegels. At the beginning of the novel, Margaret is obviously the more mature and pragmatic Schlegel sister. She can appreciate the wisdom of Mrs. Wilcox's deep connection with Howards End and her refusal to confuse her life with politics. Yet she can become passionately engaged in questions of social justice and feels the pain of failure when she does not make a connection with Leonard Bast on their first meeting. She walks delicately between the extremes and seeks to find a way that connects the best of both. With her appreciation of duty and certain English values, Margaret is poised to accept Henry Wilcox's marriage proposal, yet she hopes to make something better over time with the connection they forge. Margaret represents the middle way between the humanism and liberalism that drives Helen to extreme and irrational action and the heartless mercantilism on which Henry's life and work are built. At the conclusion of the novel, one sees the fruit of the connections that Margaret has made: Leonard's and Helen's son will inherit Howards End, while Wilcoxes will continue to breed and prosper. Furthermore, Helen and Henry and all of the differences they represent now coexist peacefully with Margaret at Howards End.

Helen Schlegel is revealed in the very beginning of the novel to be passionate and flighty. Her misalliance with Paul Wilcox is the result of the degree to which she allowed romance and sentimentality to overshadow reason. In fact, her easy dismissal of her own passionately held socialist and feminist beliefs in the face of Henry Wilcox's mocking pragmatism early in the novel reveals her inconstancy. Ultimately, she comes to represent an extreme in the novel: She is the example of extreme humanism and liberalism without a firm foundation; she represents feelings without pragmatism. Her wild flight to the wedding at Oniton with the starving Basts in tow is an example of this extremism, as is her fling with Leonard. She acts impulsively and fails to consider the broader picture as she makes her judgments of the world and people around her. In fact, Helen appears quite selfish and solitary in her conviction that we should privilege relationships and social justice. She ends up embarrassing and hurting people, isolating herself from those who love her and refusing to see the subtleties of the world around her if they require her to acknowledge that the approach of men like Henry Wilcox might have some merits.

Henry Wilcox, for his part, becomes the extreme example of mercantilism and conservative social and political values; he represents pragmatism without feeling. He is clearly a successful and established business man, an example of what duty and hard work and class can earn in the world. He upholds all the "right" values, reinforces the ethics of Empire, and tends to his family as he might a flock of sheep. Yet, his contact with the Schlegels changes him. He comes to appreciate a quieter and more connected life, one that roots him to the land. Although it can be argued that Henry Wilcox is not so much changed by the end of the novel as broken, his decision to leave Howards End to Margaret, so that she might leave it to Helen's child, is that of a man with hope for the future.

Leonard Bast is a tragic character, like his wife Jacky. On the extreme edge of the middle class, he represents the many who struggle life-long to reach the comforts that others are given at birth. His death symbolizes the crushing of the "little man" by the machinery of progress, which is driven by the Wilcoxes of the world. It leaves the reader wondering what Forster wanted us to make of this character. Does he serve merely to represent a set of ideas, a social problem? Or is he a full and developed character with passions or concerns independent of any agenda that the novel might promote? Leonard is revealed to us as a man who, before he connects with the Schlegels, might have had the chance to slowly improve his station in life. One can imagine that he would gradually rise in his company to a more secure and tenured position and that he and Jacky might be able to find better lodgings and a more comfortable domestic life. Bast is killed by passions, feelings, ideals. He is killed by the sword, representing impulse, and by books, representing ideas. The death of this young idealist at the hands of passion and ideals conveys the message that when humans cannot forgive, they kill.

Schlegels or not, Leonard Bast is trapped by the circumstances of the world he was born into and the one bad choice he made: his relationship with Jacky. Where Jacky might shackle a man like Leonard, Henry Wilcox could shake her off and forget about her as he might forget other "exotic" adventures he had while in Cyprus. Jacky is also a victim of economic and historical forces. A more agrarian time might have offered her a good living on the land, when she could have enjoyed a house and a family. Her gender also counts against her. Jacky is the victim of a patriarchal society. She has been marked by her "use" at the hands of men like Henry Wilcox: There is no future for such a woman unless, of course, she was to choose to make a "profession" out of her experience as a lover of wealthy men. Jacky may be one of the most unfairly treated characters in the novel. She is mocked by the Schlegel sisters, used by Henry Wilcox, and, ultimately, left to her own devices after Leonard dies. Not even Forster pays her much attention. Contemporary sensibilities might well lead readers to protest that Forster has not been fair to this character. She is scorned by all, even her author.

Ruth Wilcox is an enigmatic character. She is, on the one hand, an example of a passing generation—the values it held for the land and for the communal connections of country life. She is, on the other hand, an example of the obedient wife who willingly allows her husband to make all decisions relating to economics and politics. As such, she is a troubling figure for Margaret, who would find a path that allows her more autonomy and self-direction. Still, it is Margaret who recognizes a deeper wisdom within Mrs. Wilcox. After Mrs. Wilcox's death Margaret repeatedly feels her presence and grants it a sort of mystical power and authority. Indeed, the transformations in the novel are all set into motion by Ruth Wilcox's death and by her request that Howards End be left to Margaret Schlegel. She is a shadowy figure who is instrumental in shifting the reins of power from the hands of the conservative and patriarchal Henry to the gentler hands of Margaret Schlegel, thus ensuring a future for the Bast-Schlegel child.

Charles Wilcox is neither as savvy and capable as his father, nor as gentle and patient as his mother. Indeed, he is a pompous, reactive prig whom one enjoys disliking. One might argue that Forster has created an insignificant or flat character upon whom to pin the evils of the British public school and mercantilist class. Charles does take a beating for this group. Because he is never quite a complete character to begin with, one cannot be sure that he is transformed by experience one way or another. Like Charles, his wife Dolly, sister Evie, and brother Paul are minor characters who represent their class and upbringing more than anything else. Tibby Schlegel and Aunt Juley are also relatively minor characters who do not change in the course of the novel but function to allow insight into the worlds inhabited by the central characters. These characters represent the stable worlds from which the central characters emerge.

THEMES, SYMBOLS, AND MOTIFS

Howards End is a deft exploration of critical issues facing England during Forster's time: the erosion of liberal values, urban and imperial expansion, and the division between classes. In part, this novel is important because it deals with so many dichotomies found in modern existence: liberalism versus conservativism, culture versus capitalism, and country life versus city life. But, most importantly, this novel deals with the dichotomy between passion and pragmatism. When Lionel Trilling first offered his careful reading of this novel half a century ago, he saw these dichotomies as caught within the key question, "Who shall inherit England?" In his interpretation, these dualities come down to a question of class struggle: Will the Wilcoxes or the

Basts inherit England, or will the liberal intellectual class, represented by the Schlegels, offer a middle way? One might also posit the question in terms of the ideals of pragmatism and feelings: Which will inherit England: pragmatism or passion? Or will Margaret Schlegel help to create a middle way? No matter which question you choose, the novel explores the possibility of connection and balance. With *Howards End*, Forster clearly envisions a change wrought by attention to relationships rather than attention to political or social movements, a change achieved by an adherence to a moral philosophy like G. E. Moore's, which was so influential in Forster's life.

The novel begins with the two enigmatic words "Only connect." The reader is not allowed to forget this theme as it is embraced and reiterated by Margaret and Helen Schlegel throughout the novel. Indeed, this edict is at the center of Margaret Schlegel's personal philosophy: When her sister broods on the conflict between the visible features of the world (the material) and the unseen (the spiritual and symbolic), Margaret reminds her, "our business is not to contrast the two, but to reconcile them" (108). "Connection" is Margaret's approach to Henry Wilcox as she tries to lead him to see the "salvation that was latent in his own soul." As Forster says, "Only connect! That was the whole of her sermon. Only connect the prose and the passion, and both will be exalted, and human love will be seen at its heights" (195). Throughout the novel, characters are evaluated by how well they do or do not connect, reiterating the dichotomous nature of the world around them.

But the novel makes other connections. Helen's and Leonard's physical connection brings both the death of Leonard and the birth of a child. One might logically ask whether Leonard had to die so that his son might one day inherit Howards End. Does Forster mean to suggest that one class must die in order to give way to a new and, as Trilling would argue, "classless" society? If so, we might also interpret Henry Wilcox's broken state at the end of the novel as a form of death, as he said to Margaret when he heard of Charles' imminent incarceration: "I'm broken—I'm ended" (350). With Charles in prison, Henry subdued, and Leonard dead, they become noncombatants in class struggle. Rising out of these changed circumstances is a curious menagerie at Howard's End: Henry Wilcox, the broken symbol of pure pragmatism; Helen Schlegel, the one-time representation of pure liberal ideals; Margaret Schlegel, the one who represents the balance of pragmatism and idealism; and Helen and Leonard's offspring, who is in a position to inherit the country estate. Clearly connections have been made and the unseen made visible. The child who is born as a symbol of "connection" will inherit England.

But England is a large and changing country, and this novel was written in a time when change was everywhere. The peace that Howards End comes to represent is a hopeful ideal with a limited chance of success. Indeed, Paul Wilcox comments at the end of the novel that it is "not really the country, and it's not the town," suggesting that urban sprawl has already begun to encroach upon this idyll. The changing demographics of the country are elsewhere reflected in the novel repeatedly: The Schlegels are forced to vacate the house they have lived in since they were children because the landlord wants to build new flats. Henry Wilcox occupies three houses in the course of the novel and is in search of a fourth when circumstances send him to Howards End. And Leonard and Jacky are examples of the difficulties of finding adequate, inexpensive housing in an urban center as they move from poverty to destitution. These changes in housing reflect the larger economic changes in England of the time. As imperialism was decreasing, capitalism and mercantilism were expanding, and a new, business-driven imperialism was emerging. The novel repeatedly draws our attention to the modern pleasure in "bigness" and speed, where the automobile is ever bigger, ever faster. Yet the novel is also critical of these as elements of the seen world that obscure the unseen: The elements of progress get in the way of meaningful human relationships.

Even as this novel concludes with an image of connection and the change it can bring, however tenuous, it is replete with dualities that seem irreconcilable. Margaret and Helen both repeatedly observe the differences between wealthy and poor: "To trust people is a luxury in which only the wealthy can indulge; the poor cannot afford it" is what Margaret realizes when she first encounters Leonard Bast's distrust over the affair with the umbrella (36). Life diminished by poverty is represented in Margaret's thoughts as an "abyss" or "squalor" conveyed through the motif of goblins. Insight into this abyss and squalor is what the sisters and Leonard share. Indeed, as Daniel Born has argued, the term "the abyss" had a very specific and historically relevant definition that would have been familiar to Forster's first audience. It was the term that the liberal journalist C. F. G. Masterman coined in 1902 for the urban poor living in London. Jack London also wrote about the inhabitants of the "abyss" in *The People of the Abyss*, a narrative of his experience living in London in 1903 (Born). Clearly, Forster was rooting his description of Leonard and the world he sought to escape in familiar descriptions of the contemporary London scene. The Schlegels can see the abyss because they are sensitive and intellectually curious. Thus, Helen observes, "I began to think that the very soul of the world is economic and that the lowest abyss is not the absence of love, but the absence of coin" (63). Throughout the novel this abyss is variously referred to as "beneath the waves," "the submerged," or "greyness." The Schlegels and Leonard Bast turn away from their glimpses of this squalor; it contrasts starkly with the small and "obscure" life and world "gilded with tranquility" that they have created at Howards End by the end of the novel (352).

Though they may rarely see the abyss or the goblins, the work of the industrialist Wilcoxes and their ilk contributes to creating them: "But the imperialist is not what he thinks or seems. He is a destroyer. He prepares the way for cosmopolitanism, and though his ambitions may be fulfilled, the earth he inherits will be grey" the narrator tells us (339). There is some implication at the end of the novel that Henry Wilcox is not only broken by his son's incarceration for the murder of Leonard Bast but also by his glimpse of the unseen world. Margaret tells Helen that Henry is tired: "He has worked very hard all his life and noticed nothing. Those are the people who collapse when they do notice a thing" (352). Having noticed something of the "unseen world," Henry has collapsed. Henry's "collapse" is a step toward the future that Helen's and Leonard's child represents—both pure pragmatism and pure idealism must die for a balance to survive.

One central theme around which much of the imagery and symbolism of this novel revolves is the contrast between the abyss and economic stability. Thus, the goblin footfall that Helen hears when she listens to Beethoven's Fifth Symphony is a threat that chaos and emptiness lie beneath the beauty of life. "They were not aggressive creatures; it was that that made them so terrible to Helen. They merely observed in passing that there was no such thing as splendour or heroism in the world" (34). "Panic and emptiness" are the two words often repeated by the sisters when they glimpse this world without splendor. For both Helen and Margaret, the goblins lurk when their vision of the world seems particularly threatened or fragile, and they are reminded that their very comfort is in part bought by the Leonard Basts of the world.

Leonard, then, is a symbolic character insofar as he represents that proximity of the abyss and the squalor that goes with it. He reminds both Helen and Margaret that their life of comfort and ease is purchased at his expense. To this, Helen responds with her characteristic, impulsive passion, seeking to secure him a safer position with a new company before Porphyrion folds. And it is Helen who is headlong in her pursuit of Henry Wilcox as the one responsible for Bast's economic fall when he loses that new position. She clearly sees the connection between the secure and safe world of Henry Wilcox and the precarious existence of Leonard Bast. In seeing this, she invites the readers to see both Bast and Wilcox as symbolic of larger communities toiling in the same struggle between power and powerlessness.

Another theme essential to the novel is the contrasting imagery and symbolism of the seen and the unseen, wherein the seen is the everyday surface business of life, and the unseen is the life of the spirit and the soul. Margaret and Helen have access to the unseen; indeed, it is the work of their life to "reconcile" the seen and unseen. The Wilcoxes, save Ruth, are symbolic of those who observe only the "seen" world, the world of propriety, business, and manners. They "avoided the personal note in life. All Wilcoxes did. It did not seem to them of supreme importance" (96).

The novel offers another, perhaps lesser, dichotomy in the contrast between London and the "progress" it represents and the simple life of the country. London is fast changing: "And month by month the roads smelt more strongly of petrol, and were more difficult to cross, and human beings heard each other speak with greater difficulty, breathed less of the air, and saw less of the sky" (112). The progress that so many applauded with the advent of the modern is much disparaged throughout Forster's treatment of the city as a fast-paced place where people only speak in short, clipped sentences and "potted expressions." This place of haste and destruction is contrasted to the grand English countryside that Margaret falls in love with when she first visits Howards End. In the novel, Howards End becomes explicitly symbolic of the fecundity of the natural world, a world of a possible future wherein people who embody connected dichotomies have a say in the future of England.

This future may not come to pass for any but the lucky few, but Forster does unabashedly ask us to imagine it. The novel ends with unrepentant Wilcoxes offering what sounds very much like final farewells and the new inhabitants of Howards End celebrating the harvesting of the hay. Clearly a symbolic ending, this nevertheless leaves the reader wondering about the future of these people, if not the future of England. And it is in an exploration of the narrative techniques that Forster uses that we can discern the degree to which he intended to create this anxiety in his readers.

LITERARY STYLE

E. M. Forster has commonly been considered a "novelist of manners" like Jane Austen, a writer to whom he acknowledged a great debt. Mannerists explored the social customs of a specific social group in detail, showing the enormous control these customs or manners have over their characters. Although often satirical, the novel of manners is always realistic. Certainly Forster's first three novels engaged intimately with the social interaction of a specific class in a particular place, usually, in Forster's case, the English middle class abroad. His novels are perhaps also mannerist in their realistic and occasionally satiric style.

Forster is a modern figure, caught up in a historical moment of profound global and national change. His prose features some of the curious shifts in narrative perspective and the reliance upon symbolism that we might expect of Modernist authors, but Forster does not see that through to any radical break with traditional prose. Rather, Forster's Modernism was in his moral philosophy and his refusal to pin down the various dichotomies of Modern existence to which his fiction gives voice. He sought to unveil the moral and philosophical challenges of modernity without necessarily foreclosing on the multiplicity of conclusions one might draw from that unveiling.

Forster's liberalism was not so much a political stance as a personal moral philosophy that supported individual freedom. Forster was deeply distrustful of collective movements and organizations. He believed in the individual above all and felt that collectives tended to diminish the beauty and power of the individual. It is to Forster's liberalism, specifically his belief in the value of individuals and human relationships, that this realistic novel gives voice. It does so by focusing on three households and the interactions of the members of those households, most importantly Henry Wilcox, Margaret and Helen Schlegel, and Leonard Bast. These characters are symbolic of polarized social values, like conservative mercantilism and liberal humanism. They are also important to the novel as individuals, and for the relationships they forge, relationships that foster a community that is not based on familial inheritance or class as much as in a commitment to balance and personal connection.

The narrative begins with a gesture that one might interpret as either a throwback to Victorian novelistic techniques or narratorial "intrusion," whereby the narrator calls attention to his omniscient position and directs how the reader is to receive the forthcoming story: "One may as well begin with Helen's letters to her sister" (3). This introductory sentence preceding the three letters from Helen to Margaret suggests several things. On the one hand, it suggests that the action is now finished and that where one takes up the story is relatively insignificant. It also suggests that the narrator knows the meaning of the story in its entirety and is in a position to make these judgments about where to begin. The narrator is inviting the reader to trust his decision to begin with Helen's letters.

This sort of narratorial intrusion recurs throughout the novel, "puzzling" the reader, or merely leading her to "hesitate," as Virginia Woolf observed at the time. Upon receiving the note from his deceased wife, indicating that she would have him leave Howards End to Margaret Schlegel, for example, Henry and the Wilcox family engage in a discussion from which we are removed by the narrator's comment "and the discussion moved towards its close. To follow it is unnecessary. It is rather a moment when the commentator should step forward" (102). The narrator does step forward and asks whether the Wilcoxes should have offered their home to Margaret. He concludes that they should not have. The episode leads us to wonder about the ethical responsibilities that the living have to uphold the requests of the deceased. The narrator's intrusion does not settle our anxiety but rather provokes it, inviting us to consider the matter further and taking us away from an engagement with the characters. This is a gesture for which Virginia Woolf and others have criticized Forster. But it is quite possible that Forster wanted to provoke this sort of discomfort and distrust to remind his reader that, particularly in a world where so much is in chaos, including religion and moral authority, there are no single answers to such questions. What keeps the narrator's intrusions from becoming a mimicry of the Victorian narrator of old is the degree to which Forster's narrator refuses to remain authoritative. Where the intrusive narrator of Victorian prose would have us see his or her command of all the elements of the fiction, Forster's narrator freely invites us to see the story proceed without him.

Another narrative technique that is distinctly modern is the "free indirect discourse," which, as we see in the work of both Woolf and Joyce, blurs the narrative point of view and allows readers to experience the immediate perceptions of the characters without the intrusion of an omniscient narrator. Free indirect discourse is a combination of two modes of discourse: direct discourse and indirect discourse. Using direct discourse, Forster writes, for example, "'Oh, hooray!,' said Margaret" (7). As is common with direct discourse in fiction, this is a clear statement attributed by quotation marks to the named character. Indirect discourse, in contrast, is not usually spoken by the character it addresses; usually it is a character or the narrator paraphrasing what another has said. Free indirect discourse, then, occurs when characters' thoughts are woven into the narrative fabric in such a way that it becomes difficult to tell whether the prose reflects the narrator's perspective, the thoughts of a character, or the thoughts of someone else about that character. Thus, the narrator follows the above direct discourse with this: "But she did not want to receive anything expensive.... She did not want to be thought a second Helen, who would snatch presents since she could not snatch young men" (83). This free-indirect discourse allows the narrator's comments and Margaret's thoughts to merge in such a way that it is difficult to discern whose perspective is being advanced. Is Margaret genuinely anxious about how she might be perceived by the Wilcoxes, or is this an opportunity for the narrator to reveal the Wilcox view of the Schlegel sisters? Or is it both? This is the destabilizing beauty of free-indirect discourse.

Yet another destabilizing narrative technique employed by Forster is the "double turn," a term first advanced by the critic Lionel Trilling. Trilling tells us that this technique emphasizes the "something else that lies behind" and springs from Forster's respect for "two facts co-existing" (*HE* Norton 329). Forster's tendency to represent two coexisting facts through the double turn is evidenced throughout *Howards End*. A notable example of this occurs as we watch Leonard Bast struggling to "form his style on Ruskin" (51). The comic tone is clear as Leonard tries to work a Ruskin passage describing a Venetian church into a description of his shabby basement flat. But Forster offers the double turn when he has Leonard interrupt his own efforts: "'My flat is dark as well as stuffy.' Those were the words for him" (51). Here, the fact of Leonard's real life collides uncomfortably with the fact that he seeks to improve himself through his study of Ruskin, a man "who had never been dirty or hungry, and had not guessed successfully what dirt and hunger are" (52). Indeed, this double turn leads us further to reflect on Forster, the author of independent means and a secure position in the middle class depicting the life of a man of the extreme lower middle class.

The narrator not only calls attention to his presence and challenges us to see the competing facts at work in this novel; he often seems to be directing our attention to the staged quality of this drama. For example, in the scene following their evening debate at the women's club, Margaret and Helen take a seat on a bench by the Chealsea Embankment. The narrator relates, "As Margaret and Helen sat down, the city behind them seemed to be a vast theatre, an opera-house in which some endless trilogy was performing, and they themselves a pair of satisfied subscribers" (135). Here the narrative invites us to see Margaret and Helen as, in a sense, ourselves, although they are the subscribers to a theatre production whereas we are readers. Similarly, in a scene in which Charles is holding forth about the Schlegels and their supposed desire to get Howards End, the narrator draws a close to Charles's speech by stating, "The interlude closes. It has taken place in Charles's garden at Hilton. He and Dolly are sitting in deck-chairs" (193). This shift introduces the language of stage directions and refuses to offer the smooth prose transitions that might invite the reader to remain inside the fictional world. Instead, we are called outside to observe its staging. We are thereby reminded that Charles and Dolly are characters in a fiction. Both of these scenes call the reader to attend to the staging of the fiction we are "reading" and remind us to be alert to layers of meaning.

HISTORICAL CONTEXT

The specific context for this novel is late Edwardian England, a time and place of social change and growing apprehension about a possible war in

Europe. The Edwardians were confidently dismantling the pillars of Victorian propriety, challenging the rule of God and the strict moral code known today as simply "Victorian." Women were actively pursuing the right to vote. The liberals in government were losing their authority, and socialism was on the rise. In London there was widespread and rapid economic and social change that led to "urban sprawl" and diminished the importance of the countryside and the country life. In this world Forster is a sensitive observer, noting the changes and, in part, longing for an earlier time and values that pertained to it.

This nostalgia is not unique to Forster. His desires are directly related to the historical circumstances of the early twentieth-century expansion and change in British society. Many Modernists struggled with the rapid changes in social, moral, and political structure in their world. Although none would embrace a simple return to the stability of, say, the Victorian world, most Modernists found themselves critical of many aspects of change that they observed. Thus, Forster was not comfortable with the expansion of the city and the squalor that it generated. This is the world from which Margaret Schlegel willingly retreats.

3

James Joyce
A Portrait of the Artist as a Young Man
(1916)

BIOGRAPHICAL CONTEXT

James Joyce was born in Dublin, Ireland, on February 2, 1882. As the oldest of 10 children, he was the only one to benefit from his father's fast diminishing prosperity. Because he was the eldest, there was still money available for him to attend some of Dublin's best schools and establish a reputation for academic excellence, which afforded him scholarships and access to University College well after his father's fortune had been wasted. When he finished college, Joyce went to Paris for a time, intending to study medicine. He soon found himself more interested in writing, spending a great deal of his time in Paris formulating his aesthetic theories. Joyce returned to Dublin in 1903, when he learned of his mother's fatal illness.

Joyce began work on self-portraiture in prose form shortly after the death of his mother, in 1903. His first effort was an essay titled "A Portrait of the Artist," which had been commissioned by the magazine *Dana*. The editor rejected it, claiming that the essay was incomprehensible. This rejection led Joyce to his decision to expand the essay into a novel. First titled *Stephen Hero*, after 10 years of sporadic work, the novel finally became the much revised *A Portrait of the Artist as a Young Man*. Although critics argue about the merits of this first novel, it is arguably an essential first step in the path into experimental Modernism for Joyce. The novel is a bildungsroman in that it traces the growth and education of its central character, Stephen Dedalus. But it is much more than that. As we observe Stephen's life from infancy to young adulthood, the stylistic changes within the prose allow us to experience his developing consciousness. The Modernism of this gesture is evident: The prose probes and reflects the consciousness of the individual. In Joyce's later works, this reflection of consciousness through prose becomes radical as he continues to experiment. Perhaps the unifying desire behind Joyce's focus on individual consciousness in all his work is a desire to break from the constraints of history, society, country, and family. In A *Portrait*, Stephen Dedalus's concerns are consistent with this focus. Once he understands the restrictive nature of these institutions, he is essentially concerned with finding a way out. Indeed, in all that Joyce writes, one notices not only his effort to break away from the linguistic and psychological constraints of family, church, and state, but one is struck by the degree to which these institutions have shaped and influenced his voice.

What is biographically important about A *Portrait of the Artist as a Young Man* is its reflection, though fictionally transformed, of Joyce's early life and his history. Although this novel is by no means an autobiography, it is still highly autobiographical. Like Stephen Dedalus, James Joyce attended the prestigious Clongowes College until he was forced to withdraw because of his father's reduced financial circumstances. Joyce also attended Belvedere College and won a national award for an essay he wrote. Moreover, the increasing poverty of the Dedalus family and the father's trouble with drink and sloth mirror the Joyce household of James's youth. Most importantly, the growing antipathy that Stephen feels for the Catholic Church, for the institution of family, for British Imperialism in Ireland, and for Irish nationalism reflects Joyce's own frustration with the constraints Ireland placed on an artist.

Joyce met and courted Nora Barnacle in 1904. Unwilling to embrace marriage or the standards imposed by Irish society, which would have been violated by their living together as an unmarried couple, Joyce and Nora eloped to Pola in October of that same year. (At that time, Pola was a part of the Balkan coast belonging to the Austro-Hungarian Empire.) Ultimately, the couple moved to Trieste, where Joyce taught English in the Berlitz School. In July 1905, Nora gave birth to George. Thus began many years of struggle for Joyce. He tried to better support his family, moving them to Rome in 1906, where he was more lucratively employed as a bank clerk. The family returned to Trieste in March 1907, when Joyce felt he could not tolerate the bank job any longer. In July of that same year, Lucia Joyce was born. By all accounts, life in Italy during these years was marked by poverty and crowding for the family; they lived in poor quarters, which they were forced to change regularly when they could not pay the rent. Variously, they shared living space with Joyce's brother Stanislaus or friends who generously helped sustain the family.

In the midst of all this, Joyce continued to write. Between 1905 and 1907, Joyce worked on the stories that would ultimately compose *Dubliners,* a collection of stories that critics have argued "virtually invented the modern short story" (Wollaeger 3). Shortly after his first collection of poems, *Chamber Music,* was published in 1907, Joyce returned to work on the idea of portraiture in prose in *A Portrait of the Artist as a Young Man.* Joyce worked on this novel for the next seven years. In 1913, the American poet Ezra Pound sent a letter to Joyce seeking permission to publish one of the poems from *Chamber Music.* Thus began an important relationship for Joyce. Pound was enthusiastic about Joyce's writing and was instrumental in securing the first publication of *A Portrait,* a serialized version that appeared in an important London Journal, *The Egoist,* in 1914 and 1915. Finally, the novel was published in its entirety by the American publisher B.W. Huebsch in 1916.

PLOT SUMMARY

Composed of five chapters that trace Stephen Dedalus from infancy to young adulthood, the novel is structured episodically. Each chapter takes us through certain periods of Stephen's young life, introducing key events and focusing almost exclusively on Stephen's reactions, thoughts, and feelings. Most importantly, as Seamus Deane has pointed out in his excellent introduction to the 1992 Penguin edition, each chapter traces the protagonist's ability to articulate himself. The novel begins with other voices dominating Stephen's young consciousness. It is only as the novel progresses that we begin to witness Stephen's discovery of his own voice and his rejection of the definition put upon him by the voices of others, most notably by family, church, and state. As this shift occurs, the text becomes less dominated by others' voices and we hear more and more from Stephen Dedalus.

In chapter 1, however, we are in the thick of voices competing for Stephen's consciousness. The first lines of the novel are those of a story that Stephen's father tells him: "Once upon a time and a very good time it was there was a moocow coming down the road" (3). The narrative shifts from brief, orienting phrases from the infant Stephen to other fragments of song and speech that float into his consciousness from those around him: mother, father, Uncle Charles, and Dante Riordan (an aunt figure who appears to function as a governess in the Dedalus household).

The key to following the narrative flow of this chapter (if not the entire novel) is to watch Stephen's consciousness make meaning of spoken words and events he encounters. Thus, when we meet Dante Riordan on the first page, we immediately enter Stephen's consciousness as he offers information that he will later understand more completely: "Dante had two brushes in her press. The brush with the maroon velvet back was for Michael Davitt and the brush with the green velvet back was for Parnell" (3–4). Dante's nationalism is apparent in the velvet on her brushes: both Davitt and Parnell were Irish nationalists who fought for Home Rule. It is here evident that the young Stephen is sifting through physical and lexical signs to make sense of the world around him with the simplicity of a child's voice and consciousness. We are expected to heed these physical and lexical signs, for they are the details that make Stephen Dedalus who he is.

Signaled by ellipses, the chapter moves forward abruptly from cradle to youth. Now away at a boarding school, Stephen contemplates the "wide playgrounds" that are "swarming" with boys at Clongowes College, the best preparatory school in Ireland at the time. Stephen feels weak, small, and blind. He contemplates fellow classmates like Roddy Kickham, Nasty Roche, Wells, and Fleming, boys that frighten and tease young Stephen. Their words and mockeries are repeated in the text, and Stephen focuses on expressions and words that catch his interest: "Suck was a queer word," Stephen reflects when a classmate calls another by that name (8). As is his wont, Stephen traces his verbal and sensory associations with this word. It is largely because of this attention to the "obscene" details of life that the novel was originally considered by many to be lewd and indecent. For example, Stephen moves from thoughts about the ugly sound "suck" makes when spoken to memories of dirty water going down a drain and the sound it made going down. He then moves from mental reactions to physical: "To remember that and the white look of the lavatory made him feel cold and then hot…. And the air in the corridor chilled him too. It was queer and wettish" (8). This series of reflections, memories, and sensory reactions is quite typical of Stephen's narrative. In fact, when a classmate, Wells, mocks him for saying that he kisses his mother good night, Stephen's thoughts return to the previous day when Wells knocked him into the ditch by the playing fields. As the boys laugh at him for his sweetness, Stephen remembers the details of the ditch and the physical discomfort he experienced: "And how cold and slimy the water had been! And a fellow had once seen a big rat jump plop into the scum…. The cold slime of the ditch covered his whole body" (11). Stephen's descriptions of his physical sensations and perceptions reinforce the emotional discomfort he experiences at the hands of his rough schoolmates.

Structured like the disjointed and confused reactions of a child, chapter 1 delivers many such details about Stephen's life at Clongowes College and at home. We hear how small and weak Stephen feels among the other boys; we hear the sensory details of night prayers in the chapel; we hear of the discomforts and fears of bedtime in the dormitory. In one instance, the prose captures the feverish dreams of a sick Stephen in the infirmary. While there Stephen hears the priests talking about the death of Charles Stewart Parnell (which establishes the year of Stephen's attendance at Clongowes as 1891, the year that Joyce himself was nine years old). Parnell was an Irish political leader who had been called by many the "uncrowned King" of Ireland. He was the leading figure in the Home Rule movement in the late 1870s and was nearly able to engineer passage of a Home Rule Bill in 1886. Unfortunately, he fell from grace and political power when the public learned that he had been conducting a 10-year-long affair with Kitty O'Shea, the wife of a fellow politician. Joyce, and his father before him, were ardent supporters of Parnell and felt that his forced departure from politics was a travesty.

From the scene in the infirmary, we are abruptly transported to the Dedalus household on Christmas Day. At the table are Stephen, his parents, Uncle Charles, Dante Riordan, and Mr. Casey, a Fenian (an Irish revolutionary) and friend of the family. Shortly after the meal begins, an argument ensues between Dante (a religious conservative who has followed the Catholic Church in denouncing Parnell) and the men at the table, especially Simon Dedalus and John Casey. Both Mr. Dedalus and Mr. Casey criticize the bishops and priests for getting involved in politics with their condemnation of Parnell. Dante is deeply offended; her stance reflects the subordinated position that Joyce felt too many Irish took to the Church. The argument escalates to the point that Mr. Casey is shouting that the priests "broke Parnell's heart and hounded him to the grave" (33). Simon Dedalus calls them "sons of bitches" and "lowlived dogs" (33). The argument comes down to a disagreement about who is most loyal to Ireland, Parnell or the priests. Dante insists that, because he broke the laws of the church, Parnell was not loyal to Ireland, thus conflating the Church with Irish nationalism. "God and morality and religion first," she tells Mr. Casey (38). Mr. Casey counters with a denunciation that leads Dante to leave the room screaming that he is a "blasphemer." He says, "No God for Ireland! We have too much God in Ireland. Away with God" (39). Stephen is exhilarated by this altercation.

Again, the scene shifts abruptly and Stephen is back at school listening to fellow classmates talk about several older boys who had stolen wine from the sacristy. Throughout the talk of crimes and punishment, Stephen reflects variously on his broken glasses (which were knocked onto the cinder path by a boy sprinting past him), his fear of being flogged for the broken glasses, and the sounds of the cricket bats on the field. This last thought leads him to think about the pandybat that the priests use to hit the boys when they require punishing. This is followed by Stephen's struggle in Latin class without his glasses. Father Dolan, the prefect of studies, comes into the Latin classroom to see if there are "any lazy idle loafers that want flogging" (49). After flogging Flemming at the behest of Father Arnall, the Latin instructor, Father Dolan spots Stephen and accuses him of purposefully breaking his glasses in order to avoid his studies. Calling him a "lazy idle little loafer," Father Dolan hits Stephen's open hands with the whalebone and leather pandybat. Forcing Stephen to kneel on the floor, he tells the class that he will be back every day to beat loafers.

Struck by the injustice of this treatment and the prospect of further beatings before his new glasses arrive (for the doctor has told Stephen not to read without glasses), Stephen takes the advice of his classmates and goes to see the rector after dinner. With thoughts of Roman senatorial decrees and tales of ancient Rome in his head, Stephen climbs the stairs to the castle to speak to Rector Connee, who agrees to speak to Father Dolan. When he returns to his schoolmates, Stephen and Rector Connee are praised and cheered. The chapter concludes with Stephen's sense of relief and his attention to the sounds of the cricket bats on the field: "pick, pack, pock, puck" (61).

Chapter 1 has set the themes for the novel: Stephen's education in (and break from) family, church, and nationalism. It has also revealed a few of Stephen's traits that will develop throughout the novel: his sense of his physical weakness, his intellectual ability, his sense of honor, and his willingness to speak up and defend himself and his views. In addition, this chapter introduces us to Stephen's reliance upon sensory perceptions and memory as he makes sense of the world around him.

Chapter 2 begins in the summer. As a result of his father's reduced finances, Stephen is no longer at Clongowes College. He is at home with his family in Blackrock, a comfortable suburb of Dublin. The tone of this chapter is subtly different from the first. Stephen is apparently more confident and more aware of changes in the world around him. For example, he is wary of the merits of the old trainer, Mike Flynn, whom his father claims "had trained some of the best runners in modern time" (63). After his morning run, under the eye of Mike Flynn, Stephen often "glanced with mistrust at his trainer's flabby stubblecovered face" (63). This, and other such observations, signals Stephen's developing awareness that the world is not always as his father or other authority figures claim it is. Stephen spends a great deal of time with his uncle and his father, listening to their talk of politics and family history. As he catches words he does not understand, Stephen repeats them to himself. The narrator notes that it is through these unfamiliar words that Stephen "had glimpses of the real world about him" (64). Stephen senses that a "great part" awaits him in life, and influenced by his reading of *The Count of Monte Cristo*, he goes through his summer days imagining himself as a great adventurer, reciting love poems to fair Mercedes, the heroine of the novel.

Even as he imagines a rogue future and has boyish adventures with his neighborhood friend, Stephen is uncomfortable with the artificial nature of this imaginary life. Although he plays happily among the cows in the summer, by fall the sight of them in the filthy cowyard sickens him. This and other misgivings "dissipated any vision of the future" for Stephen (66). Thus, we see the tentative and fragile quality of Stephen's budding sense of his own potential future. Furthermore, it is clear that the vision is easily stained by the dirt and tedium of the everyday life. The narrative of this chapter traces Stephen's misgivings back to his vague awareness of his father's financial troubles. Stephen grows restless as his "boyish conception of the world" is shocked by the changes in his family's circumstances. Stephen is no longer content with daydreaming. It is no longer adequate for him to imagine a heroine in some romantic daydream: "He wanted to meet in the real world the unsubstantiated image which his soul so constantly beheld" (67).

The family is again forced to move. This time, they leave the comforts of Blackrock and move into the bleaker and crowded environs of the city of Dublin, where Stephen is left free to explore on his own. He continues to feel both a vague dissatisfaction and a sense that his future awaits him as he wanders throughout the city, aware of only "squalor and insincerity" (69). Stephen grows more and more detached from the life going on around him: "He chronicled with patience what he saw, detaching himself from it" (69–70). No longer taking part in games and fantasy, Stephen grows more and more lonely. He has an interaction with Emma, a young girl to whom he is attracted, but feels only the failed nature of their connection and berates himself for his shyness and cowardice.

Stephen's father has a chance meeting with the past rector of Clongowes, Father Connee, who has become the Provincial of the Jesuit order and has agreed to arrange for Stephen to attend the prestigious Belvedere College. The narrative jumps forward in time from this news to the night of the Whitsuntide play at Belvedere during Stephen's second year there. Stephen and Vincent Heron are rivals at the top of their class at Belvedere. Awaiting his part in the play, Stephen wanders out into the schoolyard where he finds Heron smoking with a friend. Heron teases Stephen about the young woman, Emma, who is attending the play with Stephen's family, mocking Stephen for his affected lack of interest in girls and other such diversions. Bored with such false familiarity, Stephen flashes back to his first term at Belvedere and an altercation with Heron and two other boys one afternoon as Stephen was walking home from school. The boys ask Stephen to name the greatest writers of prose and poetry. They argue over Lord Byron's supposed heresy and the boys attack Stephen, who defends Byron and refuses to admit that he is no good (whether or not he is a heretic). The narrative shifts back to the present in the school yard and Stephen's wondering that he bears no grudge against Heron and the others for their previous torment.

Stephen is called in to dress for his part in the play by a younger student and obediently turns to go in. Heron, however, grouses about the manner in which he had been summoned. Stephen again senses that the companionship of "upper class men" that Heron offers is insincere and a sign of what awaits him in the future: untrustworthy comrades and isolation. Stephen does not care about "honour" and rules with hollow meanings. Already, he has begun to sense the falsehood inherent in allegiance with fellow men, family, church, and country. He catalogs for himself the voices that he has heard all his life urging him to "be a gentleman," to "be a good catholic," to "be strong and manly," to "be true to his country." These "hollowsounding" voices "made him halt irresolutely in the pursuit of phantoms" (88–89). Stephen finds that he is happiest when he is far from these voices and their demands.

Yet, curiously, Stephen shifts to embrace fellowship as he prepares to go onstage for his part in the play. "For one rare moment he seemed to be clothed in the real apparel of boyhood" (90). Yet, as is so often the case, this feeling is fleeting and leaves Stephen feeling foolish and duped. As the play ends and the audience breaks up, Stephen's "nerves cried for further adventure." He dashes from the theater, telling his family that he must take a message to George's Street and feeling "pride and hope and desire like crushed herbs in his heart" (91). Finding himself at Lotts Lane, Stephen breathes the "rank and heavy air," telling himself that the smell of "horse piss and rotted straw" will calm his heart. Again, the squalid world around him has helped to crush Stephen's romantic fantasies and leaves him feeling chastened.

The narrative shifts from this scene to a train in which Stephen and his father are seated. They are on their way to Cork to sell off more of the family estate in order to pay Simon Dedalus's growing debts. As his father talks fondly of his youth in Cork, Stephen is unmoved, thinking of his own dispossession. Once in Cork, Simon Dedalus is reminiscent and takes Stephen to Queen's College to see where he studied. The college porter, with what Stephen sees as mock sincerity, takes them to see the anatomy theatre, where Mr. Dedalus and the porter look for his initials carved into a desk. Depressed and restless, Stephen hangs back. He notices the word *foetus* carved into the desk before him, and it evokes the "absent students of the college." Stephen shrinks from these absent students' ribald company and goes to his father, hiding his blush as he observes Simon Dedalus's initials. The vision of the college students and the word carved into the "dark stained wood" stay with Stephen. The more he reflects, the more the letters carved in the desk mock his "bodily weakness and futile enthusiasms," leading him to loathe himself (96). As Mr. Dedalus waxes nostalgic over his youth, Stephen too reviews his life, trying to hold on to what he now realizes is his lost youth. In his agitation, Stephen's memory of his life is reduced to only names: "Dante, Parnell, Clane, Clongowes" (98). Stephen reflects that he had not died, "but he had faded out like a film in the sun," thus obliquely evoking the myth of Icarus, the son of Daedalus in the Greek myth (99). In this myth, Daedalus fashions wings of wax that will allow him and his son, Icarus, to escape imprisonment. When Icarus's wax wings were melted by the sun, he fell to his death. Stephen has one last vision of himself as a "little boy in a grey belted suit" and with it, he senses that his youth is over (99). On the day that the property is sold and "one humiliation succeeded another," Stephen stands by as his father drinks with old cronies and he realizes that "his mind seemed older than theirs" (102). Unlike them, he "had known neither the pleasure of comradeship with others nor the vigour of rude male health nor filial piety" (102). Even as he seems to celebrate his own wisdom, which exceeds that of his elders, Stephen feels sorry for himself. In this moment, Stephen repeats what we have already gleaned: "His childhood was dead" (102).

Again the narrative shifts abruptly. We are back in Dublin and Stephen is cashing a check he has been awarded for winning an essay contest. With his sudden wealth, Stephen engages in grand gestures and enjoys a "swift season of merrymaking" (104). He is generous to himself and his family, but his resources come to a sudden end. He realizes that he had attempted to build a dam against the "sordid tide of life" (104). Recognizing both his motivation and his failure, Stephen feels his "futile isolation" once again. He is returned to feeling like a foster child, alienated from parents and siblings, alone in the world.

Increasingly, Stephen is tormented and confused by desire and lust. The women he sees as pious by day visit him in his dreams as "lecherous" and "cunning." Stephen wakes to humiliation and shame. He begins wandering the streets of Dublin at night, remembering his youthful visions of Mercedes (the heroine from *The Count of Monte Cristo*). But these memories are replaced by "the wasting fires of lust" (106). Wandering one evening in a feverish and animal state of desire, Stephen meets a prostitute and succumbs to his desire for her. The chapter ends with this scene. In a very broad sense, one might make the argument that in chapter 2 Stephen rejects the nets of family and boyhood. He knows that his family cannot guide him to the future that he only glimpses. He enters manhood feeling alienated, humiliated, and confused.

In chapter 3, Stephen grapples with religion and its demands upon him. In the beginning of this chapter, Stephen presents himself as pure animal, rough and brutish: The chapter opens with Stephen's hungry belly counseling him to "stuff" his dinner in. We learn that Stephen visits the brothels nightly, prowling the streets to satisfy his "sinloving soul," and that this life of secret "sin" has left Stephen feeling indifferent (109). Knowing that his behavior has placed him in the category of grievous sinners, Stephen develops contempt for himself and others; he knows he is a hypocrite and sees hypocrisy all around him. Feeling that he is beyond redemption, Stephen scoffs at all pieties. Yet, when he learns that all boys at the college must attend a three-day religious retreat in honor of Saint Francis Xavier, "Stephen's heart began slowly to fold and fade with fear" (115).

On the first day of the retreat, Father Arnall, Stephen's old master from Clongowes College, starts off the sermon by stating the subjects to be covered over the course of the retreat: death, judgment, hell, and heaven. Thus begin three days of guilty torment for Stephen. As he hears the sermon on death and judgment, Stephen feels that "every word of it was for him" (123). He thinks guiltily of his boyish love for Emma and feels himself to be a brute and a beast, too far gone from God. As though the priest has read Stephen's "sinful soul," he next details the abode of sinners: hell. His description is vivid and highly sensory, a description that might lead even a nonbeliever to break out in a cold sweat. Stephen is reduced to terror.

Returning to his room on the evening of the first day of this retreat, Stephen is physically ill from his spiritual torment. He imagines that God has shown him a vision of "the hell reserved for his sins: stinking, bestial, malignant, a hell of lecherous goatish fiends" (149). Sweating and aching, Stephen vomits in agony. When his illness passes, he offers an abject prayer and weeps for the "innocence he had lost" (150). Stephen then sets out into the damp night with the conviction that he must confess his sins. He finds a chapel where he is unknown and confesses to the priest. The voice of the old priest who hears his confession implores Stephen to give up the sin of fornication. Stephen leaves the church "conscious of an invisible grace pervading and making light his limbs" (157). The chapter ends with Stephen feeling cleansed and peaceful, as though he has been given a new life.

Chapter 4 takes the reader through Stephen's self-torturing regime to atone for his sins by living in a devoutly religious manner, to his ultimate rejection of the authority of the church in defining his life. The chapter begins with a list of the holy images or mysteries before which Stephen "hallowed himself" every single day. Stephen seeks to mortify himself in order to "undo the sinful past" (162). In this way, he brings each of his senses under a "rigourous discipline," depriving himself of pleasures and subjecting himself to numerous discomforts.

Stephen's regime is noticed by the director, who asks him to consider joining the priesthood. In a speech that relies heavily on the words *pride* and *power*, the priest tells Stephen that to receive the call to join the priest-hood is the "greatest honour" that God can "bestow upon a man" (171). He delineates the powers of a priest. Stephen allows himself "proud musings" on the possibility of "wielding calmly and humbly the awful power" (171). He grows aware of the "secret knowledge" his entrance into the priesthood would allow him. When Stephen shakes the director's hand as he departs, he notices that he gave his hand "as if already a companion in the spiritual life" (173). This noticing of comradeship is a warning, for every time that Stephen has previously felt the pull of companionship in a cause or belief, he has found it hollow or false.

Indeed, as Stephen walks away from his visit with the director, "some instinct" awakens memories that "armed him against acquiescence" (174). Feeling "repelled" by the life of the order, Stephen passes the Jesuit house in Gardiner Street and wonders vaguely "which window would be his if he joined the order" (175). He recognizes in this remote wondering that his soul is detached. He knows he will not become a priest: "His destiny was to be elusive of social or religious orders" (175). In this moment of insight and determination, Stephen also knows that he will sin again. He casts this as "falling" and uses the word many times to imagine his future. The repeti-tion of the word again evokes images of Icarus, son of Daedalus, who fell to the earth when his wax wings were melted by the sun. Stephen returns to his father's home and "smiled to think that it was this disorder, the misrule and confusion of his father's house … which was to win the day in his soul" (176). Stephen will not embrace the cold, ordered life of the priesthood with its power and its mystery.

The narrative shifts abruptly. Stephen waits impatiently for his father and his tutor to come out of the University and give him news about his admit-tance. Finally, unable to wait any longer, Stephen sets off walking toward the sea. He contemplates his "wayward instinct" that led him to refuse the call of the priesthood. He begins to reflect on words and his love of them, their colors, their rhythmic rise and fall. He senses music, a "longdrawn" note calling him. He comes upon his adolescent classmates romping in the water, calling to him, "Stephanos Dedalos! Bous Stephanoumenos!" (182). He is flattered by their play with his name and "Now, as never before, his strange name seemed to him a prophecy" (183). He senses his true calling in the "fabulous artificer" that is Daedalus, the artificer who made the wax wings that allowed him to fly free from constraints (183). Suddenly, Stephen's soul is "soaring sunward" and he is "purified in a breath and delivered of incertitude" (183). He longs to cry out like a hawk or eagle, recognizing that "this was the call of life," not the "world of duties" or the "inhuman voice" of the priesthood (184). Rejecting both his worldly and his spiritual fathers, Stephen embraces the mythic father, Daedalus.

In this moment, Stephen's fear of the ocean abates and he wades into the sea. There, among the seaweed, he notes that he is alone, "unheeded, happy and near to the wild heart of life" (185). At that moment, Stephen observes a girl standing before him and looking out to sea. "She seemed like one whom magic had changed into the likeness of a strange and beautiful sea-bird" (185). Aware of Stephen's gaze, the girl turns and gazes back, "without shame or wantonness" (186). Stephen's soul leaps in an "outburst of profane joy" (186). Stephen's observation of the girl is the epiphany that confirms the "advent of the life that had cried to him" (186). She is a "wild angel" who has appeared and thrown open for him the "gates of all the ways of error and glory" (186). Stephen turns away and finds a sandy cleft where he lies down. When he awakens, it is evening and he sees the "rim of the young moon" (187). Ending chapter 4, this epiphany sets the trajectory for the final chapter. Stephen has now found a path from which he will not turn.

Chapter 5 traces Stephen's break from the nets that have been used to hold him: family, church, and nation. In this chapter, he makes a telling comment about the constraints that Ireland places upon a "soul": "When the soul of a man is born in this country there are nets flung at it to hold it back in flight. You talk to me of nationality, language, religion. I shall try to fly by those nets" (220). Stephen Dedalus, whose name alludes to of the myth of Icarus and the artificer who created wings so that he might escape, will try his own wings to escape the nets that Ireland would use to hold him. The chapter begins with Stephen finishing his watery tea in the impoverished kitchen of his family home. The scene of family life is so disintegrated that we can no longer identify the gentility that once marked the family. Late again for University classes, Stephen leaves the mess of his family home that offends his soul. As he walks through Dublin, key places evoke authors and philosophers he has read, giving the reader insight into Stephen's idiosyncratic experience of the world.

Late for French class, Stephen enters the theater for his next class and finds the dean lighting the fire. As they fall into discussion, they alight upon the topic of the tundish (a word that means funnel). The dean did not know this name for the funnel before, coming, as he does, from England. He is pleased and curious to have been told it. Stephen, in contrast, notes their national differences and observes to himself that "the language which we are speaking is his before it is mine.... My soul frets in the shadows of his language" (205). In this English priest, Stephen finds the embodiment of his dual oppressors: England and the Catholic Church.

In a discussion with his friend Davin, in which Davin urges him to be more of an Irishman, Stephen notes "my ancestors threw off their language [and] ... allowed a handful of foreigners to subject them" (220). With this evidence, Stephen refuses the nationalist cause. Davin counters that Stephen should give himself to the nationalist cause for the sake of Irish freedom. Stephen's response is unequivocal: He reminds Davin of those "honourable and sincere" men who gave themselves up for the nation only to be "sold" to the enemy, "failed" by their countrymen, or "reviled." He asks: "And you invite me to be one of you. I'd see you damned first" (220). When Davin persists, Stephen ends the discussion by telling Davin that "Ireland is the old sow that eats her farrow" (220).

Stephen walks off with his friend Lynch and launches into an explanation of his aesthetic theory. He tells Lynch that Thomas Aquinas's theories serve him only so far because they tell him nothing about being the artist: "When we come to the phenomena of artistic conception, artistic gestation and artistic reproduction I require a new terminology and a new personal experience" (227). This comment points to the final direction that Stephen will take as he rejects the voices that have sought to restrain him and he begins to forge his own language—his own life. He goes on to explain his idea of the artist and his act of creation to Lynch, concluding that the artist, "like the God of the creation," remains invisible, "refined out of existence," thus giving us a clue as to how to read the work before us (233). We are not to seek Joyce or clues to his life in this autobiographically inspired book but to see "life purified in and reprojected from the human imagination" (233).

Noteworthy in this long speech to Lynch is the way that Joyce has replaced the presumed role of the Catholic Church in his life with the role of art. He has become like "the God of the creation." He wonders why Emma listens to a priest rather than to him, "a priest of eternal imagination" (240). The very language that Stephen uses to describe his aesthetic theory and his role as artist borrows liberally from the language of the Catholic Church, which he is rejecting. For, as he tells Davin much earlier, "This race and this country and this life produced me.... I shall express myself as I am" (220). Stephen the artist, though he has rejected the voices of family, nation, and church, is still made up of these—his soul may "fret in the shadow" of the languages of nation, family, and church, but he is forced to use these languages to create. This point is made by Stephen's friend Cranly when he points out that Stephen's "mind is supersaturated with the religion in which you say you disbelieve" (261).

Having delineated his reasons for rejecting nationalism to Davin and having outlined his rejection of the church and his preference for art to Lynch, Stephen turns to his friend Cranly to explain his rejection of the family's demands and expectations. Stephen's mother has asked him to take his Easter religious duties and he has refused. He is troubled by how sad this makes her and consults with Cranly. Cranly advises that he take communion, seeing as how doing so will make his poor mother happy. But Stephen refuses to pay false homage and concludes: "I will not serve that in which I no longer believe whether it call itself my home, my fatherland or my church" (268). He tells Cranly that he will be leaving Ireland so that he can express himself freely using "silence, exile, and cunning" (269).

At this point in the chapter, the style shifts from conversations with close friends to Stephen's entries in his diary, sporadically entered from March 20 to April 27. These entries catalog thoughts and conversations he has in the last few months of University, before he leaves Ireland for Paris. In the second to last entry, he writes the lines that are now famous: "Welcome, O Life! I go to encounter for the millionth time the reality of experience and to forge in the smithy of my soul the uncreated conscience of my race" (275–76). In his final entry and the final sentence of the novel, Stephen asks his mythic father for his blessing: "Old father, old artificer, stand me now and ever in good stead" (276).

CHARACTER DEVELOPMENT

This novel traces the development of a cerebral, interior artist, Stephen Dedalus. Stephen's growth over the course of the novel sets its pace and structure. Indeed, all other characters appear relevant only insofar as they allow us to witness the development of Stephen's character. Still, as such, several characters are critical to the plot; most significant among these characters are Stephen's father Simon Dedalus; Stephen's friends Davin, Lynch, and Cranly; and Emma, a young girl whom Stephen wishes to know intimately.

The novel opens with Stephen Dedalus as an infant and traces him through University to the brink of his departure for Paris. Naturally, when a work traces a character over such a long span, there will be both dramatic changes and emerging consistencies in that character. In this novel there are key moments of growth that are marked by a shift in narrative voice and perspective. Although the Stephen at the end of the novel is still a young man caught up in the vanity and solipsism of youth, he is dramatically evolved from the "baby tuckoo" who begins the novel.

It is only appropriate that the focus on Stephen as an infant does not allow us to hear his voice. Rather, we are given access to his character by the narrator's recording of physical and sensory perceptions of experiences. He observes that his father had a hairy face and that the bed gets warm and then cold when one wets it. He notes the smell of the oil cloth on the bed and the smell of his mother. These perceptual observations serve to evoke the reader's sensual memories. But, more importantly, they mark a trait of Stephen Dedalus: Stephen is acutely sensitive to his sensual perceptions, especially smell. This is introduced at the very beginning because this is the "language" of infancy; but the trait persists throughout the novel. It is one of the qualities that leads Stephen to art, for his alertness to sensory details and, later, his verbal acuity combine to create his desire to be an artist.

As Stephen grows and develops, it is clear that this sensitivity to the world around him is connected to his timidity and fragility. Once he is away at school and among other boys his own age, Stephen repeatedly observes that his body is "small and weak." This quality sets him apart from the other boys at school. He notices their physical strength and size, their ease in the company of other boys, and he longs to be at home with his mother. Although Stephen does grow more independent as the novel progresses, he is never a particularly athletic or muscular man. These "deficits" lead him to feel isolated from boys and men around him and, even as he longs to fit in, he distrusts groups. In fact, he often shrinks from what he feels is the false companionship of boys and men.

Another aspect of Stephen's character that is constant in the novel is his sensitivity to words and language. This is apparent at the very beginning of the novel when the text reflects the number of songs and stories that filled Stephen's preverbal world. The first line of the novel quotes a sort of fairy tale that Simon Dedalus tells to his son. It gives us the sense of an infant's memory and ability to make sense of narrative. Later, at school, Stephen's attention continues to be drawn to language: to the sentences in his spelling book that remind him of poetry; to the evocative sound of the word *suck*; to the specific words of the prefect's prayer. A key example of this alertness to language and its power is reflected in Stephen's memory of the beautiful song that Brigid had taught him. He notes that the song made him want to cry, "not for himself: for the words so beautiful and sad, like music" (22).

Stephen's acute sensitivity to language is a feature of his character that will remain constant throughout the novel. It contributes to his interiority, his comfort with ideas more than with people, and his intellectual curiosity. It is also intimately connected with his ultimate commitment to art over church, family, and nation.

Two related qualities of Stephen's character that emerge early in the novel and remain are his intolerance of hypocrisy and his stalwart commitment to truth. These traits might come in part from his father's early commands "never to peach on a fellow" (6). Early in his career at school, Stephen is bullied several times. Yet he is proud that he never informs on them. He faces the punishment as if no one else deserved blame. This trait grows beyond a fidelity to comrades, to a fidelity to oneself and one's philosophies. Though Stephen longs to enjoy the easy company of his fellows, his sense of the hypocrisy involved in pretending that he fits in always leads him to reject that company. As he grows, we see the emergence of Stephen's resolve to find his own way in the world, independent of the edicts of institutions that, as he sees it, seek to conscript him. It is important to remember that though he is heroic, noble, and serious, Stephen is also very young. Like many youths, he is shortsighted, vain, and highly dramatic. He is not necessarily a likeable character. He takes himself very seriously and is dismissive of others. But he is consistent: He seeks truth on his own terms, and he will not compromise himself.

Other key characters in the novel are only developed through Stephen's eyes, for he is the narrator and "artificer" of the novel. Thus, it is through Stephen's growing awareness of his father as a flawed human being that we come to see Simon Dedalus as a failed businessman, a limited father and husband, and a sentimental drunk. Like Stephen, our first views of Simon reflect a large figure who sings beautiful songs, tells comic stories, and states his religious and political views with passion and humor. But as Stephen grows, and as the family's circumstances slide toward poverty, we see the flaws in Simon Dedalus's character. He talks a good game, but he is not a man of action. He appears to be living in a past where old Ireland was a more congenial place and where Michael Davitt and John Stewart Parnell were in power. Unable, apparently, to accept the loss of this world, Simon Dedalus slowly retreats. By the final scene we merely hear his "shrill whistle" from his upstairs room and his query to one of Stephen's siblings: "Has your lazy bitch of a brother gone out yet?" (189). Simon Dedalus's demise matches Stephen's rejection of the values that he represents: family and country. Upon leaving the family home, following his father's shrill whistle and rough question, Stephen rejects their hold on him: "His father's whistle, his mother's mutterings, the screech of an unseen maniac were to him now so many voices offending and threatening to humble the pride of his youth. He drove their echoes even out of his heart with an execration" (190).

Just as Stephen rejects the hold of his father's values on his soul, he must free himself of the other constraints that check his flight and threaten to ground him forever. One of those constraints is represented by the director of the Jesuit order, the priest who asks Stephen if he feels the calling to join the order and become a priest. Because Stephen has been through a period of self-denial and pious observance of the edicts of the church (after his "conversion" from his previous habit of visiting prostitutes and rejecting the laws of the church), the director has seen in him the potential of a priest. He offers Stephen the "secret knowledge and secret power" that the priesthood holds, and Stephen at first warms to the idea of joining this company of knowledgeable, powerful men. Yet Stephen knows that he will reject this company as well for, "waking ... within him at every near approach to that life, an instinct ... armed him against acquiescence" (174). The priesthood, then, no matter how much power it might offer Stephen, is portrayed as an institution that would require him to submit himself to standards that are not his own. Stephen is emerging as a young man who cannot submit to others but who must determine his own path in life. Turning away from the nets of church, family, and, ultimately, nation, Stephen recognizes that he is "destined to learn his own wisdom apart from others" (175).

The final snare that threatens to restrain him is the company of friends who embody the central constraints that Ireland represents for the maturing hero of this novel: nation, church, and family. Davin, Stephen's classmate at University College, is a fervent nationalist; in this way, he is Stephen's opposite and serves to highlight Stephen's searing critique of Irish nationalism. When Stephen mocks Davin's nationalism, Davin asks, "What with your name and your ideas ... Are you Irish at all?" (219). Stephen reminds Davin that "this race and this country and this life produced me" (220). To which Davin exhorts him to "try to be one of us" (220). Hinting at the treatment that Parnell received by fellow nationalists, Stephen reminds Davin that the nationalists have always failed or reviled those who give themselves to the cause. Stephen's allusion to John Stewart Parnell here deserves attention: Throughout this novel, Parnell's story serves as an example of the treatment Ireland offers its most devoted advocates. As mentioned previously, Parnell was the leading figure in the Home Rule Movement and was denounced by the church when his affair was discovered. He died soon after this in 1891, a broken man. Those who supported Parnell, like Joyce's father, bitterly criticized the Irish people for betraying Parnell. By refusing the join the cause, Stephen refuses to risk being sacrificed as Parnell was before him.

As his aesthetic theory takes shape and Stephen begins to commit himself to art above all else, his friend Vincent Lynch hears Stephen's disquisition on this subject. Narratively, Vincent Lynch is not much more than an opportunity for Stephen to hold forth: Their conversation is very close to a monologue on Stephen's part. Stephen draws heavily on the theories of Thomas Aquinas to arrive at this key observation: "When we come to the phenomena of artistic conception, artistic gestation and artistic reproduction I require a new terminology and a new personal experience" (227). Thus, Stephen is poised on the cusp of developing this new terminology and of having new experiences that will enhance and refine his aesthetic theory. He is poised to fly. Lynch (a character who reappears in Joyce's novel *Ulysses*) is sympathetic to Stephen's plight as an artist and ultimately asks him, "What do you mean ... by prating about beauty and the imagination in this miserable God-forsaken island?" (233). This question will lead us to Stephen's final conversation with his friend Cranly, in which he reveals his plan to leave Ireland for Paris.

Stephen turns to Cranly on the subject of his mother's frustration with his rejection of religious practice. Cranly questions Stephen about his beliefs and reminds Stephen that his mind is "supersaturated with the religion" in which he says he disbelieves (261). Even so, it is clear that Stephen is not confused on the subject of religion: It may inform his language insofar as it appears in the metaphors and references that pepper it, but he does not pretend to believe in the church that he elsewhere calls the "scullerymaid of all Christendom" (239). Cranly appeals to Stephen's filial responsibilities and advises him to save his mother from more suffering by fulfilling his Easter religious duty. He attempts to demonstrate for Stephen that many supposed saints of the church have acted falsely and so might Stephen without a bad conscience. Stephen responds that he does not so much fear punishment from a God he does not believe in as the reaction in his own soul to a falsehood. As Cranly presses him to accept that he would be in the company of good believers to challenge the rules of the church, Stephen reminds Cranly of what he wishes to do in life. He wishes to "discover the mode of life or of art whereby [his] spirit could express itself in unfettered freedom" (267). As if challenging this fundamentally, Cranly counters that Stephen has the freedom to take communion without believing in it. Cranly's facile promotion of falsehood to one's own beliefs in order to soothe another in effect ends his friendship with Stephen. As a narrative device, it allows Stephen the opportunity to express his fidelity to art, freedom, and self-expression.

It is through the character of Emma that we see Stephen's growing understanding of love and companionship. By the time the novel ends, he has far to go toward finding love, but he has grown in his understanding of women. It is upon Emma that he projects his hope and anxiety about being loved. When first he meets her, he cannot bring himself to speak as he likes or act upon his desires. He is like the unnamed adolescent narrator in Joyce's short story "Araby": chastising himself for his foolishness and his reverence of his beloved. As he grows, Stephen seems no better at approaching the object of his great affection; she still renders him mute and tortured with self-consciousness. But his final reflections upon her, which are triggered by a "dream or vision," he recalls vividly upon waking from an "enchanted" night (235). Stephen holds the feeling of the dream and begins to compose a villanelle, a poem. Upon writing it down, he begins to think of Emma and takes himself through the range of emotions he has felt in her presence. He finally acknowledges to himself that his rage at her flirtations with a young priest, which he has observed on a few occasions, is also a form of "homage." But he tells himself that "she was a figure of the womanhood of her country, a batlike soul waking to the consciousness of itself in darkness and secrecy and loneliness" (239–40). This thought leads him back to bitterness that she, like many of the women of her country, would "unveil her soul's shy nakedness" to a priest, "rather than to him, a priest of the eternal imagination, transmuting the daily bread of experience into the radiant body of everliving life" (240). Stephen's aesthetic theories and commitment to art have advanced so far that art is the spiritual devotion; art turns experience into everlasting life.

THEMES, SYMBOLS, AND MOTIFS

Joyce's use of symbols and motifs to convey essential themes is fundamental to the emerging portrait of the artist. A *motif* is a word or an image that repeats throughout the work to such a degree that it upholds or enhances a central theme. Thus, one significant motif in this novel that is evident early on and develops throughout is blindness. Early in the first chapter, the narrative relates a rhyme that Dante repeats when young Stephen is called upon to apologize for some misdeed: "Pull out his eyes, /Apologise, / Apologise, / Pull out his eyes" (4). Here, the threat of blindness is used to reform the young boy's behavior at the same time that apology is equated with enforced blindness. Later, Stephen will observe that the central institutions of his world (family, church, and country) all require a kind of blindness to himself and to the logic of his own heart and mind.

Stephen's weak sight is also reflective of his naiveté and initial lack of insight into the ways of the world around him. Early in the novel we learn of Stephen's weak eyes and his "blindness" without the aid of glasses. Later, Stephen is beaten with a pandybat by Father Dolan, the prefect of studies at the school he attends, for allegedly breaking his glasses and, therefore, for willfully causing his inability to see well enough to complete his lessons. In many ways, the novel elaborates on both Stephen's shortsightedness and initial emerging insight into his world. But, by the end, although Stephen may have seen into the pitfalls that Ireland holds for the artist, he is still weak-sighted and in need of glasses, a point that leads readers to consider just how enlightened Stephen has become as a young man.

Just as the motif of blindness serves to introduce the theme of the limitations placed upon the artist by church, nationalism, and personal limitations, the repetition of voices and words leads to the development of another theme. Stephen is profoundly attentive to voices and words throughout the novel; it begins, in fact, with fragments of the voices most central to Stephen in his infancy. Stephen grows to awareness in large part through his meditation on voices and words. These early snatches of the supposedly real world come together to reveal a world that Stephen finds increasingly discouraging and depressing. Yet words remain a central fascination for Stephen, and ultimately, they will be his art. Stephen reflects upon words when he has at last rejected numerous false paths: "Did he love the rhythmic rise and fall of words better than their associations of legend and colour? Or was it that, being as weak of sight as he was shy of mind, he drew less pleasure from the reflection of the glowing sensible world through the prism of a language manycoloured and richly storied than from the contemplation of an inner world of individual emotions mirrored perfectly in a lucid supple periodic prose?" (180–81). As an artist, Stephen reflects the Modernist fascination with language and the "inner world of individual emotions." He has left behind the traces of Victorian and Edwardian realism and fidelity to plot and begun to explore the associative qualities of language and prose that attempts to capture the fluid quality of individual consciousness.

As Stephen sees into his father's failures, the church's deceptions, and his own shattered hopes of finding companionship, his increasing isolation reinforces his study of words. But this study does not relieve him of his sense of duty to family, church, and state. Indeed, Stephen's uneasy alienation is an important theme throughout the novel. His emerging confidence in his own insights does not alleviate this isolation. In fact, Stephen's growing acceptance of isolation leads him to visions of flight and escape. In his journey to discovering his future, the "end he had been born to serve" (178), Stephen takes many wrong turns: He rejects the path of his father, subtly ashamed by his father's retreat to alcohol and poverty even as he occasionally affects an easy camaraderie with "false friends." He rejects the path of nationalism, which his father and his friend Davin exhort him to follow. Even after a sustained experiment in religious piety, Stephen rejects the path of the priesthood, recognizing its false power and piety. In each case, Stephen ultimately recognizes the error of the path and seeks escape. But escape becomes "flight" as Stephen has an epiphany and begins to see his future in art. This is where the repeated and subtle references to flight and the myth of Icarus come together to convey a vision of Stephen's future as an expatriate man of letters.

Considering his recent rejections of the call to become a priest that his mother, among others, would have him embrace, Stephen notes that "the end he had been born to serve yet did not see had led him to escape by an unseen path" (178). This escape conjures images of Icarus and the means of escape that he used. Stephen observes that the "end he had been born to serve beckons him like music," music that he likens to "triplebranching flames leaping fitfully, flame after flame, out of a midnight wood" (179). This reference to flame so suddenly following his consideration of escape echoes Icarus's escape with wax wings that his father, Daedalus, fashioned. For Icarus flew too close to the sun's flames and his wings were melted, tragically ending his flight. Whether Stephen will crash like Icarus or succeed like Daedalus, both of whom escaped by flight, remains to be seen.

As Stephen reflects on his choices and, therefore, on people he has rejected, it occurs to him as never before that his name, Dedalus, is a "prophecy." It is a prophecy of "the end he had been born to serve … a symbol of the artist forging anew in his workshop of the sluggish matter of the earth a new soaring impalpable, imperishable being" (183). Stephen will serve his spiritual father's path, turning life into art through writing. The references to flight that follow Stephen's insight are numerous, leaving the accrued impression that Stephen has at last found his calling and will be able to escape the ties that Ireland would use to hold him back. As he has his great insight into the destiny he has been seeking, the language he uses is rich and repetitive with images of escape by flight: "His heart trembled, his breath came faster and a wild spirit passed over his limbs as though he were soaring sunward. His heart trembled in an ecstasy of fear and his soul was in flight. His soul was soaring in an air beyond the world" (183). As Stephen soars, he realizes the "call of life" for him is not bound in the "dull gross voice of the world of duties and despair," nor in the "inhuman voice" that would call him to the "pale service of the altar." Stephen is metaphorically "reborn" in this moment, aware of his life's calling to "create proudly out of the freedom and power of his soul," just as the "great artificer whose name he bore" had done (184). Stephen embraces his namesake and the grand mythic destiny that he represents.

These insights coalesce in an epiphany that reiterates the expansiveness of the life Stephen has chosen: The path he will follow will not lead to a sterile and cloistered life, but will lead to a quest for the spiritual within the physical world. The key moment of his epiphany is conveyed when Stephen observes a young girl standing in the waves and "gazing out to sea" (185). Stephen sees her as transformed by magic into a sea bird or a dove. They exchange a lengthy gaze that reveals a new world to Stephen, and he sees his life's path: "To live, to err, to fall, to triumph, to recreate life out of life / A wild angel had appeared to him" (186). Thus, returning to the myth of Icarus and embracing his spiritual and mythical father Daedalus, in this epiphanic scene Stephen's future is revealed: a life in the world that will be committed to art and engage the very "stuff" of life.

Finally, "the artist" is both an abstract concept and an actual person that Joyce's novel evokes and considers. It may indeed convey a portrait of an actual young artist, Stephen Dedalus, but it also invites readers to contemplate the nature of "the artist" in the abstract. It suggests that the artist has the harder path, for he must cast off all conventional rules and live by his own strict rules, to express himself "in some mode of life or art as freely as I can and as wholly as I can, using for my defense the only arms I allow myself to use—silence, exile, and cunning" (269). When Stephen tells this to his friend Cranly, he also adds that he does not fear the isolation and rejection that this fidelity will no doubt cause. He knows that he has chosen the hardest path, the path that is not chosen by many. Thus, he calls his mythic father to stand him in "good stead" as he seeks to do no less than forge "the uncreated conscience" of his race (269).

NARRATIVE STYLE

A *Portrait* is rich with literary technique. Joyce was experimenting with the structure of the *kunstleroman* (the novel of or about the artist), conveying the narrative through the perspective of the growing artist, literally from infancy to adulthood. His syntactical and grammatical style maps both the development of the mind and abilities of the young artist, beginning with the fragmented and simple style and associative logic of a child, and moving to the complex logic and subtle perception of a sensitive and artistic young man.

James Joyce is, of course, best known for his radical stylistic experimentalism, which came to its ultimate realization in his final work, *Finnegan's*

Wake. Yet, even in this early novel, we see Joyce's nascent experimentalism. Here, Joyce uses a unique episodic development of the narrative to reveal the emerging character of the artist as a young man. He employs free indirect discourse, which allows for a slippery point of view throughout the novel. He employs an epiphany, Joyce's own term for this sudden sort of insight, to convey the moment of revelation when the young artist sees and embraces his calling. Finally, Joyce uses repetitive patterns and phrasings to layer meaning and understanding. Joyce's experimentalism here is young, like the writer he was and the artist he is portraying, but it is consistent throughout the novel and successful in telling the "story" in an appropriately unconventional way. By the use of the word *unconventional*, one means to signal not just Stephen's refusal to abide by the "rules" of his country, but Joyce's refusal to convey Stephen's refusal in anything like a typical story.

Thus, the very structure of Joyce's novel is noteworthy: He portrays Stephen's growth to manhood through key episodes of his youth. In part, in order to cover so much of his youth, Joyce tells Stephen's story in episodes, focusing on the most formative events or moments in Stephen's life. Through these episodes, we become familiar with Stephen's key characteristics—his weak sight, his sensitivity to the music and meaning of words. These episodes also afford insight into Stephen's fierce refusal to quietly comply with the values and expectations of others. The novel is structured by these formative experiences of Stephen's life: his alienation from others, his intelligence, his rejection of a calling to the priesthood, his refusal to blindly serve family and nation.

The novel is composed in a stream of consciousness style, which allows the story to unfold directly through the thoughts and comments of the central character, Stephen Dedalus. This style further reinforces the purpose of the novel to convey a portrait of Dedalus, the artist, as a young man, for we see the world through his eyes, uninterrupted by an omniscient narrative perspective. Yet this stream of consciousness style is further complicated by Joyce's use of free indirect discourse. Because free indirect discourse allows telling of the narrative to slip from the direct statements of characters to a more omniscient intelligence authoring the text, it makes it difficult to discern who is "telling" the story. At the very beginning of the novel, for example, we are introduced to a "once upon a time" sort of opening that rapidly unravels into numerous narrative points of view under one organizing narrative consciousness. This pattern continues throughout the novel, leading readers to experience the very same tension of multiple and competing voices with which Stephen struggles. Yet, almost as a tool for coherence amidst this unsettling narrative technique, Joyce uses repetitive words and motifs such as "weak," "blind," and "flight" that reinforce key ideas and insights throughout the novel.

A feature of Joyce's prose that is particularly idiosyncratic but also revealing is his unique use of the language and imagery of Catholicism. Over and over as Stephen struggles to see his life's calling, he uses the language of Catholicism to describe his experiences. Through this, we see how informed Stephen's (and Joyce's) consciousness is by his religious background, for Catholicism is clearly everywhere he turns: in his home with Dante Riordan and his mother, in schools run by Catholic priests, and in the confusion of nationalism and Catholicism in Irish politics. Thus, when Stephen at last begins to forge his own philosophy, his language is distinctly religious. Borrowing from and altering the language of the Catholic Church, Joyce often uses the term *epiphany* (adopted from the Catholic religion to signify a moment of transformative insight experienced by a character). Epiphanies function in Joyce's prose to signal a moment of secular, transformative insight for his characters. Though secular, these epiphanies are described in terms that come directly from Joyce's religious background. For example, Stephen's epiphany in this novel is described with repeated reference to God and Church. Seeing the young girl who is central to his epiphany, Stephen experiences a "holy silence" of ecstasy. He describes her as a "wild angel" and cries to God in "profane joy" (186). The work is replete with examples of Joyce drawing on the language of Catholic experience to describe his secular insights.

HISTORICAL CONTEXT

Joyce worked intermittently on this novel between 1903 and 1915, with his most concentrated writing done between 1907 and 1915. These years, like so many in the Modernist period, were witness to radical changes. In 1907 two key artistic developments would have been significant to Joyce and his efforts to create a new fictional form. In that year, the first exhibition of Cubist painting was held in Paris. In Cubist paintings, one finds a corollary to the portraiture that Modernist writers like Joyce were attempting. Cubist paintings do not represent objects from a single or fixed angle; instead, objects are represented from multiple angles simultaneously as the artist attempts to render a more "complete" portrait of the object or person. Although cubist paintings are often jarring to view, like the Modernist portrait, they seek to capture an individual object or person in a multidimensional way. 1907 is also the year that Filippo Marinetti published his "Futurist Manifesto." With this text, Marinetti attempted to declare the thoughts and beliefs of the "Futurists," an avant-garde group of mostly Italian artists who sought to address the role of art in the new century, when Italy was attempting to elevate its status in Europe and "progress" was the word on everyone's lips. Aggressively embracing "progress," Marinetti's text reflects a violent streak that would ultimately lead to the connection between Futurism and Fascism. Living in Italy at the time, Joyce was no doubt familiar with the publication of this manifesto.

Other significant historical events occurred while Joyce worked on *A Portrait of the Artist as a Young Man*. One was the sinking of the "unsinkable" Titanic, an event that shook confidence in progress and technology. In 1913, the first Charlie Chaplin movie was released, signaling the emerging dominance of film as an influential form of art and entertainment. Also in 1913, D. H. Lawrence published his novel *Sons and Lovers* and was hailed as an important new voice on the literary scene.

Of course, the most profound event of the period was the start of World War I in 1914. Many artists of the time found themselves completely disheartened by the outbreak of war, though most had seen it coming. The war would change the face of Europe, leaving its inhabitants with a "well of tears," to use Virginia Woolf's term. It would also hasten the changes in literary style that Joyce, among others, was beginning to initiate with *A Portrait*. After the war, Joyce, like other Modernist writers, would pursue his interest in fractured narrative reflecting the modern consciousness with a new clarity and purpose.

4

D. H. Lawrence
Women in Love
(1919)

BIOGRAPHICAL CONTEXT

David Herbert Richard Lawrence was born in Eastwood, Nottinghamshire, England, on September 11, 1885. Nottinghamshire, in the English midlands, is coal country. Lawrence's father, Arthur John Lawrence, was a miner who married Lydia Beardsall, a distant cousin, in 1875. The Lawrences had five children, three boys and two girls, and D. H. was the next to youngest child. Lydia was very religious and considered herself superior to her husband and other mining families. As a result, John and Lydia Lawrence had an unhappy marriage, and this had a profound influence on their children. As the family moved from poorer to yet poorer quarters for the first six years of Lawrence's life, Lydia attempted to keep herself apart from her neighbors. The strained relationship with her husband increased as he developed a habit of stopping by the local pub on the way home from the mines and arriving home drunk. They often had violent fights. As her marriage soured, Lydia Lawrence denigrated her husband and attempted to keep her children from working in the mines or as maids by educating them.

Lawrence received the weight of his mother's needy affection when his elder brother, Ernest, died of complications from pneumonia in 1901. As she began to recover from the grief of this loss, Lydia transferred all her hopes and expectations to David Herbert. When he too became ill with pneumonia, she nursed him back to health. In turn, she expected the sort of devotion from him that she had not received from her husband; her son obliged. Devoted to his mother, Lawrence obediently rejected his father, though later in his life he regretted this. He was a gifted student, and with his mother's emphatic encouragement, he undertook a program of reading and studying the classics of music, literature, and art. Ultimately, Lawrence began teaching at a boys' school in the London suburb of Croydon.

While he was teaching at Croydon, Lawrence was also writing. His close friend from that time, Jessie Chambers, sent some of his writing to *The English Review* without telling Lawrence. This led to his introduction to the editor of *The Review*, Ford Madox Hueffer (later known as Ford Madox Ford), and to several other important literary personalities, including W. B. Yeats, Ezra Pound, and H. G. Wells. Ford Madox Hueffer recommended Lawrence's first novel, *The White Peacock*, to a publisher. It was subsequently accepted for publication.

In 1910, shortly after the publication of *The White Peacock*, Lawrence's mother died of cancer. The 25-year-old Lawrence was devastated, stricken for a third time with pneumonia, and suffered a long convalescence. Eventually, however, her absence allowed Lawrence to take greater freedom in his writing. Indeed, the death of his mother marked what many consider a radical change in Lawrence's life and work. His next novel, *Sons and Lovers*, is in many ways a fictional working out of his relationship with his mother. Exploring the impact of an extremely possessive mother on the central character, Paul Morel, this novel was Lawrence's first great success.

As though the writing of this novel exorcised his mother, Lawrence embarked on his controversial third novel, *The Rainbow*. *Women in Love* (the sequel to *The Rainbow*) was written almost in its entirety between April and October of 1916. The publication history of *The Rainbow* sets the stage for the trouble Lawrence would have publishing *Women in Love*: Finished in 1915, *The Rainbow* was published by Methuen in September of that same year. In October, *The Rainbow* was charged with obscenity by the British government and suppressed. In November it was banned in England. Although Lawrence finished writing *Women in Love* in 1916, it was rejected by publishers until 1920. Written during World War I and in the early years of Lawrence's marriage, *Women in Love* reflects his interest in exploring the unconscious depths of character that influence human relationships. He came to believe that identity is shifting and unstable, and that humans are far more controlled by unconscious drives and desires than by rational thought. Lawrence's growing belief in the instability of personality and self, combined with the sexually frank and explicit nature of his texts, resulted in the continued rejection of his work by many publishers and the persecution of Lawrence himself.

In March 1912, Lawrence met Frieda Weekley, the wife of a Classics professor at the University College of Nottingham and the mother of three children.

In the beginning of May 1912, they eloped to Germany. Lawrence committed himself to making his marriage to Frieda work although, by all accounts, it was a fiery and difficult relationship that took a toll on them both. Lawrence and Frieda fought intensely. Frieda was miserable about abandoning her children, and Lawrence was impatient with her for this. They were too poor to emigrate, which is what they wanted to do, so they moved to Cornwall and set up house. Lawrence wrote *Women in Love* while they lived in Cornwall.

Written in the middle of the First World War, *Women in Love* is, as many have argued, a war novel. It is set in peacetime, but the central characters and themes reflect the violence and conflict of the world in which it was composed. In the midst of this war, Lawrence grew increasingly alienated from British society. As the son of a coal miner who had escaped the colliery, Lawrence had always felt like an outsider among the artists, intellectuals, and patrons with whom he mingled. When he met and fell in love with (and ultimately married) Frieda Weekley, he estranged himself even further from society. By the middle of the war, Frieda and Lawrence were falsely accused of spying (most likely because Frieda was German) and were expelled from Cornwall in 1917. Ultimately, Lawrence and Frieda would leave England. Until his death in 1930, the Lawrences traveled widely to such places as Ceylon, Australia, Greece, and the United States, only returning to England a few times. Lawrence died of tuberculosis in Vence, France, in 1930.

PLOT SUMMARY

Women in Love owes its genesis to an earlier novel, tentatively titled *The Sisters*, which Lawrence began writing in 1913, after the successful publication and reception of his novel *Sons and Lovers*. As Lawrence worked on *The Sisters*, which eventually became two novels (*The Rainbow* and *Women in Love*), he began to articulate the philosophy that would guide his writing for the rest of his life. Like his other great works, *Women in Love* is the exploration of characters who are always changing. Through 32 chapters, we follow four central characters (the sisters Ursula and Gudrun Brangwen and their lovers Rupert Birkin and Gerald Crich) as they come to know each other and themselves. The point of view shifts from chapter to chapter, allowing us insight into the developing relationships of these characters and others.

In the first chapter, we meet Ursula and Gudrun Brangwen and the men they will ultimately choose. The elder sister, Gudrun, is an artist who has recently returned from London to her family home in the colliery town of Beldover in the midlands of England. The sisters reveal their independent and unique characters as they discuss the merits and drawbacks of marriage,

love, and children. They set out on a walk to observe the wedding of Laura
Crich, a daughter of the local mine owner, Thomas Crich. As they walk
through Beldover, Gudrun recoils at the life and setting she observes, protesting to herself that it is a "defaced" countryside where everything is "sordid"
and the people are all "ghouls" (11). Her sensitivity to what she considers
the colorless and purposeless toiling of these people leads her to feel tortured. The local colliery people remark on the sisters' colorful stockings and
provoke rage in Gudrun. Compared to Gudrun's summation and dismissal
of them, the way the local people observe the sisters sets up a stark contrast
of class and culture that is furthered as the Crich family enters the scene,
representing the class of landed gentry.

Observing the wedding party from the sidelines, each sister sights the
man she is "fated" for. Gudrun observes Gerald Crich, the eldest son of the
mine owner Thomas Crich, and feels destined to "know more of that man"
(15). Her first reactions are indicative of the nature of their fated struggle:
She is drawn to his masculinity and the "lurking danger of his unsubdued
temper" (14). She concludes that his totem is the wolf, intimating her early
sense of his dominating and aggressive nature. For her part, Ursula observes
Rupert Birkin, an inspector in the school where she teaches, whom she has
met before. She notes his "clever and separate" nature and acknowledges to
herself that she "wanted to know him" (20). Her reactions to Birkin are of a
less aggressive nature than those of Gudrun to Gerald. Where Gudrun feels
a violent attraction, Ursula feels that she and Birkin have "some kinship"—a
common language or understanding.

The second chapter takes us to the wedding party at the Crich home
and introduces the friendship of Rupert Birkin and Gerald Crich. Theirs
appears to be a friendship of opposites. Birkin emerges as an iconoclast who
can play the social game in the upper classes, even while he despises the
implicit falsehood of social proprieties. He acknowledges to Gerald Crich
that he would prefer to live in a world where people acted as spontaneous
individuals. Gerald claims that such a world would lead to chaos and murder,
and Birkin turns this claim upon him, suggesting that it means that Gerald,
who accidentally shot and killed his brother as a young boy, has a desire to
be murdered. The chapter concludes with an acknowledgement of the deep
attraction and yet animosity these men feel for each other and a suggestion
that they cannot acknowledge these feelings and, thus, cannot have a deeper
and more fulfilling friendship. This early interaction between Birkin and
Crich sets the stage for conflicts that reappear throughout this novel.

The next two chapters focus on the relationships of the sisters and these two
men, developing points of connection and fascination from the perspectives

of the sisters. In chapter 3, Ursula is startled and frightened to discover that Rupert Birkin has entered her classroom as she is giving a lesson on catkins. He instructs Ursula to hand out crayons for the children to draw the colors of the male and female catkins. He argues that what the drawings must emphasize is not the outline of the plants, but the red of the female flowers and yellow of the male. This, he says, is the critical fact that must be attended to. His instruction is interrupted by the entrance of Hermione Roddice, a member of the "slack aristocracy that keeps touch with the arts" (16) and erstwhile lover of Rupert Birkin. Her entrance sets the scene for an unspoken three-way conflict between Birkin, who rejects Hermione's possessiveness, and the women who recognize each other as foes. This conflict proceeds at a suggestive level. The chapter draws to a close with the departure of Birkin and Hermione together and concludes with Ursula weeping and confused in the darkened and empty classroom.

The next chapter introduces the virile figure of Gerald Crich as he plunges naked into a pond that the sisters happen to be passing. Where the relationship between Rupert and Ursula appears to be advancing with mutual exploration, that between Gerald and Gudrun continues to evoke images and suggestions of violent opposition, as if one must always assume a dominant position over the other. Thus, as Gudrun observes Gerald free and powerful, she envies him terribly. She wants the same freedom and mobility that he possesses by virtue of his gender. Observing Shortlands, the Crich estate, the sisters talk of Gerald's effort to make all the latest improvements to the estate. In a foreshadowing that is often repeated in various forms throughout the novel, Ursula comments that Gerald will "have to die soon, when he's made every possible improvement, and there will be nothing more to improve.—He's got to *go,* anyhow" (48). She then tells her sister the story of how Gerald accidentally shot and killed his brother as a young boy.

The next three chapters focus on Rupert Birkin and Gerald Crich in London as they mix with a set of artists and intellectuals (whom Lawrence skewers). These chapters introduce Birkin's flatmate in London, Halliday, and the people of his set, specifically, a young woman known as "the Pussum" and a Russian named Maxim. Gerald stays at the flat for several days and spends drunken evenings with these people. The chapters serve to reveal the hollow nature of the art world that Birkin is seeking to escape by spending most of his time in the country. The concerns of this group seem to be petty and trivial, focusing on their personal and sexual freedom, fetishizing primitive arts as somehow more essential than contemporary art, and condemning anyone who disagrees with their critical and aesthetic point of view.

In chapter 8, the sisters visit Breadalby, the country estate of Hermione Roddice. The party of visitors includes Rupert Birkin, Gerald Crich, and several others. The chapter features a tense conflict between Birkin and Hermione Roddice. One-time lovers, these two are now pitted against each other, illuminating the strange and cerebral connection they have forged. Hermione is keen to claim Birkin as her own, whereas Birkin is repulsed by her possessiveness. These two are engaged in a fierce disagreement in which every encounter between them is fraught with rage and violence. This violence finally erupts at the end of the chapter when Hermione takes up a heavy paperweight and slams it twice onto Birkin's head as he sits reading. He escapes a third blow by grabbing her arm and fleeing into the countryside, where he strips naked and mingles with the soothing and dew-wet vegetation around him. He concludes the chapter with the resolution that he does not need people or a woman; he simply needs the natural world. This conclusion sanctions the world of nature over the talk, theory, and politics that dominate Hermione's world. Rupert Birkin has made the escape from Hermione Roddice and her powerful desire to possess him.

The next chapter opens with a contrasting scene of a man dominating nature rather than joining with it. As Ursula and Gudrun walk home from teaching at the local school, they witness Gerald riding a mare. As they are forced to wait for a passing train, they observe Gerald forcing the frightened animal to stand close to the passing train, subduing her and forcing his spurs into her bloody sides. Ursula, in "pure opposition," is horrified by this scene. Gudrun is grotesquely fascinated by the brutal subjugation of this powerful animal to Gerald's will. It feeds her increasing enchantment with Gerald Crich. The sisters walk on, Ursula reeling with horror and Gudrun cold and indifferent to her sister's feelings. As they pass through the colliery town, two men working on the road appraise the sisters as they might animals up for sale, disagreeing whether five minutes with Gudrun would be worth a week's wages. She observes them with a withering glance, dismissing them as "her sinister creatures" and thereby asserting her superiority over them (112). The chapter concludes with a description of the colliery town of Beldover, Gudrun's loathing for it, and her habit of nevertheless walking the streets in the evening with a like-minded young man friend. Together they observe the masses of humanity with disgust and a scientific detachment. Gudrun fantasizes escaping from Beldover and yet recognizes its powerful hold over her.

The next three chapters bring the sisters and the men they are interested in closer together. In one scene, as Gudrun sketches by a pond, Gerald Crich and Hermione Roddice row up in a small boat and ask to see her sketches. In the course of the exchange, the sketchbook is dropped in the water and retrieved. This act is the deliberate fault of Hermione, and Gudrun's offhand dismissal of Hermione and her caper excite the observant Gerald, who notes that he and

Gudrun are alike. They both have a cold and hostile power within them. In stark contrast to this emerging antagonistic relationship between Gudrun and Gerald, we witness Rupert Birkin's and Ursula's first efforts to articulate a connection. This begins with Rupert sharing his despair at the state of humanity in the modern world and his doubts about the possibility of real love, when the word itself has become "vulgarized." Trying to understand him, Ursula repeats that love is essential and possible. They circle this topic, alternately admiring and hating each other as they move closer to acknowledging a bond that already exists between them, a bond that Ursula realizes will either break them or release them into a new life. The chapter concludes with Birkin telling Ursula that his affair with Hermione is over, even as Hermione approaches with Gerald Crich to visit the mill house into which Rupert has just moved.

As they meet Hermione and Gerald at the mill, Ursula challenges Gerald on his abuse of the mare earlier. An argument follows in which Ursula insists that Gerald's actions were a cruel abuse of his power while Hermione and Gerald defend the position that one must use one's will to master animals and baser creatures or instincts. Birkin, who despises Hermione for her use of will to control herself, goes so far as to assert that women, like horses, have two wills (one will to "subject herself utterly" and the other to "bolt"). He cautions that it is a dangerous thing to "domesticate" "even horses, let alone women" (140). Hermione and Ursula leave the men at this point and form a curious bond of mutual mistrust and respect. Ursula departs, feeling both firm in her position about the abuse of will and foolish in the eyes of the others.

In chapter 14, titled "The Water Party," a series of events further define the characters of Gudrun and Gerald and emphasize the fate that awaits them. The Brangwen sisters attend the colliery owner's annual "water party," an event that all the families of the region are invited to attend. Upon arriving, they ask Gerald if they might have a boat and a basket of food so that they can row over to a small island and have a quiet and private picnic. He supplies them with a canoe and sends them off. The sisters land on a quiet bank and bathe and dine, happy to be alone. While her sister sings, Gudrun begins dancing rhythmically. They are interrupted by a group of Highland cattle that wander into their picnic area. Gudrun insists that Ursula continue to sing while she begins to dance toward the cattle. Her mesmerizing dance is interrupted by a shout from Gerald that disperses the cattle. Gudrun is enraged with Gerald and strikes him in the face. He responds by stating that she has struck the first blow. "And I shall strike the last," Gudrun retorts, foreshadowing their relationship and its demise.

Meanwhile, Birkin has taken up a mocking, gyrating dance in front of Ursula. She is baffled and frightened by his behavior and demands that he stop. They fall into a philosophical conversation about the nature of relationships between men and women. Birkin diagnoses Gudrun and Gerald as engaged in the process of "destructive creation," calling them "fleurs du mal," flowers of destruction. Even as they create a bond, they are ensuring destruction, he says. When Ursula asks if she and Birkin are also flowers of destruction, he responds: "Some people are pure flowers of dark corruption—lilies. But there ought to be some roses, warm and flamey" (173). And Ursula insists that she is a "rose of happiness" (173). With these metaphors, the scene is set: We shall watch Gudrun and Gerald, the "pure flowers of dark corruption," battle; we shall watch Rupert and Ursula struggle to realize the possibility of happiness in a world where destruction is commonplace.

As the couples row back to the main party in the dark, they hear screams of panic. Diana Crich has disappeared in the dark, muddy water of the lake. A local doctor who dove in to search for her is also missing. Gerald dives again and again into the bone-chilling water, but he cannot find the two. The lake must be drained. In the morning, when the bodies are found at the bottom of the empty lake, Diana has her arms tightly around the neck of the young man beside her.

In the next chapter, we witness Ursula in a dark and despairing mood. Visited by Birkin, she is "absent" from him—changed. This mood results in her temporary but profound hatred of Birkin. In chapter 16, "Man to Man," Birkin is ill and meditates on his aversion to the love offered by Ursula, a love he considers to be a "dreadful bondage, a sort of conscription" (199). As Birkin reflects on the traditional love that Ursula offers, he defines his desires as different from this traditional arrangement: He wants a love that leaves both partners free, a love that is not as intent upon possession and control as he assumes Ursula's love to be. Birkin sees Ursula's love as typical of women: "Woman was always so horrible and clutching, she had such a lust for possession" (200).

While Birkin is sick in bed, Gerald Crich comes to visit him. They discuss the night of the accident and their relations with the Brangwen sisters. Gerald reveals that his father is devastated by the death of his daughter and has focused all his attention on his youngest child, Winifred, an artistic and sensitive child. As they discuss Winifred's possible future, Gerald points out that Hermione Roddice had suggested that Gudrun Brangwen might privately tutor Winifred in art. They discuss Gudrun and her possible reaction to this. Both men become abstracted and contemplative. Birkin realizes his love for Gerald and proposes that they take a vow of brotherhood and "swear to love each other" (206). Although pleased by the proposal, Gerald remains reserved, proposing that they wait.

Chapter 17, "The Industrial Magnate," begins by briefly returning focus to the Brangwen sisters, both of whom have turned away, if only for a time, from the men who interest them. Gudrun is busy trying to implement a scheme for leaving England. She would like to go to St. Petersburg or Munich to sculpt. Then the focus turns to the Crich family and the differences between the dying father and his son Gerald, who is taking over the family business. The bulk of the chapter focuses on Gerald as an "industrial magnate," revealing his business philosophy as both efficient and inhumane. As his father fades both from the business and his life, Gerald vigorously reforms the business of the mines, removing all excesses of humanitarianism and implementing a new and strictly efficient business model. Gerald is depicted as a high priest of industry, a divinity of sorts, whose achievement is not humane but it is lucrative. We are told that he had made the "industry into a new and ter- rible purity" through which there was more coal than ever. And though the miners' lives have been stripped of joy and hope, though they have become mechanized, they have submitted to Gerald's will and even seem satisfied "to belong to the great and wonderful machine, even whilst it destroyed them" (231). The chapter concludes by allowing us insight into the terror Gerald sometimes feels when he sees himself clearly. He feels increasingly empty, hollow, and unmotivated by the world around him.

Moving from attention to Gerald and his life, chapter 18 focuses on Gudrun's choice to become Winifred's tutor. She knows that this is forcing the relationship with Gerald, about which she is so ambivalent, but her curi- osity leads her to accept. Gerald meets Gudrun and Winifred by chance on one particular morning when they are planning to do a portrait of Winifred's pet rabbit, Bismarck. Gerald is "caressed" by Gudrun's words and gestures and feels himself "in love with her" (239). As Gudrun tries to take the rabbit from its pen, it struggles violently and tears the skin on her wrists. Gerald intercedes and takes the rabbit from her and subdues the screaming rabbit that has also torn his flesh. In a flash, both Gerald and Gudrun recognize that they share a common knowledge of "abhorrent mysteries." They both recognize in the other a fascination with power and dominance.

With chapter 19, "Moony," the narrative returns to focus on Birkin and Ursula. Feeling misanthropic, Ursula sets out for a walk one evening. She wanders into the wood by the mill and notices Birkin sitting by the pond, a full moon reflected on the water. While she sits nearby, unnoticed and silent, Birkin attempts to destroy the moon by throwing stones into the water. With each shattering strike of a stone, Ursula feels the violation. Yet the narrative notes the persistent return of the moon with the settling of the water. Finally, Ursula approaches him and asks him to desist. Their conversation turns to the topic of love. He tells her that she has a "golden light" within her that he wants her to give him. She counters that she wants him to "serve her spirit" but that he wants her to serve him. They argue about their different definitions of love: He wants her to "surrender her spirit" whereas she wants to "have him as her own, utterly"; he wants "mutual unison in separateness" and she wants "unspeakable intimacies" (264). Saddened by their differences but more in love, they part for the night.

The next day, Birkin doubts his insistence upon Ursula's surrender and goes to ask her to marry him. Ursula is not home, so Birkin tells her father of his desire to marry her. They quarrel because Mr. Brangwen sees Birkin, and Ursula for that matter, as representative of a new and sinful generation that does not take marriage as a sacred commitment. Birkin, meanwhile, sees Mr. Brangwen as an uninspired bag of clichés and traditions. When Ursula returns home to their tense meeting, she is affronted by the marriage proposal and feels "bullied" by both men awaiting her response. Birkin leaves quickly and Ursula retreats for several days into a cold, detached, and self-contained manner that torments her father.

In chapter 20, "Gladiatorial," Birkin leaves the fiasco with Ursula and goes straight to his friend Gerald at Shortlands. There, he finds Gerald restless and tormented, "like a machine that is without power" (266). Gerald had not been able to find anything to lift him from his utterly unfamiliar and terrifying boredom. The arrival of Birkin is a bright promise of community to Gerald. Gerald confesses his inertia and Birkin counsels that he should try hitting something. To the duo of work and love that cure boredom, Birkin adds fighting. He succeeds in interesting Gerald in a round of Japanese wrestling. Both men strip naked and engage in the fight. The fighting frees them of thought and provides each with a focus and essential unity. At last, they lie back on the carpet exhausted, their limbs entwined. As they dress and review their wrestling, Birkin feels that in addition to the pleasure of the physical engagement of wrestling, he takes pleasure in Gerald's physical beauty. But as they linger, Ursula returns to his mind and he tells Gerald that he has just proposed to her. Gerald is startled by this news. Birkin tells him that he thinks that he loves Ursula. Gerald responds that he has always believed in love but never felt it. He wonders whether he will ever feel true love.

As if following on this question, chapter 21 opens with Gudrun reading a letter from Winifred in which she introduces the idea that she and Winifred will have an art studio built for them at Shortlands. This would allow Gudrun to give up her teaching at the Grammar School and spend her days in the studio. Gudrun acknowledges this as Gerald's intention to have her "attached" to the household at Shortlands but concedes that she is quite happy with the arrangement if it allows her to create art.

In chapter 22, "Woman to Woman," Gudrun, Winifred, and Ursula are to have tea with Birkin in his apartment. Ursula arrives to find Hermione Roddice making herself at home in the drawing-room. They are tense, but they fall into conversation about Birkin's marriage proposal to Ursula. Ursula tells Hermione that she is not as keen on the idea of marriage as Birkin. She finds his views of marriage distasteful and confused. "He wants me to give myself up," she tells Hermione (294). Hermione, who is privately enthralled with the idea of giving herself up to Birkin, of becoming his "slave," asks Ursula more about Birkin's theories of marriage. Finally, in a pseudo-altruistic gesture, Hermione states that she thinks it would be disastrous for Birkin and Ursula to marry. She tells Ursula that she is too impatient for the sensitive and creative Birkin. Hermione suggests that Ursula is naïve and inexperienced, whereas Rupert is of an older "race," and succeeds in insulting and intimidating Ursula. At this point, Birkin enters the room and affects a bluff and cheerful manner that only irritates Ursula further. The three of them have tea, during which Hermione manages to engage Birkin in conversation about topics and people they are both intimate with, to make herself at home with Birkin's cat, and to demonstrate her worldliness by chatting alternately in Italian and English. Ursula leaves abruptly after tea, "outraged" with both Hermione and Birkin.

The next chapter is climactic and critical. "Excurse" begins with Birkin seeking Ursula. They set out for a ride in the country; both are tense and reserved with each other. Birkin gives Ursula three rings that he has bought for her. Recognizing that accepting these will signal a pledge, Ursula relents and tells him she is pleased with the rings. As they ride along, Ursula is happy and cheery. Birkin, in contrast, is brooding over the nature of their relationship. He wants her to "accept him in the quick of death" just as he has "taken her at the roots of her darkness and shame" (304). As Ursula proposes that they have a late tea and drive home in the dark, Birkin is forced to concede that he is to dine at Shortlands and that Hermione will be there. Immediately, Ursula draws away, "closed in a violent silence" (305). Birkin asks Ursula if she minds that he will dine with Hermione, and she retorts that she does not, that he "belongs" to Hermione and her "dead show" (306).

Birkin stops the car in the middle of the road so that they might attend to their "crisis of war" (306). Ursula accuses him of wanting her for "daily use" while he keeps his "spiritual bride" in the background. She tells him that he is entranced by Hermione's "sham spirituality." Throwing his rings in the dirt of the roadside, Ursula walks away. Birkin picks up the dirty rings and sits down to reflect on the truth of what she has said. He acknowledges that his spirituality is self-destructive—depraved. But, he counters, isn't her desire for emotional and physical conjoining, for "fusion," equally perverse? Isn't it a sort of tyranny that does not leave the other free? He reflects that Hermione wants men to worship her as an "Idea," but that Ursula wants men to come to her as the "perfect Womb" (309). He detests both absolutes. Still, Birkin sits there wishing that Ursula would return to him, which she does. They have a gentle reconciliation and feel the force of their love for each other all the more. Relaxing after their "battle," Birkin feels as if he were "born out of the cramp of a womb" (311). They take up their drive again, peaceful and happy in their love.

Birkin and Ursula stop to have tea at an inn. As they wait in a parlor to be taken to their meal, Ursula kneels before Birkin on the hearth rug and embraces "his loins, and put[s] her face against his thighs" and discovers his "mysterious life-flow" (313). In this position, she comes to awareness of him beyond her previous knowledge. She "discovered" him as "one of the Sons of God such as were in the beginning of the world" (313). As they dine, they come to the conclusion that they must quit their jobs at once and travel away from their current lives—away from the "old thing" (315). They have paper and pen delivered to them and proceed to write their formal resignation letters. They leave the inn and stop for provisions at a little village along the way. Then, they find a forest and spend the night together, making love and then sleeping.

In chapter 24, "Death and Love," the narrative returns to the dying Thomas Crich and the story of Gerald and Gudrun. Gerald is exhausted with anxiety related to his dying father. He feels bound up in his father's dying and intent upon seeing him through it. Yet, every day, as the father grows more weak, his son grows more anxious and detached from all else in his life. Unable to take more of this tension, Gerald seeks out Gudrun. He follows her and Winifred to their studio and invites Gudrun to dinner. Gudrun is hesitant to accept: "She felt as if she were caught at last by fate, imprisoned in some horrible and fatal trap" (325). After dinner that night, Gerald walks Gudrun home to Beldover and they pause where the colliery railroad bridges the road. Here, "where the young colliers stood in the darkness with their sweethearts," Gerald and Gudrun embrace for the first time. Both are transported by this embrace. Gerald finds a balance he has been seeking. Gudrun, who feels the fatal nature of their relationship, sees Gerald as "an unutterable enemy, yet glistening with uncanny white fire" (332). They part, and Gerald returns to Shortlands and his dying father.

Soon his father is dead and Gerald is left virtually alone in the house. He has not seen Gudrun for days and is growing increasingly anxious. One evening, unable to bear his misery any longer, he sets out into the night and finds himself at his father's grave. Yet this does not offer him peace, so he sets out to find Gudrun. It is late and the family has retired. Gerald slips into the house and stealthily ascends the stairs to find Gudrun's room. Alarmed and startled, Gudrun asks him why he has come to her and he replies simply, "Because—it has to be so.—If there weren't you in the world, then *I* shouldn't be in the world either" (343). In fascination, Gudrun embraces him. They make love and he feels an "infinite relief." He feels restored, "a man again, strong and rounded" (344). Gerald falls into a deep and peaceful sleep and Gudrun lies awake until dawn, tormented and wishing that his beauty "did not so fatally put a spell on her, compel her and subjugate her"(348). Quietly and awkwardly, Gerald leaves at dawn.

The next three chapters focus on marriage, both the idea of marriage and the actual marriage of Rupert Birkin and Ursula Brangwen. In Chapter 25, Gerald and Rupert discuss the idea of marriage when Gerald proposes semi-seriously that they make it a "double-barreled affair" in which both couples marry at the same time. Birkin again asserts his views on marriage and invites Gerald to join him in a union, man to man, that is in addition to the union of man and woman. Again, Gerald gently rejects the offer. The narrator reflects that Gerald would be willing to "condemn himself in marriage," but that "he would not make any pure relationship with any other soul" (353). For Gerald, marriage would be merely a formal bow to tradition, not a mystical union.

In the next chapter, "A Chair," Rupert and Ursula explore this same territory. That is, they attempt to determine whether they share the same understanding of marriage. They both agree that they do not want to be confined by objects and possessions; they want to be free of social trappings and social restrictions. They conclude that they would prefer to be without a home, free to travel and shed traditions that might accrue should they stay in one location for too long.

At the beginning of Chapter 27, Ursula announces brightly to her family that she is going to marry Rupert Birkin the next day. This breezy assertion leads to a severe break between Ursula and her father, who accuses her of being selfish and secretive about the marriage. Ursula retorts that he bullies her in the name of love and does not care about her happiness. Her father slaps her and Ursula leaves the house for good. She goes to Birkin's home. The next day they are married and she sends a letter to her parents. In these very early days of her married life, Ursula stays close to home with Birkin and sees only Gerald and Gudrun. Gerald proposes to Ursula and Birkin that the four of them take a trip to the Tyrol together.

In Chapter 29, the couples meet up in Switzerland and set out for their destination in the Alps. Birkin and Ursula are in a trance-like state, borne away from the familiar England and anticipating the future. Both feel childlike, as if they are about to become someone else or about to enter a new life. Chapter 30, "Snow," is the longest in the novel and focuses on the two couples in the Tyrolean Alps. When they arrive, all are struck by the vast expanse of snow, cold, and sky and by the isolation of the place. Ursula and Birkin cleave to each other, while Gudrun and Gerald turn toward the fatalism that has been foreshadowed throughout the novel. Gudrun shuts herself off from Gerald, recognizing that "a deep resolve" had formed in her to "combat him" (413). Gerald, sensing her absence and coldness, is caught within his inescapable desire to possess her.

At the inn where they are staying, the couples meet an artist, Loerke, and his homosexual partner, Leitner. Both Gudrun and Ursula are interested in Loerke, but there is between Gudrun and Loerke an immediate and inevitable attraction. She sees him as the "rock bottom of all life," as a man who has no illusions. Both Birkin and Gerald dislike Loerke. Birkin describes Loerke as a "little obscene monster of darkness," a "gnawing little negation, gnawing at the roots of life" (428). Neither Gerald nor Birkin can understand why Loerke is so attractive to the women. Ursula and Gudrun discuss art with Loerke. He shows them a photograph of a sculpture he did in bronze of a girl sitting sideways on a stiff and massive horse. Gudrun is deeply affected by the image; she feels like a supplicant before Loerke. Ursula takes exception to the stiff and oversized horse, accusing Loerke of depicting one of his mistresses in the girl and his own "brutality" in the horse. Gudrun and Loerke turn on her, insisting that art and life are two separate realms. Ursula leaves them and goes out into the snow, only to realize that she wants to go away, to escape the cold and snow and the false light it casts on everyone. Ursula and Birkin decide to go south; they will leave the next day.

In Chapter 31, with Birkin and Ursula gone, Gerald's and Gudrun's "vital conflict" begins. Gudrun remains cold to Gerald, and he will not leave her alone. She feels oppressed by his constant presence and reminds him that she never loved him. She tells him that she only took pity on him. She torments him by challenging that he never loved her, that he merely desires her, and forces him to repeat the words "I will love you always" (443). With his numb and dark desire, he crushes her in love-making, leaving her gasping, "Shall I die?" (444). Their battle is "an eternal see-saw, one destroyed that the other might exist" (445). As the battle between Gerald and Gudrun rages silently, Loerke and Gudrun forge an allegiance, "something insidious and traitorous" (447). Their allegiance forms around their discussions of art, yet it has a curiously "suggestive" quality. Meanwhile, Gerald waits patiently, unable to give up his abjection before his own desire, yet promising himself that he can kill Gudrun to put an end to it all.

One evening when Gerald is arguing with Loerke about Italy, disparaging all that Loerke asserts, Gudrun grows enraged and reveals that she is not Gerald's wife. This pivotal revelation enhances Loerke's interest in Gudrun and forces the issue with Gerald, who asks Gudrun why she "subjugates" herself to "that little scum of a sculptor" (455). She taunts Gerald, telling him that he is a fool and that Loerke understands women. Unaware that Gerald's patience is wearing thin, Gudrun torments him one night, telling him that it is over between them, asserting that he cannot love and she cannot love him. As he turns to strangle her, she senses his rage and dashes out of the room. She acknowledges that their fight is "to the death" and that she is walking on the "edge of an abyss" with him (462). But she cannot break the bond with him until she proves to both of them that she is not afraid of him.

The next day, when Loerke and Gudrun are out tobogganing and having a picnic in the snow, Gerald comes upon them silently. Loerke offers him schnapps. Knocking the bottle from his hand, Gerald hits him on the side of the head, twice. When Gudrun strikes out to stop him, he begins to strangle her. He watches her change color and slide into unconsciousness and suddenly loses his desire to kill her. He drops her and wanders off in the snowy twilight, murmuring that he has had enough. He wanders on and on in the night, lit only by the moon. He falls in the snow in a hollow surrounded by sheer slopes, his spirit broken, and he dies there.

In the final chapter, "Exeunt," Rupert and Ursula have returned to Switzerland to see Gudrun and make arrangements for Gerald's burial. When Ursula visits Gudrun, she finds her cold and tearless, fighting the knowledge that she killed Gerald. Rupert enters the room and Gudrun sees that he knows she killed Gerald. He agrees to take care of the details of Gerald's burial and leaves the room. Rupert meditates on Gerald's death, mourning his friend and the love Gerald would not accept from him. He concludes that if Gerald had embraced this final love between them, his death would not have mattered. Ursula challenges Rupert, saying that it would not have made a difference if Gerald had returned his love. Later, she asks him if she is not enough for him, and he responds, "You are all women to me. But I wanted a man friend, as eternal as you and I are eternal" (481). Ursula tells him that this is impossible. The book ends with Rupert asserting, "I don't believe that" (481).

CHARACTER DEVELOPMENT

Lawrence was keenly interested in the subconscious life of the individual. He wanted to bring those subconscious desires and motivations to the surface. We see these motivations arise as the characters pair off and build unions, each gaining a sense of a future for him- or herself in the modern world. Each central character in this novel is weary of old and false truths. To use a phrase from the character Hermione, each character feels "imprisoned within a limited, false set of concepts" (41). What Lawrence's exploration of characters and couples allows us to see are the difficulties, successes, and failures of their various attempts to find a meaningful way out of and beyond the set of "false concepts" belonging to the previous generation and questioned in this novel.

The Brangwen sisters, on whom the novel initially focuses, are on two separate paths toward self-discovery. Through their relationships with others, Lawrence is able to propose two models for rejecting the false concepts that these characters have inherited from their predecessors. One model, exemplified by Gerald, Gudrun, and Hermione, is cruel, deliberate, and predicated purely upon understanding something with one's mind. This approach is clearly demonstrated in Gerald's reform of his family's mining business; when Gerald has "modernized" the firm, we are told that "there was a new world, a new order, strict, terrible, inhuman, but satisfying in its very destructiveness" (231). Yet we are warned away from this path not only by Gerald's ultimate fate in the novel, but also by the fact that when he has achieved this transformation, Gerald is left with the same emptiness he has always felt. It is only his powerful will that sustains Gerald in the face of this growing knowledge of his own emptiness.

Rupert's and Ursula's search for a union that is based on "blood knowledge" and "learning not to be" is the second model for rejecting the old world and its worn-out traditions. This approach is in direct contrast to the model that Gerald and Gudrun represent, which is predicated on a dominating will: Gerald's will to reform the mining industry; Hermione's will to know the primitive; Gudrun's will to conquer Gerald. All of these fail in their way. But Rupert's and Ursula's efforts to escape the trappings of Victorian middle-class domesticity that places man over woman and reason over passion, though always tenuous, seem far more successful than the others. In the end of the novel, there is some hope for these two, who, although still disagreeing on many topics, have found relative peace outside the social structures that they have been fighting. They are not employed in "dead-end" jobs that stifle their spirits; they have chosen to live without all the physical markers of bourgeois domesticity; and they are open to a productive struggle to know and understand themselves and each other, even if that might prove impossible.

It is by contrast to each other that we first see the sisters: Gudrun is described as "diffident" and cool, whereas Ursula reflects a "sensitive expectancy" (8). As the novel progresses and the sisters develop relationships, these distinct manners are developed, explored, and contrasted. The novel directs our attention to Gudrun first. Gudrun's path in the novel is intimated early by her diffident character and her desire for power. She will struggle with questions of dominance and authority, refusing the path of compromise that her sister takes. She will pursue a path fraught with conflict generated by her own will to power. We first encounter her in conversation with Ursula, sharing her reactions to the constraints of marriage, and to the mining country where she has grown up. In her discussion of marriage as the "inevitable next step," Gudrun reflects that she has come home in order to prepare for a jump into some new experience: Gudrun is poised for change. In fact, when her sister wonders where one can "jump to," Gudrun foreshadows the extremity of her next experience when she says, "If one jumps over the edge, one is bound to land somewhere" (10).

What Gudrun wants to escape is made clear as the sisters walk through the mining town of Beldover. Gudrun is disgusted by the signs of middle- and working-class toil. Reflecting one aspect of Lawrence's own reactions to the mining country of his youth, Gudrun tells Ursula that the "people are all ghouls, and everything ghostly. Everything is a ghoulish replica of the real world, a replica, a ghoul, all soiled, everything sordid" (11). To Gudrun, there is no life in the repetition of labor. Belying her cold and competent demeanor, Gudrun grows frightened as they walk through the town, clinging to Ursula who, we are told, is inured to this "hostile world" (12). Here we see that Gudrun's tough exterior imperfectly hides a fragile interior.

As if in answer to what Gudrun's new experience might be, upon observing Gerald Crich, she is at once "magnetised." Her first observations of Gerald will be reiterated throughout the novel; she recognizes him as associated with cold and ice and tells herself that his totem is the wolf. She asserts self-confidently that she will "know more of that man" (14). The nature of her relationship with Gerald Crich will develop in conflict. In Gerald, Gudrun finds a potent male whom she will seek to conquer. She is as much drawn to his cold, northern beauty as she is to the "lurking danger of his unsubdued temper" (14). Thus, from the beginning, we have hints that their relationship will be a struggle for power and dominance, a struggle to the icy end.

In contrast to Gudrun, Gerald lacks insight into himself. He is only comfortable in action. Where Gudrun is the artist, disgusted with the trappings of the workaday world and seeking new experience, Gerald is constrained by the class and country to which he is heir: He is the golden son of a wealthy industrialist. Soon to be master of the estate and the industry, Gerald knows himself best as a man of action. He is not introspective, and he fears a life without the definition of his social position. Gerald is like a machine, to which he is often compared in the novel. He is not torn by awareness of human discomfort and social disparities. He is efficient, cold, and poised. He dominates and subdues difficult situations, be they human or industrial. Thus, when he takes over the mine as his father slowly dies, his approach is based on efficiency and productivity, not on humanism. His takeover of the mine is associated with death: "As soon as Gerald entered the firm, the con-vulsion of death ran through the old system.... Terrible and inhuman were his examinations into every detail; there was no privacy he would spare, no old sentiment but he would turn it over" (229).

Yet, like Gudrun, Gerald is poised for some great change: "He would have to go in some direction, shortly, to find relief" (232). They will "jump" together into a mortal battle. Gudrun and Gerald pursue their power struggle to the bitter end. Ultimately, it is Gerald who is defeated in this battle when he cannot either bring himself to subdue Gudrun by force or break through his own reliance upon the tradition of male authority in order to discover himself. He ultimately commits suicide by wandering away into the Alps and freezing to death.

For her part, Gudrun pursues a relationship with the German sculptor Loerke, whom she meets at the hotel in the Alps where she has gone with Gerald. Loerke is a nihilistic figure. He has rejected all social morals and beliefs and set his own terms for existence through and for art. Gudrun, fol-lowing her trajectory away from all social conventions, departs with Loerke to Dresden at the end of the novel, clearly ready to pursue all that this path out of conventional society can offer her.

Ursula and Rupert pursue a path of growth and compromise that, though hard won, is not a violent battle to death. The narrator tells us repeatedly that with her sensitive and open manner, Ursula has the "strange brightness of an essential flame" (9). Rupert speaks of this as her inner "golden light." We learn that Ursula is "prescient" of something "yet to come," some real-ization of life defined by her own terms. Commonly, Ursula (like Rupert) is described as being like an "infant in the womb" about to be born. And, appropriately, when Ursula first recognizes "some kinship," she acknowledges that "she wanted to know him" (20). But Ursula's thoughts are balanced and cautious in comparison with Gudrun's conviction that there is a fated destiny between her and Gerald. Ursula seems measured in her assessment of Birkin, more thoughtful, and less willing to plunge into something without knowing where she is headed.

Ursula's attraction to Rupert Birkin is based upon her sense that there is a "richness" and "liberty" in him that is searching for expression. Still, Ursula seems quite conscious of Birkin's flaws. She knows of his longtime relationship with Hermione Roddice and has observed them together. To Ursula, their relationship appears strained, cerebral, and false. Ursula recognizes Hermione as a "man's woman" and notes the way she tries to take possession of Rupert, even as he fights her off. Based loosely on Lady Ottoline Morel (a prominent arts patron, socialite and one-time friend and supporter of D. H. Lawrence), Hermione is an example of the overly cerebral and ego-centered type of person that Lawrence consistently derides. Birkin's relationship with Hermione is set up in direct contrast to the potential relationship he might have with Ursula. In the scene when Birkin and Hermione interrupt Ursula's class, Rupert describes Hermione best when he attacks her, saying, "You have no sensuality. You have only your will and your conceit of consciousness, and your lust for power, to *know*" (42). It is this self-conscious examination of everything that Birkin is turning away from; for, this is another way of having and owning. In contrast to this, Ursula represents for Birkin the sensual, unselfconscious world that he seeks; she owns only herself.

As a character, Rupert Birkin is based loosely on D. H. Lawrence (just as Ursula Brangwen is based on Frieda Lawrence). Although one cannot read the novel as autobiography, the theories that Rupert puts forward, and even his habit of bullying with talk, are very like Lawrence's. The "blood knowledge" that Rupert seeks is quite consistent with Lawrence's theories of unselfconscious being. In the classroom scene after he has argued with Hermione for her "will to know," Ursula asks Rupert if he really wants sensuality, a question suggested by his stiff and intellectual interactions with Hermione. He responds that he wants nothing else: "it is a fulfillment—the great dark knowledge you can't have in your head—the dark involuntary being" (43). When Ursula asks how you can have knowledge that is not in your head, he responds that you have it "in the blood." Rupert seeks this knowledge throughout the novel. In this early chapter, Rupert states what will become the model for relationship that he and Ursula share. He tells Ursula, "You've got to lapse out before you can know what sensual reality is, lapse into unknowingness, and give up your volition. You've got to do it. You've got to learn not-to-be, before you can come into being" (44).

THEMES

It is important to remember that this work was written in a time of great personal and social turmoil. Lawrence had just been through the banning and burning of his previous book, *The Rainbow*, which was said to be "pornographic." Europe was at the height of the bloodiest war ever. In 1916 there were thousands of deaths reported in the newspapers each day. Lawrence was living in Cornwall during the war and was harassed daily for his marriage to a German and his suspicious behavior, which made him all the more paranoid and isolated from his fellow Englishmen. In the midst of all of this, he was struggling to overturn traditions and values that not only did he feel had led to the war in the first place but that he also found personally suffocating. Lawrence felt that the rise of industrialism, everywhere apparent in the modern and mechanized world, was essentially destroying the possibility of genuine connection and intimacy among people. Written under the pressure of all these roiling conflicts, *Women in Love* reflects conflict thematically.

Throughout the novel, Lawrence presents us with oppositions that we must seek to reconcile or make sense of. One of the most prominent dichotomies manifests in the theme of life versus death, which plays out in numerous ways and serves to remind us that oppositions are not as clear as we might at first assume. For example, where Birkin and Ursula are typified as flowers of life, Gerald and Gudrun are "pure flowers of dark corruption" and represent death (173). The clarity of these symbolic opposites appears when Gerald and Gudrun do battle to the death. It is also evident when Ursula and Birkin have found a new life, one relatively free of the social trappings that they despise, but in the process they have been through a form of death and rebirth. Lawrence constantly reminds us that opposites are intimately connected, and that with death there is life and with life there is death.

The theme of violent conflict is most apparent in the relationship between Gudrun and Gerald. The very nature of their mutual attraction is predicated upon the violence each senses in the other. This attraction to violence in the other stimulates in each a will to dominate and subdue. Gerald notices in Gudrun a "cold power" and a "dangerous hostile spirit" (122). He is drawn by a "diabolical freemasonry" between them (122). Similarly, Gudrun recognizes in Gerald a desire to "lapse into sheer unrestraint, brutal and licentious" (287). Each of these characters has a barely restrained rage and will to dominate that reinforces the theme of violence. This theme has several sources: the war in Europe, Lawrence's conviction that he was living in a "collapsing civilization," and Lawrence's own rage at these and other realities.

Gerald and Gudrun are only the most obvious examples of violence. This theme is present throughout the novel and in many other characters. Every character in this novel, even the mild Ursula, has moments of blinding, violent rage. Hermione bashes Birkin on the head with a lapis lazuli paper weight. When Diana Crich's body is pulled from the lake and her arms are still around the neck of the doctor who died trying to save her, Gerald pronounces that "she killed him" (189). These scenes illustrate that love, need, and violence are all intertwined. They also illustrate the failure of the connection between people. Hermione's violent act comes when it is clear that she has lost control over Birkin. It is an act of violent despair in the face of the inevitable. Similarly, Diana Crich's act, whether or not she did in fact "kill" the doctor, reflects desperation and a desire for connection.

The theme of violence is also connected to characters' desires for power over each other and the natural world. It is not only humans who come in for abuse. Gerald's scene with the horse is perhaps the most obvious example of this. His attempt to dominate the mare is savage: As she rears frantically, he "forces" her to stand near the passing train. "It was a repulsive sight. But he held on her unrelaxed, with an almost mechanical relentlessness, keen as a sword pressing in to her" (111). Symbolized as mechanized power and cold sunshine, Gerald here is pure dominance. He represents man over matter in the purest and most violent sense. But there are other scenes that demonstrate the strong dominating the weak: Gudrun tries to take the rabbit Bismarck from its pen and its violent struggle leads Gerald to silence the animal in "white edged wrath," and in another scene Gudrun torments cattle (241). Like the futile violence characters inflict upon each other, more than anything else, these scenes speak to Lawrence's questions about relationships that result from both a desire for connection and a deep rage and desire to control other beings.

Another theme in the novel is Lawrence's challenging of traditions. In their discussion of marriage, the Brangwen sisters articulate a perception of the institution of marriage that was not unique to Lawrence. Many people in the early part of the century had begun to challenge traditional notions of the family and, specifically, marriage. (We have already seen this in Forster's *Howards End*, for example.) What Lawrence brings to this emerging debate is a focus on individual character and the impulses that live under the surface of our consciousness. The Brangwen sisters express distaste for traditional marriage when they return to their near-empty childhood house. Observing that their own parents' marriage seems hollow and empty, Ursula shudders at the thought of reliving it. She tells Gudrun that if she thought that her married life would be like theirs, "I should run" (373). Although this may be a common sentiment today, it was a radical thought at the time Lawrence wrote this novel. Gudrun, aware that Ursula and Birkin have a chance to escape this tradition, shares her own despair of finding freedom in marriage: "To marry, one must have a free lance, or nothing, a comrade-in-arms, a Glucksritter. A man with a position in the social world—well, it is just impossible, impossible" (374). And this "position in the social world" is precisely what Gerald Crich has and cannot escape. He is an industrialist, an estate owner, and a man who promotes the commerce of his nation.

But Ursula and Birkin do promote the possibility of escaping the confines and constrictions of middle-class values and traditions. The chapter that most effectively articulates this theme of rejecting traditions might well be "The Chair," a chapter that allows them to explore the meaning of "housekeeping" or "setting up house." The symbol for the traditional notion of marriage becomes a secondhand chair that they impulsively buy at an outdoor market. Intending to decorate their home, they at first are charmed by the chair. Rupert likes it for its representation of history: "My beloved country—it had something to express even when it made that chair.... And now, we can only fish among the rubbish heaps of the remnants of their old expression. There is no production in us now, only sordid and foul mechanicalness" (355). Ursula is irritated by this view and asserts that she does not want an old chair that "preaches" the past. They both agree that they do not want to "go on living on the old bones of beauty," even if the present is dull repetition. They determine to live free of the restrictions of household and possessions that "turn you into a generalisation" (356). They give the chair to a young couple, the woman obviously pregnant and the man sullen and trapped. Birkin and Ursula assert to each other their desire to be "disinherited" and live without the trappings of house and home and all they signify in society.

In fact, at the end of the novel, Ursula and Birkin have achieved some form of "disinheritance," leaving England for the Alps, and then the Alps for Italy. In the sisters' final discussion before Ursula leaves for Italy, Gudrun asks Ursula if she is really leaving behind the old world—the world of family and country and home. Ursula responds tentatively that she agrees with Rupert, that "one wants a new space to be in," to fall away from the old (437). Gudrun counters that a new world can only develop from "this world," and all else is illusion. Gudrun persists, asking whether it isn't an illusion to think you can get out of the world you live in, no matter where you go. And Ursula counters that one can "see it through in one's soul," given the chance (437).

SYMBOLS

In this novel, symbols commonly adhere to characters. Thus, Ursula is symbolized as a rose and a warm light. Gudrun is symbolized by ice and cold, as is Gerald, who is also commonly symbolized as Cain, as mechanized energy, and as crystal. These symbols are omnipresent, but they are often complicated by contradictory symbolism, reminding readers that opposites coexist. For example, immediately following the scene in which Birkin describes Gerald as a force of pure destruction, Gerald attempts to rescue his sister and the doctor from the lake, at great risk to himself. Clearly, this force of destruction carries with it the ability to do good. This is particularly evident in the descriptions of Gerald's reform of the mining business. He is savagely efficient with human resources but builds a powerful business.

More than through singular symbols, the main ideas in this novel are conveyed through symbolic acts and characters. For example, key acts and characters symbolize the danger of trying to know someone (or something) entirely with your mind. As Lawrence has said in his essay on Edgar Allen Poe, "Man does so horribly want to master the secret of life and of individuality *with his mind*. It is like the analysis of protoplasm. You can only analyze *dead* protoplasm, and know its constituents. It is a death process" (138). In the novel this idea is demonstrated in part through the character of Hermione. For example, in the scene just before Hermione and Rupert have the violent clash that signals the end of their relationship, Hermione pushes harder to know Rupert intellectually: "She was at once roused, she laid as it were violent hands on him to extract his secrets from him. She *must* know. It was a dreadful tyranny, an obsession in her, to know all he knew" (145). The tyranny and violence of intellectual knowing is Hermione's obsession. As we repeatedly see Hermione's intellectualism criticized, it comes to be portrayed as a force of death: Hermione becomes symbolic of this "death process." But she is not the only symbol of this idea.

Lawrence relies heavily upon symbols in this novel when he sets out to demonstrate the violent dominance of one's will. The scene with the mare and the scene with the rabbit both stand out as symbolic of this violent use of force. This is perhaps most fully explored in the scene in which Loerke shows the sisters an image of his sculpture of a naked girl on a huge horse. This sculpture comes to symbolize the domination of one by another. The girl sits on the "massive, magnificent stallion, rigid with pent up power" in a position of "shame and grief" (524). Indeed, we learn that Loerke "had to" beat his young model to get her to sit still for this sculpture. Subjected to Loerke's will and forever captured in the sculpture, as naked and ashamed, this female figure symbolizes the violence of the will to dominate. Clearly, we can see throughout the novel that Lawrence is fascinated with domination and power. But each symbolic representation of it in the novel ultimately reveals deadliness. In the end, the only hope is contained within the relationship of Birkin and Ursula, a relationship that is, however tentatively, predicated upon mutuality.

NARRATIVE STYLE

Like other Modernists, Lawrence found himself struggling with the limitations of the language and literary styles he had inherited. As he sought to explore the psychological depths of character and psyche, depths of which Lawrence believed people had very little awareness, he forged a style that reflected what had not yet been articulated in fiction. Lawrence's style is full of repetition, rhythm, dialogue, and innuendo. Like Joyce, Woolf, and other Modernists, Lawrence felt he was inventing a new language, a language that articulated the subterranean depths of our psyches, which he considered a critical component governing our lives and actions. But unlike Joyce and Woolf, Lawrence was relatively comfortable with the form of the novel; it was the content and subject explored in the novel that Lawrence felt must break from the past. He addresses the psychic depths of his characters; he examines their sexual drives and ambivalences. This is the "new" in Lawrence's writing. Repetition allowed Lawrence to drive home the nature of subconscious drives and desires, which return to motivate a character's actions and choices. One of the hallmarks of this style is repetition, for which Lawrence has been criticized. Yet, if we understand his style in the context of his intentions as a writer, we might come to appreciate it. Lawrence wanted to reveal the influence of the subconscious life on the conscious. Just as words repeat in his fiction, driving a point or idea home, so too do subconscious drives and desires reappear and shape our conscious actions, he believed. Thus, for example Gudrun's and Gerald's violent drives reemerge throughout, driving forward to their inevitable ends.

Quite like Sigmund Freud, who was working at the same time on his theories of psychology and sexuality, Lawrence believed that our subconscious sexual drives are far more central to our actions in our conscious life than society had ever acknowledged. He felt compelled to articulate and demonstrate this centrality in his fiction. In 1919, he wrote a foreword for the American publication of *Women in Love*. In this forward, he defended his exploration of the spirituality within sensual passions and his effort to divine a fate dictated by the aspirations of one's soul, rather than the dictates of society. Lawrence was ostracized and persecuted for his effort to bring forth his vision of a new passion between individuals.

Lawrence turned to writing in order to articulate his understanding of human nature and convey his ideas for change. He also observed that he exorcised his own demons through writing. Lawrence wanted to teach people through his writing, to help them see the deadly constriction of the traditions they blindly embraced. Most people, Lawrence felt, did not know that they were living in a dead world. They are best described in this statement by Birkin: "Humanity itself is dry-rotten, really.... They are apples of Sodom, as a matter of fact, Dead Sea fruit, gall-apples. It isn't true that they have any significance—their innards are full of bitter, corrupt ash" (186). Lawrence hoped that his writing would help people to be freer with themselves, to come to understand a little better the impact of desires and physical drives on our actions. This was new territory in the early part of the twentieth century. No one had written so freely about sex and love before Lawrence.

The novel is staged like a drama, with chapters changing scenes and settings and highlighting the development of plotlines. This allows the narrative to move forward in episodes, which coalesce in key scenes throughout the novel. The episodic staging of the novel is enhanced by the scenes that each chapter stages. So, for example, the novel opens in the Brangwen home, takes us into the town of Beldover, thus contextualizing the Brangwen's home, and narrows again to focus on the church. Similarly, the next chapter stages the scene of Shortlands, the Crich estate. Ultimately, as the characters seek to escape the worn-out world of their past, the stage becomes Switzerland. The dramatic structure also allows Lawrence to shift abruptly from the point of view of one character to another. This takes the readers back and forth between the two central relationships of the novel. We see each relationship developing in dramatic contrast to the other, with Gudrun's and Gerald's relationship heading toward destruction as Ursula's and Birkin's moves toward connection.

There is a powerful realism to Lawrence's prose and scenery. Through his descriptive detail, Lawrence has an ability to make us see the colliery town, the lush countryside, and the constricted interior of the Crich estate, Shortlands. His description affords the reader a sense of place and location, even as the thoughts and discussions of the characters are the central focus of the prose. This serves the novel in two ways. On one hand, it saves the novel from becoming too heavily cerebral; it balances the "incessant talk" of the characters and roots the emotional and intellectual struggle of the central characters in a realistic context (Sanders 120). But the descriptive detail also serves the purpose of emphasizing the intellectual struggle or the mood of the characters. Thus, the cold and frozen landscape of Switzerland resonates with Gudrun's icy resolve to destroy Gerald, and the warm landscape of Italy beckons the "flamey" love of Ursula and Birkin.

Although Lawrence's style was not as structurally experimental as that of contemporaries like Woolf and Joyce, his exploration of the subconscious forces that drive individuals and society was an important contribution to Modernist literature. Lawrence's style is innovative in its content and refusal to resolve the contradictions of the human motivations that he so insistently examines.

HISTORICAL CONTEXT

It is impossible to talk about this novel without addressing the historical and personal context in which it was composed. Although Lawrence's marriage was a struggle, he was even more distraught over the state of Europe. World War I was raging, and Lawrence was convinced that Europeans had collectively lost their minds. The war itself was a disaster. But to Lawrence it represented the culmination of industrialism and "the mechanical principle." The war, as Sanders argues, demonstrated the capitalist view of human workers as commodities that could be exchanged or replaced. The vast machinery of war, with its thousands of casualties per day, demonstrated the dehumanization of industrialism for Lawrence. Lawrence articulates this sentiment when he writes about London during the war: "The spirit of the old London collapsed. This city, in some way, perished, perished from being the heart of the world, and became a vortex of broken passions, lusts, hopes, fears, and horrors. The integrity of London collapsed, and the genuine debasement began" (quoted in *T. S. Eliot: An Imperfect Life* 136). Although *Women in Love* is set in peacetime, one can see the impact of this profound conflict in the work. It is a novel about relationships, but it is also a novel about the extreme violence within people and the ways that violence can destroy us and those we love.

In addition to her part in the unavoidable disaster of the war in Europe, England was faced with many other conflicts in the first decades of the twentieth century. The labor movement was growing in size and becoming far more violent in its rhetoric. The suffragists had escalated their efforts to secure the right to vote, leading to violent clashes with the police. The economy of England had been in decline since the end of World War I, and poverty was on the rise. This world was the backdrop for the enormous social forces that were changing the structure of society. The world Lawrence was writing about and seeking to change with his fiction was a world of turmoil.

5

T. S. Eliot
The Love Song of J. Alfred Prufrock (1917) and *The Waste Land* (1922)

BIOGRAPHICAL CONTEXT

Thomas Stearns Eliot was born on September 26, 1888, in St. Louis, Missouri. He was the seventh and youngest child of Henry Ware Eliot and Charlotte Champe Sterns Eliot, and a grandson of William Greenleaf Eliot. T. S. Eliot's first American ancestor was a prominent citizen in Salem, Massachusetts, and a juror in the Salem witch trials. Eliot's grandfather moved from Boston to St. Louis, where he established the first Unitarian Church and was one of the founders of Washington University. Eliot's father was a successful manufacturer of pressed bricks. His mother was a religious woman, intellectually curious and interested in writing poetry. Their household was one of strict religious observance and puritan propriety. T. S. Eliot was educated at Smith Academy in St. Louis and attended Milton Academy in Massachusetts in preparation for his college work at Harvard, where he received an M.A. in 1910. Eliot attended lectures for a year at the Sorbonne in Paris. He worked on a doctorate in philosophy at Harvard and, in 1914, was awarded a Harvard traveling fellowship to study philosophy at Oxford for a year. Eliot never returned to live in the United States. Although he completed his doctoral dissertation on the philosopher F. H. Bradley, he did not go back to Harvard to defend the dissertation and therefore was not awarded his doctorate.

In 1915, Eliot met and married Vivienne Haigh-Wood (hereafter referred to as Vivien Haigh-Wood, because she changed the spelling of her name). In that same year, with the help and insistence of his new friend Ezra Pound, whom he had met in 1914, Eliot's poem *The Love Song of J. Alfred Prufrock* was published in Harriet Monroe's journal *Poetry*. This poem gained Eliot notice as a rising star in the literary avant-garde. Eliot took a job as a teacher in the High Wycombe Grammar School, an exhausting job that paid him poorly and left him very little time to write, both facts that he expressed bitterly to Pound and other intimate friends. Alleviating his financial difficulties only slightly, in 1916 Eliot was promoted to Junior Master at Highgate Junior School, began writing reviews for periodicals, and also began giving university extension lectures, much as E. M. Forster had done in his early years as a writer. In 1917, further improving his financial situation, Eliot gave up the Junior Master teaching position, though not his university extension lecturing, and took a position at Lloyds Bank in London. Also in 1917, Eliot succeeded Richard Aldington as assistant editor of the *Egoist*, a literary review in London with a small circulation but with an important and literarily well-connected audience.

In the midst of all of these changes in employment, Eliot continually tried to write poetry, secretly confessing to his brother that he feared *The Love Song of J. Alfred Prufrock* was his "swan's song" (*The Letters of T.S. Eliot*, 150). This fear was eradicated by the publication of *The Waste Land* in 1922, which established Eliot as the quintessential Modernist poet. Contrary to what he said in his letter to his brother, Eliot did write a good deal of poetry between 1915 and 1922: *Preludes* and *Rhapsody on a Windy Night* were published in Wyndham Lewis's *Blast* in July 1915; *Prufrock and Other Observations* was published in 1917; *The Sacred Wood*, which contained the poem "Gerontion," published in 1920. In 1922, Eliot won the *Dial* Award for *The Waste Land*. After *The Waste Land*, Eliot's work became more spiritual and even specifically religious in theme, as evidenced in his drama *Murder in the Cathedral* and his religious poems *Four Quartets*. In 1927 the religious focus in his poetry increased when he joined the Church of England, where he maintained active membership until his death in 1964.

In addition to poetry, Eliot was writing a great many critical essays about literature and literary method during these years. He had many essays published in *The Times Literary Supplement*, *Vanity Fair*, and *The Atheneum*. Perhaps the most important of his critical and philosophical writing of this time came in essays that defended or attempted to define his own poetic practice and that of his colleagues (e.g., Ezra Pound). These essays include "Tradition and the Individual Talent" published in *The Egoist* in 1919; "The Perfect Critic," published in 1920; "The Function of Criticism," published in 1923; and "*Ulysses*, Order, and Myth," published in *The Dial* in 1923.

Eliot's marriage to Vivien Haigh-Wood was proving disastrous. He married her almost on an impulse in June 1915 when he was trying to decide whether to return to the United States and become an academic or, as Ezra Pound was urging, stay in England and try to make his life as a poet. Apparently Pound was instrumental in bringing Vivien and Eliot together, convincing Vivien to "save Eliot for poetry" (Gordon 117). Yet Eliot's insight into the failure of his marriage was not long in coming; his biographer tells us that in his private papers Eliot claimed that out of his "marriage to Vivien came the state of mind that 'led to *The Waste Land*'" (Gordon 119). For both partners the marriage appears to have been a torment. In Eliot's presence, two weeks after their marriage, Vivien told their mutual friend, Bertrand Russell, that she had married Eliot to "stimulate" him and confessed that it was already clear that she had failed. Indeed, all evidence points to the source of Vivien's misery in the marriage being connected to Eliot's repressed sexuality and his embarrassment with her.

When Eliot married her, Vivien was a "chic and literate woman" (Gordon 134). Yet it became quickly apparent that she suffered from mental and physical illnesses. Within a year of their marriage, Vivien was increasingly sick, taxing Eliot's nerves and finances. She had only a small income of her own and was unable to work, though apparently she had tried. As early as 1916, Eliot wrote to his friend Conrad Aiken that Vivien's health had been "a great anxiety all winter and spring," observing that her problems were "nerves, complicated by physical ailments" (quoted in *The Waste Land: A Facsimile and Transcript* xi). His letters of the time all feature his struggles to help Vivien with her illnesses, his extreme fatigue in the face of too much work, and his anxiety about finances. Eliot, too, was often sick and emotionally overwrought in the first years of his marriage.

An additional strain in Eliot's life at this time was his disillusionment with the postwar world around him. Eliot had never had much faith in his fellow humans. His early poems are clear indications of this, with *The Love Song of J. Alfred Prufrock* as a vivid testament to his state of mind even before the war began (he first drafted *Prufrock* while at Harvard in the early 1900s). It is undeniable that the public world as well as his private torment contributed to *The Waste Land*. The year 1921 was one of terrible upheaval politically and economically in London, with two million unemployed and signs of poverty and despair everywhere. Although Eliot was not a pacifist and had tried very hard to get an appointment with either the United States Navy or Army, the war had horrified him. Living in Bertrand Russell's apartment in 1915, Eliot saw a wartime London "from which almost all its young men were withdrawn, and only the sick and unfit, the elderly, the women, the workers, and the few pacifist intellectuals—outcasts—remained" (Gordon 136). Jean Verdenal, Eliot's friend from his year in Paris, was killed on the battlefield in the Dardanelles; Eliot dedicated his first volume of poetry to him. With Verdenal, Eliot had shared a love of poetry and music and a belief that these could influence one's inner life for the supreme good.

In September 1921, Eliot's health was so poor that Vivien convinced him to see a specialist, who told Eliot that he must "go away *at once* for three months quite alone, and away from everyone" (quoted in *The Waste Land: A Facsimile and Transcript* xxi). Eliot took an immediate leave of absence from his job at the bank and went to Margate, on the coast of England. Following the advice of a friend, he soon sought the help of a specialist in psychology in Lausanne, Switzerland. Eliot spent the last three months of 1921 in a sanatorium in Lausanne, where he composed the first draft of *The Waste Land*. On his way back to London in 1922, Eliot stopped in Paris to leave the manuscript of the poem with Ezra Pound for his editorial assistance. Pound wrote to a mutual friend, John Quinn, that Eliot looked good and had with him "a damn good poem" (*The Waste Land: A Facsimile and Transcript* xxii). Eliot indicates his indebtedness to Pound for his help with the poem by dedicating it to him as "*il miglior fabbro*," the better fabricator.

Over these years of developing his poetic voice and style, Eliot was influenced by widely disparate writers, many of whom he references in his poems. Perhaps the most important influences were Dante Alighieri and the French Symbolists, specifically Baudelaire and Laforgue. From Baudelaire, Eliot learned that the very material of the modern city could be central to his writing. Baudelaire's poetry often takes the modern city, with all its "sordid" filth, as the subject and scenery of poetry. Laforgue, Eliot says in his essay "What Dante Means to Me," was the "first to teach me how to speak, to teach me the poetic possibilities of my own idiom of speech" (in *To Criticize the Critic* 126). In that same essay, Eliot tells us that Dante is the greatest "religious poet," and that "*The Divine Comedy* expresses everything in the way of emotion, between depravity's despair and the beatific vision, that man is capable of experiencing" (134). In Dante, Eliot had found a poet with a deep religious sensibility to match his own, a poet who does not shy from the breadth of human experience, sordid to divine.

Perhaps more than any other Modernist author, Eliot had a hand in shaping not only the future of poetry but the future of criticism. He achieved this in two ways, one of which was through his own criticism, which dictated the terms by which generations of critics have read his work. By the standards of Eliot's own critical method, as he articulated in his essay "Traditional and the Individual Talent," modern literature was to be read as a model of objective impersonality. The poet or author, according to Eliot, was to take himself out of the poetry, using what he termed an "objective correlative" to convey emotion. As he defined it, an objective correlative is an object or pattern that evokes an emotion in the reader without requiring the poet to directly state that emotion. Thus, for example, the "brown fog" over the city of London in *The Waste Land* might well serve to convey the emotion of despair, loss, and "death in life" that Eliot wanted to capture. In his critical writing, Eliot warns readers that the poet and his "feelings" are irrelevant to the work of the poem, as he attempts to direct readers away from the author. In his essay "Tradition and the Individual Talent," he writes: "Honest criticism and sensitive appreciation is directed not upon the poet but upon the poetry" (40). With this focus, he sets the direction for readers and critical theorists.

The very intertextual and historically grounded nature of Eliot's poetry shaped its critical interpretation and spawned a library of exegetical close-reading in what has come to be called the "New Critical" tradition. This school of criticism was forged by critics like John Crowe Ransom, Allen Tate, and Cleanth Brooks, to name just a few of its key advocates. New Critics focus exclusively on the work of art itself, as opposed to the author or the impressions of the critic. Advocating critical readings that engage with the inner qualities of the literature itself to find its morality and value, new critics were most interested in image, symbol, and meaning. Thus, practitioners engage in close readings of the text that reveal meaning in the allusions, literary technique, and formal coherence of the literature. By staying close to the text of Eliot's poems for their interpretations, and guiding us through their many allusions and literary-historical references, the New Critics have done invaluable work. Their studies have given us many insights into *The Waste Land*, for example, that cannot be gained without what Eliot himself called the "great labour" of gaining the "historical sense." By "historical sense," Eliot means a "perception, not only of the pastness of the past, but its presence" ("Tradition and the Individual Talent" 38). Thus, critics have engaged in a deep analysis of Eliot's poetry by exploring its roots in an historical tradition of great poets who seek regeneration of a dead and empty world. Critics working at the end of the twentieth century and since, in contrast, have begun to discuss what the text of the poems and Eliot himself seek to hide: the very personal elements of the poems that are rooted in Eliot's life and in an historical moment of enormous transition and widespread despair.

Finally, one must say a word or two about the inclusion of Eliot, an American-born poet, in a collection of essays on British Modernists. Much important critical work has been done to establish Eliot as an American poet, that is, one who is influenced by the American literary tradition and by

American philosophical and religious history. This influence on his life and work is indisputable. Yet Eliot was, at least from 1927 onward, a naturalized British citizen. Furthermore, as he lived and wrote in England from 1913 until his death in 1965, Eliot's influence on English Modernism was immediately felt in England. Thus, without disputing Eliot's American roots, and the persistent influence of America on Eliot's writing, one can justify his position within British Modernism by pointing to his profound influence on British poetry and British Modernism. Furthermore, one can look to the importance of Britain in Eliot's life as a poet, a playwright, and an essayist.

THE LOVE SONG OF J. ALFRED PRUFROCK

Summary

    Eliot's puritan upbringing and personal reticence led him to compose arch and ironic poems that work to mask emotion. His early verse is satiric and sardonic; he does not think much of human society and he holds out little hope for it. Eliot's first mature poem and, many argue, the first poem in the modern movement, was *The Love Song of J. Alfred Prufrock*. In this poem, the critic Helen Vendler argues, Eliot found his voice as a poet. She calls this an "idiolect" that is the amalgamation of many discourses (102). This idiolect allowed Eliot to express himself honestly, albeit guardedly. Through his amalgamation of voices, Eliot could articulate the deep conflicts with which he struggled: his puritanical aversion to sex and his romantic longing, his love of drama and his need for analytic distance, his longing for religion and his impatience with the hollow rhetoric of organized churches, and his sense of propriety in conflict with his "withering irony" (Vendler 84). When Eliot had previously tried to find this balance in his poetry, he had fallen into pure irony, satire, or sardonic witticism that annihilated the possibility of direct emotional honesty. Yet, though *The Love Song of J. Alfred Prufrock* does reflect this more mature style and consciousness, it remains the poem of a young writer.

    As the title suggests, this poem focuses on the central persona of J. Alfred Prufrock. The poem is not so much a love song as a dramatic monologue, employing many tones and moods to convey the emotional state and existential crisis of the speaker. In the dramatic monologue, a form used heavily by Victorian poets, the speaker addresses another person, often the reader. The dramatic monologue is traditionally ironic, as the speaker is clearly not always aware of how self-revealing his monologue is. Occasionally arch and satiric, often harshly critical, self-deprecatory, and playful, the poem begins with a query, "Shall we go then, you and I?" Addressing an unidentified "you," Prufrock's question sets in motion the "action" of the poem. The destination appears to be a social affair with people who are trivial and hollow, more concerned with appearances and proprieties than essential experiences and feelings. But it is also a trip into the poem itself, and also into the poet's psyche. The journey takes the speaker through the "half-deserted streets" of a city that is clearly decadent and devoid of joy—a city where the yellow fog lingers over cheap bars and hotel rooms and where individuals meet for empty sexual encounters.

Yet, the speaker seems to be more interested in a journey into his divided and neurotic state of mind than in a physical destination. Prufrock longs for romantic connection with a woman but is so self-conscious as to feel himself pinned to the wall like a butterfly under the eyes of the ladies who "come and go." This divided self struggles over issues of desire and propriety. As the associations in the poem grow more sensuous, Prufrock seems to become more aware of and disgusted with his own desiring self, the "you" addressed in the beginning of the poem. He asserts that he should have been a crab, a hard shelled creature that crawls along the floor of the ocean and eats carcasses and other remains.

The poem moves forward in a series of self-doubting questions that tell us a great deal about the questioner's state of mind: "Do I dare disturb the universe?" "Then how should I begin?" "Should I then presume?" "Shall I part my hair behind? Do I dare to eat a peach?" Full of longing and self-conscious doubt, unable to act even as he sees his life passing by him, Prufrock is unable to escape the stultifying world he occupies; he is unable to escape his doubt, shyness, longing, and fear to transcend the dead world of "formulated" phrases, teacups, cakes and ices. Ultimately, he descends into an etherized sort of sleep, not unlike that referred to as the city at night in the opening lines, only to be awakened to die. Clearly, Prufrock never escapes his own inability to act, to transcend his dead world, or to express his feelings.

Analysis

Beginning with the title of the poem, one can discern Eliot's mocking approach. The title might lead us to believe that this is a love song, perhaps in the tradition of Shakespearian sonnets or other love poetry. It is, however, more firmly rooted in the style of the metaphysical poets like Marvel or Donne. Revolting against the romantic conventions of Elizabethan love poetry, the metaphysical poets wrote poetry that was rough, mocking in tone, and designed to shock the reader, commonly taking philosophy and sexuality as their subjects. Eliot's tone is suggested by the name, J. Alfred Prufrock, a name that sounds suitably pompous and stiff. Moreover, this name has echoes of *prude* and *frock*, the smock worn by young boys or girls. The speaker of this dramatic monologue is no epic hero. He is the model of a shy, intellectually precocious aesthete who is more absorbed in observing himself than taking action. Thus, rather than a love song, the poem is a neurotic collection of associations that reveal the speaker's real inner torment.

The Love Song of J. Alfred Prufrock begins with a quote from Dante Alighieri's *Inferno*. The epigraph is spoken by a character, Guido Da Montefeltro, who speaks from inside the flames of his own hell. As he speaks, the flame that encases Guido vibrates. Assuming that Dante is dead, Guido tells him that only because he is speaking to someone who will not return to the land of the living is he willing to speak of his evil life without fear of infamy; he has no fear that Dante will return to life to repeat it to others who might then think less of Guido. It is noteworthy that Guido's response comes after he has been asked by Dante to identify himself, for this is precisely what Prufrock cannot do; he cannot merge his self-conscious self with his desiring self and state his identity as unified and purposeful. Indeed, Guido's concession to speak only in a context that will not reveal him as infamous seems to tell us a great deal about the hell Prufrock occupies: a hell of self-made discomfort and stifled desires. Prufrock, like Dante's character, fears how he will be perceived by others to such a degree that he cannot act.

Eliot's first lines initiate a dramatic monologue by the speaker of the poem, presumably J. Alfred Prufrock:

Let us go then, you and I,
when the evening is spread out against the sky
like a patient etherized upon a table. (3)

Addressing an unknown listener, the speaker's tone is stiff and old-fashioned, further commenting on his mocking name; only a prude in a frock—a childish person—speaks like this. These lines set the reader up to question the tone and import of the poem, to wonder if the poem is indeed in the epic mode or if it is satiric. This state of doubt is enhanced by the reference to an unidentified "you." Who is the "you" being addressed in the poem? Is it a familiar friend? If so, why the stiff and formal tone of "Let us go then, you and I"? Is the "you" the reader him- or herself? Is it some aspect of the speaker? We are left wondering as we proceed into the unfamiliar scenery of the poem. Further adding to the reader's unease is the comparison of the evening to a patient "etherized upon a table." With this line, the night has become animate yet drugged, a patient under anesthesia. This reference to evening as an anaesthetized patient suggests a city where evening is not a welcome relief from a day of work, nor is it a natural time of rest but a time to anesthetize oneself—to numb oneself. Thus, a gathering sense of inertia and gloom begins to accrue to the scenery and the speaker.

This gloom is enhanced by the journey into this etherized city night:

> Let us go, through certain half-deserted streets,
> the muttering retreats
> of restless nights in one-night cheap hotels
> and sawdust restaurants with oyster-shells. (3)

The world that the speaker and his companion travel through is a cheap place where nights are restless and the fundamentals of life—food and companionship—are found in tawdry places that serve only for one night. These streets lead, "like a tedious argument," to "an overwhelming question" that the speaker never articulates. Indeed, this overwhelming question hovers over the entire poem, seeking expression, yet is left vague at the end of the poem. It is not the only question that issues from the neurotic speaker. His life seems to be composed of trivial questions about how he looks and how he is perceived, while the essential questions of his life are never articulated.

As the speaker presumably lingers in the rooms where the "women come and go/Talking of Michelangelo," his attention is regularly brought back to either his self-doubt or to the hollow and filthy world just outside the window. The following lines illuminate this world:

> The yellow fog that rubs its back upon the window-panes,
> The yellow smoke that rubs its muzzle on the window-panes
> Licked its tongue into the corners of the evening,
> Lingered upon the pools that stand in drains. (3)

The fog/smoke here is suggestive of a poisonous gas, further reinforcing the idea of an etherized night. And this ether is not benign or used to assist healing; it becomes an animal, a sensual beast suggestive of dogs, cats, and lascivious humans when the speaker describes it as licking corners and lingering in drains. The world outside the rooms is poisonous, inhabited by vile beings. What must the world inside be like?

We do not access the scene in the room through direct description. Rather, what insight we gain is through the increasingly self-conscious assertions and questions of the speaker. Thus, the assertions of the third stanza initiate a new idea in its echo of biblical lines confirming that "to everything, there is a season." Repeating the phrase "there will be time," the speaker lists a series of actions:

There will be time
To prepare a face to meet the faces that you meet;
There will be time to murder and create,
And time for all the works and days of hands
That lift and drop a question on your plate. (4)

Of these three actions, the only one that carries force is "time to murder and create"; but sandwiched between, and thereby equated with, time "to prepare a face" and time for hands to "drop a question on your plate," it is rendered ambiguous, if not trivial. If the "time to prepare a face" is what the speaker needs to enter into the society of ladies in the room, then perhaps it is his true self that he is murdering or masking as he creates that face. In any case, the final lines of the poem pull us back from the realm of deep significance as they reinforce the idea of a world of waste where there is time:

for a hundred indecisions,
And for a hundred visions and revisions,
Before the taking of a toast and tea. (4)

This stanza evokes a world of wasted time, profound personal indecision, doubt, and an inability to act. This is the world that the speaker enters when he goes into the room, and it is his inner world—his self-doubt.

This third stanza is separated from the fourth stanza by the repetition of the lines "In the room the women come and go / Talking of Michelangelo" (4). Bringing both the reader and the speaker back to the external context of his discomfort, these lines remind us of the society that Prufrock must either impress or reject. The fourth stanza initiates the questioning that will drive the rest of the poem:

And indeed there will be time
To wonder, "Do I dare?" and, "Do I dare?"
Time to turn back and descend the stair,
With a bald spot in the middle of my hair. (4)

Here, Prufrock challenges himself to escape the society of this world, to act rather than to struggle with indecision. But he cannot act. Indeed, the next lines take on his acute self-consciousness as they note, in parentheses that suggest that this is a comment to himself, that when he finishes ascending the stairs and enters the room the women will comment to each other on his thinning hair and thin arms and legs. He is growing old in his indecision. He is wasting away without acting.

The next three stanzas move forward on the impetus of the parenthetical remarks of stanza four, which provided Prufrock's foreknowledge of how these women would react when they saw him enter the room. Thus, these three stanzas all reiterate the line "I have known" (5). Each stanza begins with this line and offers a subtle variation upon it: "For I have known them all already, known them all"; "And I have known the eyes already, known them all"; "And I have known the arms already, known them all" (5). We are left with several impressions from this series of assertions: We have a growing sense that the world these women occupy is a prescribed world of social proprieties that do not allow for individual distinction; we have a sense that Prufrock knows this social world well, that it is, after all, his world; and we have the sense that Prufrock has only gleaned his knowledge from observation, not from action or physical experience. Thus, full of questions about how he should proceed—how he should act—the stanzas add to our growing sense of Prufrock as a man who is profoundly limited, unable to act yet desperate for contact.

Following stanza seven, where Prufrock asserts that he has "known the arms already" and then lingers on the sensual vision of those arms, the reader encounters a pair of stanzas, the first of which suggests Prufrock's intimate knowledge of the loneliness and emptiness of the world outside the society in the rooms:

> Shall I say, I have gone at dusk through narrow streets
> And watched the smoke that rises from the pipes
> Of lonely men in shirt-sleeves, leaning out of windows? (5)

Again, this outside world is permeated with smoke, poisonous air, and fog. And the speaker has been there, has observed, and, perhaps, been like the lonely men in shirt sleeves. One gets the sense that Prufrock is reminding himself that the hollow emptiness inside the rooms cannot be escaped by mere exit into the outside world, for that world too is empty. This comment on lonely lives is followed by these two lines:

> I should have been a pair of ragged claws
> Scuttling across the floors of silent seas. (5)

Here the speaker seems to offer yet another form of mindless escape, another possibility for numbing himself to the alienation and isolation he is feeling. He should have been born a crab, a creature without emotions, a "scuttling" bottom feeder of the ocean. Prufrock's self-loathing is apparent in these lines. His escapist fantasies and self-awareness come together in this crab.

The tone shifts after these lines, and the speaker becomes both more resigned to his fate and more self-revealing. In the tenth stanza, still questioning whether he should act, Prufrock aligns himself with Dante's speaker from the epigraph: He admits his fear (5). He notes that although he has endured trials and seen his head "brought in on a platter" like John the Baptist, he knows that he is not a prophet:

I have seen the moment of my greatness flicker,
and have seen the eternal Footman hold my coat, and snicker,
And in short, I was afraid. (6)

Prufrock acknowledges his insignificance, lets us know that he is laughable, and issues the honest admission that he was afraid to act. In the clear, unambiguous statements of self-awareness, we find an emotional honesty that is touching and dramatic.

With the use of the perfect conditional tense, the next two stanzas mark another shift in Prufrock's awareness. In each stanza, he repeats the line, "And would it have been worth it, after all" (6) and then takes us through the trivial world of tea cups and delicacies that seems to take precedence over true emotional connection between individuals. By describing this meaningless world, he reminds us that his great moment of revelation or questioning may well have been mistaken by those who inhabit it. He suggests that it would not be worth it to act in a world that does not appreciate either your action or the great effort it takes to act. We can conclude that Prufrock has accepted his fate and has moved on to try and console himself with questions about whether it is really so bad that he was not able to act. Comparing himself to Lazarus, who rose from the dead, Prufrock suggests that the society he seeks to impress would dismissively assert "That is not what I meant at all" (6). He suggests that this world is not hospitable to profound questions or enlightened observations.

Stanza thirteen rings with a note of final and feeble protest linked to a pathetic self-awareness:

No! I am not Prince Hamlet, nor was meant to be;
Am an attendant lord, one that will do
to swell a progress, start a scene or two. (7)

Prufrock asserts in self recognition. He adds to this a clear and painful portrait of himself as the "fool":

Deferential, glad to be of use,
Politic, cautious, and meticulous;
Full of high sentence, but a bit obtuse
At times, indeed, almost ridiculous. (7)

Again, the reader is moved to see the restrained tragedy of Prufrock's life. Most readers prefer a character with self-insight to a doubting and pedantic intellectual who fastidiously checks to see that he is properly attired and speaking correctly. It appears that Prufrock has achieved a certain reconciliation with himself too late, for in the next line he tells us, "I grow old...I grow old..." (7).

Eliot twists our sense of the resolution of the poem, however, with what follows this direct and frank self assessment. In the next few lines, at nearly the end of the poem, Prufrock reverts to his trivial questions and obsession with his appearance:

Shall I part my hair behind? Do I dare to eat a peach?
I shall wear white flannel trousers, and walk upon the beach. (7)

The latter statement combines allusions to the bohemian style of wearing one's trousers rolled with allusions to retired old men who lead trivial lives. Here Prufrock reveals himself as still pathetically concerned about looking fashionable. Yet, there is something truthful in this return to type. How often does a character change entirely in the course of a piece of literature? Rarely. More often, the character, like the rest of us, continues to struggle with the issues that have always dogged him, no matter how trivial they might be. Thus, close to the end of this poem, we have before us a character not particularly likeable but real, and therefore, somehow tragic. He is not transformed or heroic. He is an "everyman," the subject of modern poetry.

The poem concludes with a reiteration of the numbed and enervated world of Prufrock. This is a world where he can observe "mermaids singing, each to each" but knows that they will not sing to him. It is a world where only the mermaids, those creatures of myth and fantasy, can ride the waves of the sea, enjoying the natural environment in an active and joyful state. It is a world where Prufrock and those of us who, like him, are unable to act on our deepest desires, merely linger beside these mermaids, "Till human voices wake us, and we drown" (7). Like sailors of folklore, he is tempted by the mermaids. But Prufrock does not take the initiative to enter the water. These images of the final stanza suggest that Prufrock instead retreats into fantasy only to be awakened from his daydream by the world of ordinary humans around him to drown in this world of poisonous fog and trivial lives.

Themes and Symbols

Throughout this poem, the reader is confronted with the constraints and paralysis that Prufrock experiences: Constrained by fear and enervating self-consciousness, he cannot act on his desire and he cannot ask his important question. The epigraph to the poem introduces the theme of paralysis and constraint. The speaker of those lines, Guido da Montefeltro, is encased within a flame in hell, unable to escape. Prufrock is paralyzed in another sort of hell, the hell of the modern city, within which his social group is equally stultifying. Unable to bring himself to act in this society of ladies who chat about art and take tea, Prufrock doubts his every move. Prufrock obsessively questions the most trivial of his actions, paralyzed by fear of intimacy. Much of his paralysis seems to originate in his desire for emotional and sexual intimacy and his inability to act on this desire. He wonders if he should "presume" to ask his question, apparently, of one of the women in the room. He fears that the women are laughing at him, commenting on his skinny body and balding head, and preparing to skewer him like a butterfly. Further on, Prufrock alludes to a well-known liter-ary example of paralysis: Hamlet. Prufrock's allusion to Hamlet's inability to articulate his own important question reminds the reader of Hamlet's indecision: "To be or not to be, that is the question." Although Prufrock is like Hamlet, unable to act, by the end of the poem he concedes that he is no Hamlet; in other words, he seems to admit that there is nothing heroic about his struggle. Instead, he presciently aligns himself with Polonius, the meddling old fool who gets himself killed precisely because he lurks at the edges rather than enter into the action in the play. Prufrock is like the etherized night; indeed, the dreamlike state he enters at the end of the poem is evocative of this etherized night.

This theme of paralysis is enhanced by a parallel theme of anxiety. Prufrock's physical appearance seems to mark him as one with sensitive nerves: He has thin arms and legs, thinning hair, and a flaccid body. Add this to his fastidious manner and obsessive concern with his appearance and we have a character who seems highly anxious. He is anxious that he should appear appealing to the women, but also anxious about his own aging, aware that the "moment" of his greatness has "flickered" out. Further, Prufrock is highly sensitive to the tawdry and hollow qualities of the world he inhabits. His attention lingers on the soiled, sad, and empty lives that he passes in the streets or that are signified by the filthy context of the city. He even identifies with them, feeling like a pariah. This exterior world, ringing with a hollow tone, distracts Prufrock and adds to his general anxiety—his fear of action. Even Prufrock's insights at the end of the poem, his admission that he is not an epic hero and that he has seen his moment of greatness pass, suggest his anxious revisiting of his own turmoil, his inability to cease self observation and act. With his anxious and obsessive revisiting of his own trivial turmoil, Prufrock never escapes anxiety; rather, he drowns in it.

Symbols

Drawing on the symbolist's belief that one could best express emotion and character through the use of symbol rather than, say, realistic description, Eliot's use of symbols in his poetry is extensive. It is the primary method by which he conveys his characters, his themes, and his social comment. For Eliot, the symbol is an "objective correlative," a term he coined in his essay "Hamlet and His Problems". Eliot tells us that the only way to express emotion in art is through the use of an objective correlative: a set of objects, a situation, events that convey the emotion independent of the artist's direct expression of that emotion. Thus, for example, the skewered butterfly is an objective correlative for Prufrock's profound social anxiety. Although symbols work throughout Eliot's poem, there are a few key symbols in this poem that resonate with and reinforce the central themes of the poem: specifically, the modern city as hell, the symbol of the sea, and the symbol of a cat.

Beginning with the epigraph, we find allusions to hell. Dante's journey into hell in *The Divine Comedy* is a point of reference to which Eliot will direct our attention at various moments in the poem. The opening stanza of the poem takes us into the modern-day hell that Prufrock occupies: the modern city, joyless and poisonous, where night is only a time of drugged numbness. This modern hell is marked by loneliness and isolation with its "half-deserted streets" where "lonely men" lean out of windows. The filth of this scene is both industrial and sexual, conveyed by the symbolism of suggestive images like "one-night cheap hotels" and a cat that lets the soot of the city air fall upon its back as it drinks from the putrid pools in the gutters. By use of repeated images of yellow fog, night, and dusk, Eliot conveys a city that never sees the daylight, obscured as it is by the hellish fog of moral and industrial decay.

The feline imagery throughout the poem is most commonly associated with the degradation of the modern city, a degradation that is industrial and moral. Cats are often evocative of feminine qualities, and Eliot's cat is not exempt from that meaning. Its lingering, licking, and rubbing are all sexually charged gestures that initiate the idea of the cat as a feminized and lascivious creature. But in this context, the cat is associated more closely with Prufrock himself than with any woman in the poem. This furthers the image of Prufrock as ambivalent about his sexual urges and their object. It is in Prufrock's monologue that the cat emerges as a symbol of the filthy city; it is Prufrock's words that describe the fog as cat-like; and it is Prufrock's gaze that becomes associated with this cat, sliding, as it does, to the window to observe the fog and the filthy street below where the fog/cat licks and lingers.

The hellishness of the modern city is not only located in the exterior environment. It is embodied in the spiritual hollowness of the city's denizens. The repetition of the line, "The women who come and go, speaking of Michelangelo" conveys an image of a society that lives on the surface, caring more for appearance than for truth. This is reinforced by the numerous references to the activities of these women: taking tea, eating cakes and ices, reading novels, and trailing their skirts along the floor. There arises from this imagery a profound sense of ennui, of social boredom. These women, who would skewer Prufrock with "formulated phrases," have no originality of thought or voice. They appear to Prufrock as placidly and apathetically ensconced in a hollow and meaningless city, a modern hell.

Regeneration and birth, the typical associations one makes with the sea as a symbol, are not possible in this world. The sea emerges in this poem as a symbol of Prufrock's paralysis, whether it suggests birth or death. The sea is first suggested when Prufrock has begun to descend into his self-pitying despair and asserts,

I should have been a pair of ragged claws
Scuttling across the floors of silent seas. (5)

Here, both the crab and the sea are suggestive of debasement and isolation: The crab is a creature that lives at the very bottom of the ocean, burrows into the sand, and eats garbage. And this sea does not appear to be teeming with life; it is a silent sea.

The poem returns to the symbolism of the sea in its final lines. Prufrock asserts that he shall walk along the beach and tells us that he has heard the mermaids sing and seen them, "combing the white hair of the waves." Refreshingly active, these images are also fantastical. Prufrock has retreated into fantasy where he can imagine a sea that is not silent and dead. The final three lines of the poem invite the reader into the fantastical world:

We have lingered in the chambers of the sea
By sea-girls wreathed with seaweed red and brown
Till human voices wake us, and we drown. (7)

For the sea of fantasy cannot be survived by the inhabitants of the modern city. When "we" are awakened by human voices, as opposed to the voices of the fantastical sea-girls, we drown. When our delusion is pointed out to us, we die. Prufrock's use of the first person plural here demands that we see ourselves as similarly flawed and paralyzed by the modern world. It is in the final moment of the poem that the poet reaches out to the universal significance of his character's turmoil.

Poetic Style and Technique

The poem is composed as a dramatic monologue, traditionally a lyric poem that reveals the soul of the speaker. Usually, the speaker of a dramatic monologue is addressing an unidentified silent listener, often the reader, and the speaker reveals more about himself and the dramatic moment in his life than he may have intended. Many modern poets had rejected the form because of its connection with the poet Robert Browning and other Victorian poets who used it extensively; the modern poets felt that Browning and the Victorians represented a world of lies which the moderns sought to escape. But Eliot's firm belief in tradition, by which he meant a literary tradition and its role in modern poetry, led him to use the form to brilliant effect. Prufrock's monologue reveals his emotional and social paralysis, rooted in his fear of intimacy, action, and failure. Prufrock begins with a tone by which he means to convey confidence and clear intention: "Let us go" is assertively repeated three times in the first stanza. Yet, he quickly begins to reveal more about his turmoil and inability to act—his inability to go anywhere beyond the streets and rooms of the decadent and deadening modern city. This becomes most apparent in the fourth stanza when Prufrock's questioning begins. He opens the stanza with a confident assertion, but never returns to that tone without the mitigating effect of his constant questioning: "Do I dare?" he asks three times in this stanza alone. His assertions even become more trivial and reveal his desperate attempt to convince himself, if not the listener, that he is confident. He asserts,

My mourning coat, my collar mounting firmly to the chin,
My necktie rich and modest, but asserted by a simple pin. (4)

It is as though he would have himself believe that these sartorial details mark him as a confident, active man, not the effeminate and paralyzed doubter that he is. Eliot is using the style of the dramatic monologue, with its tradition of revealing more about the speaker than he or she intends, to great effect here. He is revealing his character as he descends into doubt, confusion, and fear.

This concept of descent is also relevant to a discussion of Eliot's poetic technique. For the poem's structure mimics a descent into hell. The imagery of the poem begins with the skyline, "the evening spread out against the sky," and moves downward. Prufrock moves down to the "Streets that follow like a tedious argument," briefly up to the room where the "women come and go," and then back down to the street, down from there to the "pools that stand in drains" and, finally, to the "floors of silent seas." Through the imagery of the poem we descend into a world of paralysis and death that is both a comment on Prufrock's internal state and on the state of the modern world.

In order to treat this subject in a way that captures rather than repels readers, Eliot uses wit and satire, allowing us to laugh at Prufrock and ourselves whenever we might find we are uncomfortably identified with Prufrock. Indeed, throughout the poem Eliot employs elements of the mock heroic style. This is typically a form that mocks both the tradition of romances and that of epic heroes. (Apropos here is the title of the poem, *The Love Song of J. Alfred Prufrock*.) The mock heroic often treats a trivial subject, like Prufrock's inner turmoil of how to part his hair, in a grand style that overstates its significance to such a degree that the reader is led to laugh. We see this throughout the poem. For example, Prufrock sees himself as John the Baptist, a genuinely heroic biblical character. Another example occurs when Prufrock thinks that his inner turmoil will "disturb the universe."

Overall the poem has an irregular rhyme scheme, sometimes featuring rhymed sestets and tercets and sometimes descending into nonrhyming free verse. The sestets and tercets that evoke the Italian sonnet reveal not only Eliot's insistence on the importance of literary tradition within modern poetry, but also allow Eliot the traditional meaning of those forms. So, for example, when he evokes the Petrarchan sonnet in a six line stanza, or sestet, Eliot is benefiting from the traditional structure of that style. The Italian sonnet, often called the Petrarchan sonnet because Petrarch was the most masterful poet to use the style, is composed of an octave, or eight lines with rhymes that follow the pattern *abbaabba*, and a sestet, or six lines with a variety of possible rhyme patterns. Traditionally, the octave introduces a narrative, makes a statement, or offers a question and the sestet reinforces the narrative by providing comment, application of the statement, or an answer to the question. Eliot does not follow this form strictly. He plays with the opening octave, offering us an opening twelve line stanza that withholds a question at the very moment that one might expect to find it:

> To lead you to an overwhelming question …
> Oh, do not ask, "What is it?"
> Let us go and make our visit. (3)

This should be a warning to the reader that knowledge of literary tradition will not render complete understanding of the poem. Rather, traditional literary forms will be brought together in the poem to make a new form, a form that is perhaps more relevant to addressing the concerns of the modern world.

Eliot also plays with the six line component of the Italian sonnet. The poet usually makes a general statement relating to a subject that was introduced in the first octave of the poem or indicates a personal emotion relating to a subject that was raised in the opening octave. In the six line stanza, Prufrock does indeed reinforce the opening by providing the following comment:

For I have known them all already, known them all—
Have known the evenings, mornings, and afternoons,
I have measured out my life with coffee spoons. (4)

What the stanza overall, and these lines in particular, reinforces is the hollow life of the denizens of this modern city, this hell. It is a world of meaningless social ritual; Eliot will remind us of this many times in the poem. The final tercets of the poem play on the sonnet form only to contrast sharply with its traditional content and message. These lines contain the dark insights of a modern man, not an argument for or protestations of love. In this modern world, since the sonnet cannot serve its traditional role, it is slightly ironic and jarring: a constant reminder of what is lacking in the modern world.

Eliot also makes numerous references in the poem to the metaphysical poets, to the French Symbolists, and to Shakespeare. Perhaps the overarching effect of these many references is the way fragments from these writers of the past are juxtaposed to create startling moments and multiple meanings. This is a method that both Eliot and Ezra Pound, among others, insisted was distinctly modern. Pound maintained that the job of poets in the modern world was to "make it new" with the shards and fragments of the shattered world they had inherited. Those shards and fragments came from the quotidian world around them as well as from ancient world literature. So, when Eliot uses references to Marvel's poem "To His Coy Mistress" in *Prufrock*, he uses the fragment to allude to his desire for sex. Marvel writes, "Let us roll all our strength and all / Our sweetness up into one ball" whereas Prufrock asserts, "To have squeezed the universe into a ball / To roll it towards some overwhelming question" (6). Where Marvel's speaker in his poem is attempting to persuade his mistress to have sex with him since death draws near and time is running out, Prufrock cannot begin to pose a question, let alone mount a persuasive argument to seduce a woman. The bits of various poems and poetic styles reveal the fragmentation of the modern world as they become the material for a poetry that offers a new way to express impossibility of hope, love, and meaning in the fractured modern world.

THE WASTE LAND

Summary

Written in 1921–22 and depicting the moral, spiritual, and economic wasteland of Europe after World War I, *The Waste Land* is a long poem in five cantos. Critics argue that this poem launched modern poetry. Eliot's style in *The Waste Land* is profoundly allusive, echoing so many sources from such diverse historical and geographical contexts that scholars have been busy tracing these allusions since its publication. Additionally, the poem does not feature a single narrative point of view. Rather, it is composed of many voices, some more central to the trajectory of meaning, others more peripheral. It is often difficult to discern precisely whose point of view directs certain sections of the poem. Still, there is much to be gained from a careful reading of this poem, even without a scholar's background in all the texts and occasions to which it alludes.

Taking the title from Jessie L. Weston's book, *From Ritual to Romance*, Eliot begins with an allusion to her argument that the tradition of the quest for the Holy Grail is rooted in ancient vegetation and fertility myths. Weston relates how the Fisher King has been made impotent by the gods, his kingdom laid to barren waste. In some versions of the legend, she reminds us, this occurs because of an act of sexual violence the King has committed. The Fisher King awaits a knight who can begin the quest to restore his virility and release his kingdom from its barren state. The fact that Eliot's title and numerous references in the text are connected to Weston's book and the Grail legend leads readers to search for allusions to both vegetation myths and quest literature throughout the poem.

The poem begins with an epigraph from *Satyricon* by Petronius, a Roman writer known for his satire. It translates as, "For I once saw with my own eyes the Cumean Sibyl hanging in a jar, and when the boys asked her: 'Sibyl, what do you want?' she answered, 'I want to die'" (Norton Critical edition 3). In the ancient myth, the Sibyl had asked the gods for the gift of everlasting life, but forgot to ask for everlasting youth. Thus, she shriveled with age to a size and delicacy that required her to be kept in a bottle, lest she disintegrate. Her statement speaks of her weariness with life and her desire to be released from it, though she is forced to live forever as the result of her own request. In this way, she is like one of the speakers in the poem who regrets,

> The awful daring of a moment's surrender
> Which an age of prudence can never retract. (68)

This epigraph resonates with the many voices in the poem that capture the overwhelming regret of their hollow lives. The Sibyl represents the state of world-weariness that the poem explores and decries.

The first canto of the poem, titled "The Burial of the Dead," alludes to the burial ceremonies of the Anglican Church and puts the subject of death, and all its metaphoric possibilities, at the center of the poem. This canto introduces the themes of a dead world and the need for a quest to restore that world to balance. Beginning with the famous lines,

> April is the cruellest month, breeding
> Lilacs out of the dead land. (53)

The stanza takes a beloved time of year and reveals it as a time of torment that awakens memories of a better time. This canto is composed of several disparate voices including an unnamed Prufrock-like speaker, Marie, a Lithuanian German of royal descent, the hyacinth girl, and Madame Sosostris, "famous clairvoyante" (54). These voices speak of a Europe where the royal classes live dull and meaningless lives suffused with nostalgic memories, where vision and voice are impossible, and where the dead walk in the world of the living. The stanzas of this canto capture the mood of profound apathy in a dead world occupied by the living dead. Thus, the Prufrock-like persona cannot speak to or see the Hyacinth girl with her arms full of flowers. He says,

I was neither
Living nor dead, and I knew nothing. (54)

The "famous" clairvoyant of the fourth stanza, who is satirically depicted as "nevertheless" having a cold, reads the tarot cards for the hero figure, who must embark on the journey to restore the world to its generative and healthy balance. Armed with her tarot reading, he begins his journey only to encounter the crowd of the dead that "flowed over London Bridge," alluding to the many war dead from the recently ended World War I. The hero faces this horde and is overwhelmed.

The next canto is entitled "A Game of Chess" and explores the general malaise of society by examining inhabitants from either end of the spectrum of social class in this wasteland. The title of this canto suggests an idle and purposeless existence where the question "What shall we ever do?" receives an answer fit for a routine existence: hot water at ten, a ride in the car at four, followed by a game of chess. As in the first canto, life is again seen as sterile. The interior decorations of the wealthy inhabitants of this world are described in terms that leave the reader feeling the cold ostentation of this world. In this interior, chairs are burnished thrones surrounded by glass and marble, golden cupidons, jewels, satin, and ivory. This opulence is not warm and inviting; it is frigid. The only language that might offer an image of warmth is a reference to fire. But this reference leads only to allusions of witchcraft, where "synthetic perfume," "unguent," and smoke "drowned the sense in odours" (56).

Linking this cold, overwhelming interior to sexual violence, the wall of this wealth-laden interior features a depiction of the rape of Philomel by King Tereus, a mythical story conveyed in Ovid's *Metamorphoses,* in which the Greek gods turn Philomel into a nightingale so that she cannot be killed by Tereus. Mapped onto the Fisher King legend that Jessie Weston's book documents and Eliot is clearly alluding to, this reference to Philomel indirectly parallels the rape of the virgins that results in the Fisher King's court being turned into a wasteland in some versions of the Grail legend. In fact, the singing of the nightingale and the allusion to Philomel may suggest the possibility of resurrection, which always drives the literature of the quest for the Grail. Yet, there is not even a suggestion of a meaningful quest being undertaken by the occupants in Eliot's wasteland. In fact, the stanza concludes with a focus on the lower class denizens of the wasteland who cheat each other out of money and love. The moral corruption of characters at both ends of the class spectrum reiterates the theme of decay and waste rooted in human greed and sexual licentiousness.

"The Fire Sermon," the title of the third and transitional canto, is taken from a sermon preached by Buddha in which the material world and possessions are all depicted as consuming fires. Just as the first two cantos introduced the theme of moral decay with variations and illustrations, this canto recapitulates and develops these important themes before positing a possible cleansing by fire. The stanzas of this canto reiterate the root cause of the wasteland: industrial, spiritual, and moral decay. There are three scenes of abusive or lascivious sexuality in which a character's morality is undone or revealed as nonexistent: The modern figures of Mrs. Porter and her daughter again evoke the image of Philomel raped by King Tereus, echoing the degradation of the sexual act and love in the modern world; the typist and the "young man carbuncular" engage in an act of sex devoid of passion or compassion; and the seduction that destroys the virtue of a young woman is mapped onto the geography of the city of London, suggesting the widespread nature of such seductions.

The first stanza of this canto opens with references to Edmund Spenser's 1596 poem "Prothalamion," that offers the language of poetic vision and love to depict an idyllic image of river nymphs preparing for a wedding. But in Eliot's stanza, nothing is idyllic. The "nymphs are departed" and the Thames bears no "testimony of summer nights" (60). Rather, a rat creeps in the mud of the river, "dragging its slimy belly on the bank" where bodies and bones lie, while the hero fishes and hears the "rattle of bones" and "horns and motors" at his back (60). This all stands in stark contrast to Spenser's idyll, and this contrast serves to intensify Eliot's images of the dead modern river and the city it winds through.

"The Fire Sermon" brings together disparate voices and identities, including Buddha and Saint Augustine, who were both tempted by lust before they were transformed. These figures merge in the character of Tiresias, a classical Greek known for insight and truth. Tiresias emerges in this canto as the unification of the many figures of the hero from elsewhere in the poem. Tiresias witnesses a loveless and bored tryst between a typist and the young man with an infected boil. Neither participant in this sex act is portrayed as having much engagement in this act, not to mention any concern for or interest in the partner. The young man is described as,

> A small house agent's clerk, with one bold stare,
> One of the low on whom assurance sits
> As a silk hat on a Bradford millionaire. (62)

With obtuseness and unwarranted self assurance, this young man mounts his "assault" and encounters "no defence" from the typist. Indeed, for her part, the typist is "bored" and indifferent. She engages in the sex as though it is something to be endured. After the young man finishes, "And gropes his way, finding the stairs unlit," the actions of the young woman reflect her apathy:

> She turns and looks a moment in the glass,
> Hardly aware of her departed lover;
> Her brain allows one half-formed thought to pass:
> "Well now that's done: and I'm glad it's over." (62)

From this intimate and tawdry scene, through the consciousness of Tiresias, the point of view shifts from the interiors of modern lives and returns to the oily river where images of drifting logs merge with barges, tar, and sweat. We hear the song of the three Thames daughters (which are modeled after the Rhine Maidens in Wagner's *Gotterdammerung*). With each song we gain further images of violation, pollution and empty, loveless sex. These maidens are inhabitants of the wasteland as well. With their songs, we follow the river through the country past towers, "Trams and dusty trees," through Highbury, Richmond, Kew—all parts of London. Finally we arrive at the sea:

> On Margate Sands.
> I can connect
> Nothing with nothing. (64)

Now the hero is poised for some transformation. Appropriately, the final lines of the canto are evocative of both Buddha and Saint Augustine, for whom carnal desire, burning intensely, became a cleansing fire:

> Burning burning burning burning
> O Lord Thou pluckest me out .
> O Lord Thou pluckest
> burning. (64)

Perhaps the hero, Tiresias at this point, will be redeemed. Perhaps, as in
the case of Buddha and Saint Augustine, this hero will be transformed in
response to the raging lust.

The fourth and shortest canto of the poem is "Death by Water," composed
of three stanzas of three lines each. It takes us back to the "death by drowning," the fate that the clairvoyant warned of and which will ultimately lead
to rebirth. The immediately obvious contrast with the previous canto comes
in the title; here we are greeted with the symbolism of water as opposed to
fire. Fire, in the previous stanza, was lust and desire out of control. Water,
here, means the death of "Phlebas the Phoenician" who was the sailor
referred to in the tarot cards read by the clairvoyant. Water also brings us
to the Mediterranean and Carthage, where Aeneaus left Dido to kill herself
rather than live without love. In contrast to the story of Dido, in this poem
death by water makes way for the hero to be transformed so that he can complete his quest and, perhaps, bring regeneration to the wasteland.

The last canto, "What the Thunder Said," reflects a journey through a dry
land where thunder may intimate rain yet to fall. The first eight stanzas of
this final canto create an image of Dante's limbo where, as the last lines of
the first stanza indicate,

> He who was living is now dead
> We who were living are now dying
> With little patience. (66)

This is a waterless journey through a barren landscape of rock and sand.
An element of hope or possibility is suggested by the hooded figure who
walks beside the persona of the poem, suggesting the figure of Christ. Indeed,
these eight stanzas of dry and confused emptiness lead to the crow of a
rooster, often a symbol of Christ, and the following lines,

> In a flash of lightening. Then a damp gust
> Bringing rain. (68)

The rest of the canto and the poem focus on the Sanskrit terms from
Hindu religious lore—the words of the thunder: Datta, which means to give
alms; Dayadhvam, meaning to have compassion; and Damyata, which means
to practice self control. When asked what he gave, the hero tells that he
gave the "awful daring of a moment's surrender" (68). The persona reflects
on his compassion for "each in his prison" and his self control, with a heart
"beating obedient" (69). These stanzas suggest a spiritual transformation of
the hero, as though he has given alms, found compassion, and learned self
control. Following this, the poem concludes with the hero sitting on the

shore fishing "with the arid plain behind," once again evoking the legend of the Fisher King (69). What progress the hero has found is personal; he has "shored" fragments "against my ruins" and he waits for the regenerative rain, just as the reader is forced to wait. We do not know that rebirth and a new city will arise from the desert that the hero has traveled through, but the poem intimates that this is possible.

Structural Analysis

As many critics have observed, *The Waste Land* is neither an indecipherable nor a formless poem, as was argued by some of its first critics. A great deal of Eliot's meaning can be understood by examining the poem as following the "mythic method" that Eliot identified in Joyce's *Ulysses*. He writes that, "in using myth, in manipulating a continuous parallel between contemporaneity and antiquity," Joyce was giving shape to "the immense panorama of futility and anarchy which is contemporary history" (*"Ulysses*, Order, and Myth" 177). This method, Eliot argued, begins to make the modern world possible for art—for order and form. One can discern Eliot's own use of a "mythic method" in *The Waste Land*. In *The Waste Land* this method finds expression and form through the narrative tradition of the time-honored pattern designated as the literature of the quest. Specifically, as Eliot tells readers in the notes to his poem, he is alluding to Jessie L. Weston's book on the Grail Legend entitled *From Ritual to Romance*. In this book, Weston traces the Grail legend to its earliest roots in ancient and non-Christian vegetation and fertility myths and identifies the figure of the Fisher King as an early locus of the original quest: Made sexually impotent for his own excesses, the Fisher King is condemned to live in a barren kingdom. His quest, then, is for regeneration connected to healthy procreation.

An overarching theme of *The Waste Land* is that Western Civilization has been laid to waste by industrial and moral decay and that it needs to be restored to a balanced spiritual footing. To address the perception that western societies in the twentieth century are spiritually impoverished and weakened by cultural decay, Eliot suggests that each individual must embark on his or her own spiritual odyssey with the same zeal with which the knights of the Fisher King legend set out to find the Holy Grail. In the medieval tradition of quest literature, the spiritual journey to regenerate the wasteland could only be undertaken by the purest of men. To set out on such a quest in the twentieth century mandates that it be approached by a less-than-perfect hero, yet one dedicated to a moral purpose. The hero must provide a model for the remainder of humanity so that each individual may break the deadly grip of his or her wasteland. If the reader is to identify a controlling sensibility, a persona, or a narrative voice among the cacophony of numerous voices in the poem, it must be the amorphous, but unifying, sensibility of the hermaphroditic Tiresias. Tiresias, a blend of both male and female, was granted the gift of prophecy by Zeus. Eliot points readers in this direction with his comment in his "Notes on *The Waste Land*" where he states, "Tiresias, although a mere spectator and not indeed a 'character,' is yet the most important personage in the poem, uniting all the rest" (*Norton Critical* 23). Eliot goes on to say that all the male characters in the poem are one and all the female characters are one; "and the two sexes meet in Tiresias. What Tiresias *sees*, in fact, is the substance of the poem" (*Norton Critical* 23). Indeed, Tiresias is an ideal figure to be chosen as the hero of the quest, for as both male and female, he is a unified personality; this model of the unity of man and woman also has the gift of prophecy and, therefore, cannot tell a lie. He is truth embodied.

In Greek mythology, Tiresias becomes the wisest and most truthful human as a result of his blindness. As a youth, he strikes a copulating pair of snakes that turn out to be two gods. As a result, the gods turn him into a woman. Years later, he repeats the act and is turned back into a man, but with a woman's breasts. Later he is asked by the goddess Hera, who is arguing on the subject with Zeus, whether the woman or the man has more enjoyment in intercourse. He responds that the woman does, whereupon Hera promptly blinds him. Although Zeus cannot undo Hera's act, he does give Tiresias the gift of metaphorical sight and prophecy. By these means, Tiresias becomes the model of the unified personality, the embodiment of truth dedicated to restoring community.

Eliot points his readers in the direction of the quest when he tells us in the notes to the poem that "the plan and a good deal of the incidental symbolism" of the poem come from two works about quest literature: Jessie L. Weston's book on the Grail legend, *From Ritual to Romance*, and *The Golden Bough* by James Frazer (*Norton Critical* 21). If one fuses the multiple voices of the poem into a single persona, whom we may designate as the hero-adventurer, we can follow a distinctly narrative trail through the poem. Although we cannot identify the hero as a named and stable identity as one can in most Grail legends, we can identify and map the persona's quest in the poem.

Following the trail offered by the numerous allusions to the Grail legend, one can find some help in the work of Joseph Campbell, who wrote after Eliot but elucidates the tradition upon which Eliot drew. In *The Hero with a Thousand Faces*, Campbell identifies the stages that the hero-adventurer must go through, telling us that these are universal in the literature of the quest. Although one cannot, and need not, find in Eliot's poem a one-to-one correlation with the stages Campbell identifies, one can identify various stages of the quest as Campbell has identified them. By doing so, one can find thematic coherence and a narrative that make the poem accessible. Most notably, one can find the call to adventure, the hero's refusal of the call and his ultimate acceptance of it; one can find the offering of supernatural aid to the hero, and the crossing of thresholds. Typically, the quest ends with a return and the spiritual transformation (Campbell 151). However, Eliot only hints at the possibility of such a return in this poem. Exploring these stages as they relate to the evolution of the persona in *The Waste Land* provides some justification for those who favor the view that the poem's organization is essentially narrative, and thus coherent.

Denis Donaghue argues that Eliot's poems all try to "escape from the emotional condition which incited them." They do this, he argues, not by proposing the opposite of that emotional condition but by exploring a range of "alternative conditions" (*Norton Critical* 216). Given Donoghue's comment, we must be reminded not to take *The Waste Land* exclusively as an example of quest literature. This form and tradition may have allowed Eliot to explore an "alternative condition," to escape the torment of the emotional condition from which the poem was written: disgust, self-loathing, misanthropy, and fear. Yet, the fact that Eliot may have used the quest myth as a means to escape emotion at the root of the poem does not annul the significance of the quest as a structuring device. It suggests that one might look further for both thematic and structural understanding of the poem.

In its unedited state, *The Waste Land* opens with the journey of a young man into Night Town. This excised part of the poem (taken out by Eliot at Ezra Pound's urging) offers a scene that depicts the coarse immaturity of the persona in episodes focusing on public drunkenness and debauchery in brothels. In effect, the unidentified narrator is impossible to recognize as the "hero-adventurer": He is uninitiated, unguided, and purposeless. He has all the potential for anguished failure that befell his predecessor and counterpart Prufrock in an excursion into the ennui-ridden modern city. His willful selfishness might be construed as a refusal to accept any direction towards a compelling quest. Still, the urge to set out on an adventure—to accept the call to the quest—seems evident in the persona's revelatory acknowledgement which opens the published poem as we know it: "April is the cruellest month" (Collected Poems 53). April might be construed as "cruel" only by those who consciously refuse the challenge of April's primordial urges for rebirth, resurrection, and reconstitution. This is the challenge that the hero must accept: the search for the mysteries of regeneration and the better state that must be restored. The reference to April also evokes Chaucer's contrasting paean to the cyclic call to spiritual rebirth in *The Canterbury Tales,* in which Chaucer celebrates April and the onset of spring. The hero resists Chaucer's celebration of regeneration with his assertion of April's cruelty. But Chaucer's claim to an ancient tradition of rebirth might also tempt the hero to accept the quest for spiritual regeneration.

The hero must accept that he alone among the multitudes inhabiting the "unreal city" has been chosen to undertake the adventure. Worse, he must count himself among the least consequential of the inhabitants because he has knowingly avoided the restive stirring of April, the call to adventure, when he asserted his preference for the forgetfulness and ignorance of winter. This marks him as an individual chastised and shunned, like the son in Ecclesiastes, to whom this canto of the poem refers:

> Son of man
> You cannot say, or guess, for you know only
> A heap of broken images, where the sun beats,
> And the dead tree gives not shelter. (53)

More than just an unsettling opening to the poem, it seems that the opening lines are simultaneously a call to adventure and, initially, the refusal to accept that call.

The title of Canto I, *The Burial of the Dead,* may seem paradoxical in the context of the quest tradition. But it actually reinforces the idea of the hero who is marked for a special calling. In the Anglo-Catholic sense, the burial is a transitional state associated with the transference of the individual out of death to a new life implied by faith in salvation. In the Dantean sense, burial merely entombs the persona in the death-in-life around him. Dante, Eliot tells us in his notes to the poem, is referred to in the final stanza of this canto:

> Unreal City.
> Under the brown fog of a winter dawn,
> A crowd flowed over London Bridge, so many,
> I had not thought death had undone so many. (55)

The suggestion here is not only of the many dead from the war that haunt the living inhabitants of London, but these lines also evoke those who inhabit the first circle of Hell, also called Limbo, in Dante's *Inferno.* These are the living dead. Thus, although the hero-adventurer may wish to avoid undertaking the trial of the quest for regeneration, the consequences of not accepting are simply too grave. He would be abandoned to the first circle of hell and lose all hope for regeneration if he refused the quest. The hero accepts the adventure, albeit reluctantly.

Once the challenge has been accepted, the traditional hero-adventurer invariably encounters a shadowy figure, often a spiritual leader in disguise, who is mistrusted by all except the hero. From this figure, the hero-adventurer learns how to proceed through his mysterious journey and is given "gifts" to carry on that journey. In the first canto, both the memories of the "hyacinth girl" and the ambiguous directions provided by Madam Sosostris might be construed as the "gifts," or, as Campbell calls them, "supernatural aid," that the hero-adventurer takes on his quest as he enters the infernal regions of the City and his own soul (Campbell 69).

The fact that the hero accepts the quest does not guarantee either success or the strength and resourcefulness necessary to complete the adventure. These must be gained along the way. Campbell reminds us that in the tradition of the quest, the first threshold, the encountering of the first obstacle, usually implies an attempt to bypass some guardian of the nether world, some monumental beast that obstructs the adventurer from entering what Campbell defines as the zone of "magnified power," the desert, the abyss, the decaying city, the impenetrable deep which holds whatever solutions exist regarding the mysteries of a better state (77). In this case, the better state may be the contrasting hope radiating from Chaucer's April, which is evoked by Eliot's reference to April as the "cruellest month" and which poses the conviction that a miraculous regeneration is possible. Viewed from this perspective, Canto II, *The Game of Chess*, which Eliot originally had entitled *In the Cage*, presents the guardian-obstacles of the nether world—the Scylla and Charybdis figures. Scylla and Charybdis were two sea monsters of Greek legend who guarded the Strait of Messina. Both of the Greek hero-adventurers Odysseus and Jason had to pass between them in their quests. In Eliot's poem, one guardian is the Duchess, the image of obstinate, selfish, and enervating material affluence; the other is the desiccated, disenfranchised, overwrought, and disaffected wife. Between the two is encapsulated the sexually distorted spectrum of an irresponsible world where sex without love has become the passionless norm. Beyond these guardians is the entry into the fantastical world in which the crassness of its reality is even more "unreal." The hero must pass through this world and the trials it includes to gain his insight.

Willing to progress beyond the sentinels, the obstacles guarding the entry to the inner mysteries, the hero-adventurer penetrates the nether world. Here the hero-adventurer "instead of conquering or conciliating the power of the threshold, is swallowed into the unknown, and would appear to have died" (Campbell 90). Eliot's hero is lost in his fusion with Tiresias, the model of unity and embodied truth. With the merging of the flawed and desiring modern hero and Tiresias, we gain the unique fusion of "memory and desire," with Tiresias as memory and the hero as desire. This is a link to the first lines of the poem in which spring awakens "memory and desire" (53). This fusion of memory and desire allows the hero his prophetic insight into the ultimate example of the sexless relationship: the copulation of the "carbuncular" clerk and the typist. By detailing their liaison, as observed and narrated by Tiresias, Eliot is not merely demonstrating the depth of degradation possible in the "unreal city"; rather, he is depicting the nadir, the lower depths from which the miraculous transformation can and does occur. In addition, at this point in the poem, Eliot's seeker identifies with Buddha and Saint Augustine. Both Buddha and Saint Augustine faced a personal abyss in the frenzied sexuality among the "legion of the lost" only to ascend so dramatically through the cleansing purgatorial fire which transmutes the "unreal" into the supernaturally "real." The hero-adventurer realizes that the all-consuming fire of sexual passion can, and must, provide the same all-consuming zeal that transmutes the inauthentic identity into the representative of the universal capabilities of humanity—the representative of all human potential.

Buoyed by the "prophesies" of Madam Sosostris, the hero forges on. Ironically, the water, which Madam Sosostris's warning to "fear death by water" sought to avoid, produces the antithetical effect—a rebirth, a transformed identity. This rebirth is the subject of the brief Canto IV, *Death by Water*. In the transformation that the death by water affords the hero, we find a pivotal moment in the poem. Now the hero is poised to hear the sermon, understand it, and continue his quest. Only after passing through the land of the dead is the hero permitted to uncover the meaning of the sacred mysteries and listen to the inspirational meaning in the song of the sacred spirit. In this case, the hero uncovers the revelatory implications gleaned from the voice echoing the Sanskrit words of Buddha's sermon in the Thunder in Canto V, *What the Thunder Said*. Here, the clear voice is interpretable because the hero has faced all the trials and achieved the clarifying vision. He has shattered the limiting perspective of the "unreal" city and gained the prospect of replacing it with the "real" city wherein lies regeneration.

Ultimately, to extend the analogy of the hero-adventurer further in *The Waste Land* is unsatisfying because a vision of the ultimate peace, which the character arrives at, is not the same as the full achievement of that peace. We do not see the hero returning, like Buddha, to sit beneath the Bo Tree from whence he can dispense the necessary wisdom. Rather, we are left more at a Dantean stage of just having emerged from the Inferno with the ascending transformation about to be undertaken with "These fragments...shored against [his] ruins" (69). The Thunder is merely "Bringing rain." The poem is, after all, entitled *The Waste Land*. But this also seems a most appropriate conclusion to a quest in the modern world. Eliot draws on a Buddhist sermon, emphasizing the Buddhist belief in the individual journey to peace, as opposed to the collective salvation. Each flawed hero in this modern world must find his own way to peace.

Themes and Symbols

T. S. Eliot's poem is rich with theme, allusion, and suggested meanings. Any effort to reduce the poem to a single theme is complicated by the many possibilities that are suggested as one reads the poem looking for evidence of such peculiarity. Eliot's poem is a Modernist pastiche of voices, styles, and themes which resonate with the overarching urge to find meaning in a world that has been annihilated by war, undermined by moral decay, degraded by industry, and divided by rising individualism that rejected community. Yet, one can still talk about general themes in the poem. Two of these are the moral decay of the modern world, mentioned previously, and the resulting alienation experienced by inhabitants of this modern world. With these, and the numerous sub-themes that emerge from them, Eliot's poem decries the state of hollow lives in a dead world, and searches for regeneration.

To reiterate, an overarching theme of *The Waste Land* is that the post-war modern world is decadent and spiritually empty and needs to be restored to a balanced, spiritual footing. This theme is made clear from the start, with the title of the poem, to the very final images of a desert through which the hero has finally passed. Although the decay is pervasive, the specific images of passionless sex, hollow marriages, and isolated individuals suggest that both the cause of death and a cure for death can be found in relationships. That is, the modern world, in Eliot's view, is bereft of healthy relationships and meaningful lives.

In this world of moral and physical decay, identity is fractured. In large part, the fractured identity is conveyed by Eliot's use of multiple voices to convey a dramatic monologue. Whereas the traditional dramatic monologue is presented by one speaker to a silent listener, Eliot's adaptation of the form here is not one speaker, it is many in one. This also brings to mind the contemporaneous work of cubist painters who provided multiple views on an object as a way to offer more coherence. This is the incoherent identity of an individual in the modern world: fractured, composed of many voices. The theme is also driven home through the numerous allusions and references to both ancient and modern literature. The poem is resonant with the voices of Dante, Virgil, Saint Augustine, Shakespeare, and many more. Yet the overarching drive of these voices is to find a synthesis, a unity that can lead to the regeneration of the modern world and, specifically, art in the modern world. Thus, the theme of fractured identity morphs into a quest for synthesis, unity, and rebirth.

True to its roots in French Symbolist poetry, this poem is rich with symbols too numerous to account for in a brief overview. Nonetheless, there are certain key symbols that recur throughout the poem and contribute to its central themes. Of course, the overarching symbol is of a Waste Land, a land that is barren and unproductive. This symbol is so expansive that one might best approach it through various other symbols that elaborate upon it. One of these is the symbol of springtime. The poem opens with images of spring that here are symbolic of both rebirth, as in the traditional conception, and death. In this wasteland, spring is a cruel reminder of a time when regeneration was a part of the cycle, a time of new life, growth, and purity. Spring in the wasteland does not offer relief or new life, merely dull stirrings of memory and longing. In this dead world spring draws the speaker out of the drugged slumber of winter and awakens vulgar desire and cheap lust. But this memory and longing could be said to drive the poem and the "hero" on a quest in search of spring rain that might bring regeneration, rebirth, and new life. Thus, symbolically, spring works as either a symbol of hope or a symbol of death.

The symbolism of death dominates the poem from the barren soil of a desert, where spring never arrives, to the numerous allusions to rats, dead bodies, bones, and the death in life. As it is the setting of the poem, one cannot escape this dead landscape and its cancerous decay. Specific images of decay and death litter the poem. In the first stanza, when the speaker bemoans the spring as an urge to regeneration, he speaks of April "breeding Lilacs out of the dead land" (53). The incongruity of a dead land breeding lilacs is striking and puts the readers on alert. The next stanza takes this death imagery much further. Here, the tree grows out of "stony rubbish" in a desert land where the "the dead tree gives no shelter" (53). This poem conjures images of the profound destruction of World War I throughout the land.

Indeed, this symbolism of death is so pervasive in the poem that the reader begins to experience the oppressive monotony that the denizens of the unreal city express. Like the Sybil in the epigraph of the poem, the inhabitants of the wasteland experience a sort of living death where they do not know true feeling or the difference between good and evil—they feel nothing. The symbols of death, decay, and a possible spring or regeneration mirror the stages of hell that the speaker of Dante's *Divine Comedy* must journey through: hell, purgatory, and, finally, paradise. Although Eliot does not offer us a description of paradise in his poem, both the allusions to Dante and the vague promise of rain at the end of the poem suggest that it may be in the future for the seeker of the poem.

The city itself is symbolic in the poem. Although London is specifically referred to, the landscape of the poem could be any city. This fits with Eliot's larger indictment of modern civilization and the modern city, as its cancerous core. The repetition of the line "Unreal City" throughout the poem always draws us back to this scene, reminding us that the barren and waterless landscape that suffocates all life is the modern city. Specifically, the references to the city aggregate passionless and licentious sexuality, wandering souls, and industrial degradation. Of course, the symbol also suggests other cities and other times as unreal and barren spaces, populated by crowds of the dead. As we see in the first canto, this imagery is evocative of Dante's *Divine Comedy* and the circles of hell. With this allusion, Eliot can suggest literary history, a key theme in all his poetry, and reinforce his evocation of the hell and purgatory that is the modern city.

Two additional symbols are water and fire. Indeed, two of the cantos are titled with these symbols: Canto III, "The Fire Sermon," is followed by the brief Canto IV, "Death by Water." Thus juxtaposed, the symbols of fire and water stand out dramatically. Throughout the poem, fire emerges as a symbol of lust and, in Canto III, the central message is conveyed by various examples of sex without love and the hollow alienation that accompanies it. In Canto II, "A Game of Chess," the barren life and sexual degradation of the upper class woman is marked by candle flames, burning, and smoke. With this symbolic connection to lust already established, the fire sermon concludes with the lines "Burning burning burning burning / O Lord Thou pluckest me out" (64). Followed by the Canto "Death by Water," this line suggests a possible salvation. Burning in his lust, the protagonist is plucked out and "put out," so to speak. And although the intimation of death by drowning may seem negative, when read in the tradition of both Christian symbolism and quest literature, the death by drowning promises rebirth for the protagonist.

Expanding the symbolism of water as both purifying and putrid, rivers function as central symbols throughout this poem. Rivers allude to historical texts and comment on the modern scene of London, allowing the reader to see the connections that Eliot is making with quest literature and ancient poets as he seeks to find regeneration for his protagonist in the modern city. Canto III begins with a river that is in no way romanticized or idyllic. Alluding to Spenser's "Prothalamion," in which nymphs and their lovers gather by a river to prepare for a wedding, the protagonist notes that "the nymphs are all departed" (60). Where Spenser's scene is idyllic, vibrant, and pure, symbolism of death and decay is conveyed by Eliot's modern river. Alluding to yet another river, Leman in Babylon, Eliot intimates that the protagonist is trapped in this deadly land. He describes a rat that,

> crept softly through the vegetation
> Dragging its slimy belly on the bank
> while I was fishing in the dull canal. (60)

This reference to fishing alludes again to the Grail legend of the Fisher King, which Eliot pointed to in his notes as the organizing myth behind the poem. Like the Fisher King of the Grail legend, the protagonist is trapped in a barren land, sitting by a river that is no longer pure, but rather is populated by river rats and mixed with industrial waste.

Poetic Style and Technique

Since the poem was first published, an argument has raged over whether it has formal coherence. Coherence can be found in the structural roots of quest literature. Yet, it is important to know that the Modernist poetic style, of which this poem is the quintessential example, is by nature fragmented, experimental, nonsequential, allusive, and open-ended. One cannot pin Eliot to the wall like a butterfly for examination and dissection, for his poetry resists such simple analyses at every turn. Rather, one takes from Eliot's poem an insight into modern existence that is conveyed as much by theme and message as by the very style of the poem: Modern existence, according to Eliot and the Modernists, is fragmented, alienating, and inconclusive. Eliot's style reflects this stance: It is composed of the fragments of many poetic and literary traditions, voices of his contemporaries, modern music.

As mentioned previously, one can find references to the stylistic traditions of epic poetry, quest literature, and French Symbolist poetry in *The Waste Land*. The epic poem is evoked by the references and allusions to Dante's *Divine Comedy*, which is considered the best epic poem of Italian literature. Usually a long narrative poem that presents a hero engaged in a series of adventures that are central to the survival and/or history of his race or country, the epic poem is an ancient form to which Modernists were widely drawn. It allowed poets and novelists alike to consider the state of the modern world and explore the inner experience of the epic hero, often an Everyman figure in modern literature who is flawed yet perseveres. Consistent with the epic tradition, the poet remains objective and outside the vast action of the poem, merely recounting the trials and adventures of the hero. In *The Waste Land*, this "hero" is composed of multiple voices and figures, most of whom function to illustrate the trials and obstacles of modern existence, but some of whom coalesce into the central persona of the poem, the hero. This modern hero is reluctant to tackle adventure and to overcome obstacles. He is flawed by past debauchery and is not endowed with any particular strengths. Yet, the modern hero is important for just these qualities: This hero could be anyone. As the analysis of the poem clarified, *The Waste Land* is also drawing on the tradition of quest literature. The importance of Eliot's revival of this tradition is the potential it affords for finding purpose in the modern world: that purpose being both the quest for spiritual renewal and that renewal itself. Thus, both of these ancient forms allow Eliot to address his larger themes through form as well as content.

Speaking stylistically, this poem is also a pastiche of many forms. The French symbolists helped Eliot to find both his own voice and content, but they also taught him the evocative power of the symbol. His appreciation of symbols is perhaps best clarified by his emphasis on an "objective correlative," which allows the poet to capture emotion and feeling with a concrete symbol. Thus, the central symbolism of this poem imbues it with an enervating apathy that is the central plight of the modern populace that has lost a spiritual center. The Symbolists valued the symbol because of its distance from the poet and yet its ability to evoke an emotional response. Suspicious of the ability of language to convey meaning in the modern world, where meanings had become overused and clichéd, poets like Eliot and the French Symbolists began to care less for the exact meaning they articulated and more for the full expression of emotion which could be achieved through art and, specifically in this case, through the use of symbols in poetry. Both Eliot and the Symbolists were less concerned with precise meanings and more interested in symbols both for their emotional evocativeness and for their evocations of various meanings.

Eliot's poetic style is at once unique and layered with traditional forms and references. This makes his poetry dense, allusive, and notoriously difficult to decode. Indeed, "decoding" is an apt term precisely because one gathers the impression from reading his work that a careful search for all the references and styles will reveal the message of the poem. This is both true and false. It is important to understand Eliot's literary allusions and the literary forms he is borrowing from and adapting, but they will not reveal a golden nugget of truth waiting to be unveiled. Eliot's allusions and numerous stylistic references provide layers upon layers of meaning, thus making the poem dense and resistant to singular interpretations. In large part, this is typical of Modernist literature; it is notoriously inconclusive, suggesting multiple meanings more often than settling on a single truth or message. This grew out of writers' distrust of assertions of absolute truth which had been the norm of the previous century.

In terms of poetic technique, Eliot pioneers shifts in poetic form. His poem can be read as a series of fragments which can only be properly understood in juxtaposition to one another, as the critic R. P. Blackmur put it. *The Waste Land* can, therefore, be read as an act of purging the language of its accrued meanings that it might be renewed for the modern context. In another vein, the poem can be read as a modern adaptation of ancient myths that gathers together traditions and narratives that might offer meaning and insight into the modern condition and, perhaps, a way out of it. In either interpretation, one must note Eliot's techniques: He connected symbols of emotion to avoid their Victorian evocation of universal truths like God and Empire, of which Modernists were profoundly distrustful; he explored individual consciousness to capture the ennui and sterility of the inhabitants of the wasteland; and he was able to reflect the alienation of the modern moment through techniques like juxtaposition of fragments, layered allusion, and insistent repetition.

HISTORICAL CONTEXT

The two poems examined in this chapter were written in very different historical moments. *The Love Song of J. Alfred Prufrock* was published in 1917 but written and rewritten from 1909, when Eliot was studying philosophy at Harvard, until its publication. Eliot began writing the poem in the halcyon days of Teddy Roosevelt's America and King Edward's England, when both countries were economically prosperous and the populations were generally confident and optimistic about the future. Yet, many artists expressed their sense that the decadence and confidence of the time revealed an undercurrent of despair and emptiness. We certainly see this despair and emptiness in the character of J. Alfred Prufrock.

The dull balance of 1909 was overturned by World War I. The destructive war led to enormous change across the modern world. *The Love Song of J. Alfred Prufrock* was completed and published in the middle of this war, and Eliot was living in London, not Cambridge, Massachusetts. The inhabitants of London reportedly heard daily accounts of up to a thousand casualties a day from the war. In 1915, London experienced its first air attacks by the Germans. This was also the year that the Germans first used poison gas in the war. In 1916, the Battle of the Somme took the lives of over a million soldiers. And in 1917, the year *Prufrock and Other Observations* was published, the United States had finally entered the war. The stability of Europe was literally being blasted apart between 1914 and 1918. Although Eliot was horrified by the war, once the United States entered the conflict, he tried to enlist as a soldier. Unsuccessful in his efforts to get a military appointment, Eliot stayed in London and witnessed the transformation of the population of London. As people were increasingly shocked by the war and the incomprehensibility of so much death, many writers commented on their dehumanized state.

Published in 1922, *The Waste Land* was written in a very different historical moment. Not only did the world suffer from the lasting impact of the first total war on the European continent, but by 1922 most people feared that the peace achieved at the end of that war was very fragile. The economies of England and the United States were doing very poorly. Fascism gained power in Italy, positioning Benito Mussolini as the youngest Premier in that country's history. The Red Army attacked Vladivostik in 1922, revealing the growing power of soviet Communism. Europe in 1922 was an increasingly unfamiliar and ominous place as various political agendas began to consolidate and the slow march to another world war began.

6

Virginia Woolf
Mrs. Dalloway
(1925)

BIOGRAPHICAL CONTEXT

Born in 1882, Adeline Virginia Stephen grew up in a large family with three full siblings, three half siblings from her mother's first marriage to Herbert Duckworth, and a half sister from her father's first marriage to Minny Thackeray. The Stephens' was a lively Victorian household in which Julia Stephen, Virginia's mother, held together the large family and did a great deal of charity work nursing the poor while the entire household was arranged to accommodate the father's rigorous writing schedule. (In addition to his philosophical writing, Leslie Stephen, Virginia's father, was the editor of the *Dictionary of National Biography*.) In her childhood home, Virginia Stephen had much opportunity to engage in her love of reading and her talent for writing. Leslie Stephen allowed his daughter to have free access to his extensive library, where Virginia read voraciously. In her first diary, she records reading Thackeray, Dickens, George Eliot, Trollope, Hawthorne, Washington and the works of many others. Her father created a challenging reading list for his daughter as well, which included the ten volumes of Lockhart's life of Sir Walter Scott, Carlyle's *French Revolution*, and Macaulay's history of England, among many others.

When she was nine years old, Virginia Stephens started a family paper with her brother Thoby called "The Hyde Park Gate News." She writes in her diary of the extreme anticipation she experienced when her mother sat down to read each new issue. In addition to reading and writing a great deal, Woolf did try to attend classes in history and Greek at King's College

London, but her family felt her too high-strung for this. For a time, she was tutored in Greek by Clara Pater, Walter Pater's sister. Woolf was, by our standards, very well-educated. She translated Greek prose, taught herself Russian so that she might translate plays by Chekhov, and continued to read broadly in classical and contemporary literature and history throughout her life.

Woolf's mother died in 1895, triggering the first of Woolf's many nervous breakdowns. When her father died in 1904, Virginia and her siblings (Vanessa, Thoby, and Adrian) moved to 46 Gordon Square in Bloomsbury. Thoby had completed university and was studying for the bar at the time. In an effort to stay in touch with his friends from Cambridge, Thoby initiated regular Thursday evening "at homes" that were the beginning of what has come to be called the Bloomsbury Group, a gathering of young scholars and artists who examined the cultural and political implications of their world through their discussions, writing, and art. During their soirees, everything from the state of art in the modern world to local politics and world religion was discussed openly and critically by all present. This freedom of topic and company was a direct rejection of the Victorian world that the Stephen children had grown up in—a world where men and women did not speak freely and openly with each other. Woolf was also teaching literature at Morley College at this time. Her teaching, combined with the opportunity to voice her opinions and engage in healthy argument with her peers, helped Woolf shape her opinions about art, culture, and gender politics. Indeed, the freedom that this period of her life afforded her was a fresh start. Woolf could explore her mind, her writing, and her beloved London without the constraints and demands of family and propriety that had weighed her down during her Victorian upbringing.

Yet, during this period Woolf continued to struggle with her mental health. Woolf had another nervous breakdown after father's death in 1904. In November of 1906, Virginia's beloved older brother Thoby died of typhoid and, in 1907, Vanessa married Clive Bell. Both of these events marked critical losses for Woolf, who was deeply connected to Vanessa and Thoby. In 1907, Virginia and Adrian moved to Fitzroy Square, where they continued the Thursday "at homes" that Thoby had begun in 1904. It was at these soirees that Virginia met Leonard Woolf, a classmate of Thoby's and a talented journalist and political theorist in his own right. Virginia and Leonard married in October of 1912. Between 1910 and 1915, Woolf was increasingly ill and visited several nursing homes in an attempt to manage her illness. Indeed, in 1913, just a little over a year after her marriage, Woolf attempted suicide and spent time in a nursing home. In 1915, her illness was so severe that she developed a violent aversion to men, Leonard in particular, and spent a long period away from him in a nursing home.

Virginia Woolf's struggle with mental illness was life-long. Leonard was her support throughout their married life. He tried to help make her days calm and to curtail her manic phases when she could not give herself necessary rest. In fact, it was Leonard's idea that a printing press would be a healthy distraction for Virginia—thus began their very successful publishing career. Their Hogarth press was established in 1917 and the first run featured works by both Leonard and Virginia. This press became a very successful, if not particularly lucrative, endeavor and functioned well beyond Virginia's death in 1941. In fact, it has been argued that a certain amount of the posthumous success that many of the Bloomsbury writers have enjoyed is in part due to Hogarth Press and Leonard's careful release of texts over the years.

In the1920s, Woolf was becoming a well-known voice of the new generation of writers. In 1922, she was at work on a collection of essays, "The Common Reader"; this was ultimately published in 1925 by the Hogarth Press. This collection of essays reflects Woolf's thoughts on how to read literature of the past and how to bridge the present and the past. Among the many essays in the volume one can find "On Not Knowing Greek," "Notes on an Elizabethan Play," "Modern Fiction," and "How It Strikes a Contemporary." Perhaps more than any other writer of her generation, Woolf was engaged in reviewing current literature and writing essays. Between 1922 and 1925 while she was writing *Mrs. Dalloway*, for example, she wrote seven short stories, numerous reviews of new literature, critical essays, and gave talks. In 1923, Woolf wrote one of her best known essays on her generation of writers. Published in the *Literary Review*, "Mr. Bennett and Mrs. Brown," assails the Edwardians (specifically Arnold Bennett) for their heavy-handed characterizations and overblown descriptions. Woolf maintained that her generation had to break the mold of the novel in order to speak of the radically changed world around them.

Published in 1925, Virginia Woolf's fourth novel, *Mrs. Dalloway*, did break the mold of the novel. It established her as a powerful force in the British Modernist literary scene and was the first of her experimental works which include *To the Lighthouse, The Waves, Orlando*, and *Between the Acts*. Written in 1923 and 1924, *Mrs. Dalloway* reflects in both content and style Woolf's growing conviction that her generation (which she calls the Georgians after King George) had a great deal to offer in the context of a radically altered cultural and literary scene. This novel, therefore, tackles a complexity of issues ranging from the social changes of post-war England to a questioning of the polarization of the sexes in British society, to an intimate exploration of the interconnectedness of individual lives.

In addition to reflecting these themes, the novel echoes with the various literary texts that influenced Woolf as she was writing. Woolf was reading James Joyce's *Ulysses* at the time that she was writing *Mrs. Dalloway*. Both *Ulysses* and *Mrs. Dalloway* take place in a single day, an unusual enough feature for a novel of that time and one that might suggest that Woolf was perhaps challenging Joyce. Also at that time, Woolf was reading Marcel Proust's *Remembrance of Things Past*, Peacock's *Nightmare Abbey*, Scott's *Old Mortality*, and books by Thackeray, Chaucer, Homer, Plato, Ibsen, and Euripides. In addition, there are allusions to Shakespeare and Greek myth in the novel offering structure to an otherwise uniquely open text. Like Eliot and Joyce, among other Modernist writers, Woolf was thinking through ancient literature, acknowledging that although the modern writer must "make it new," as Pound asserted, she must also use tradition to do so.

Mrs. Dalloway is a singular achievement that draws on literary tradition and Woolf's own innovations in style to capture the extraordinarily delicate and shifting nature of individual consciousness. The novel guides the reader through the course of one June day in1923 in the life of Clarissa Dalloway and her "double," Septimus Warren Smith. In her notes on the novel, Woolf described this work as a study of sanity and insanity specifically in terms of the doubling of Clarissa and Septimus: "Suppose it to be connected in this way: Sanity and insanity. Mrs. D. seeing the truth, SS seeing the insane truth" (quoted in Showalter 138). Clarissa Dalloway, an upper class politician's wife, provides the "sane" consciousness; Septimus Warren Smith, a shell-shocked young soldier, provides the "insane." Although these characters never meet, the narrative technique that Woolf creates weaves them together as if they are two sides of the same consciousness. The development of these two characters and others in the novel also allows Woolf to "criticize the social system" (Diary Vol. II 248). She was particularly critical of the way that the gender polarization of British society contributed to war and led to extraordinary suffering. The narrative point of view travels with the characters of the novel, handed off, as it is, from one to the other when the slightest contact occurs. Through this we see a wide array of perspectives on the society that Woolf would illuminate and criticize.

PLOT SUMMARY

The novel begins by tracing the consciousness of the eponymous central character, Clarissa Dalloway: "And then, thought Clarissa Dalloway, what a morning—fresh as if issued to children on a beach. What a lark! What a plunge!" This is Mrs. Dalloway's thought as she emerges onto her doorstep and sets out into the London scene to purchase flowers for the party she will be hosting in the evening, a party which will be attended by the Prime Minister of England (3). As Clarissa emerges into this London morning, she remembers opening the French doors in her parents' country home, Bourton, to "plunge" into the fresh air. This memory leads her, as many other moments and experiences in the course of this novel will, to reflect on her young suitor, Peter Walsh, whose marriage proposal she rejected over thirty years before. Thus, in the first few paragraphs of the novel, we are introduced to the pattern of Woolf's design: The stream of consciousness of the central characters will lead us from present to past with only the most idiosyncratic trigger. We must allow ourselves to be led through the weave of this design, learning to identify both the markers of memory and the textual patterns that will signal a shift in point of view or time.

As Clarissa steps out into the street, Big Ben strikes the hour, leading Clarissa to reflect on how much she loves London. This is the first of many references throughout the novel to the striking of either Big Ben or other, smaller, public clocks. These clocks will mark the hours of the day and the development of the plot (It is noteworthy that Woolf's working title for the novel was *The Hours*.) Upon entering St. James's Park, Clarissa meets a friend from her youth, Hugh Whitbread. Hugh tells her that his wife Evelyn is ill, but that he will try to attend Clarissa's party in the evening. This encounter leads Clarissa's thoughts back to Bourton and those—including Hugh—who were there the summer that she rejected Peter Walsh's marriage proposal. Her memories carry her through the park, revealing the conflicts and disagreements she had with Peter Walsh even as they reveal her abiding affection for him.

Dreamily reflecting on the invigorating experience of walking in London, Clarissa finds herself looking into the window of Hatchard's shop and considering what gift she might purchase for the ailing Evelyn Whitbread. Her eyes rest upon an open copy of Shakespeare's *Cymbeline* and she reads the following lines, "Fear no more the heat o' the sun / Nor the furious winter's rages." These lines lead Clarissa to reflect on the sadness of her post-World War I world and the "well of tears" it has bred (9). Dissatisfied with the possible gifts available at Hatchard's, Clarissa moves on toward Bond Street and reflects on her life and character in a mood of mid-life finality. She concludes that she would rather have been different: "slow and stately," "rather large," "interested in politics like a man" (10). She describes herself as a "narrow pea-stick figure; a ridiculous little face, beaked like a bird's" (10). This description of Mrs. Dalloway as birdlike recurs throughout the novel and will ultimately be one of the many links between her and Septimus Warren Smith, the shell-shocked veteran of World War.

Clarissa enters Mulberry's flower shop to select the flowers for her party. The sound of a car back-firing in the street startles Clarissa and leads her to think that a shot has been fired. Hearing the "violent explosion" and noticing the car with its blinds drawn, the people on the sidewalk speculate on the whether the car is transporting the Prime Minister. This same car and its explosion serve as a transition for the narrative point of view from Clarissa to her double, Septimus Warren Smith. Also a witness to the "explosion," Septimus becomes frightened and confused, convinced that the crowd has gathered because he is blocking the way; he fears that they are all looking and pointing at him. Indeed, the gathering crowd and the focus on the automobile threaten his equilibrium as he experiences "this gradual drawing together of everything to one centre before his eyes, as if some horror had come almost to the surface and was about to burst into flames, terrified him" (15). Then the narrative point of view moves back to Clarissa, as she meditates on the occupants of the motor car.

"It is probably the Queen, thought Mrs. Dalloway, coming out of Mulberry's with her flowers" (16). Quite in contrast to Septimus's alarm at the possibility of some "horror" about to "burst into flames," Clarissa happily reflects on the focus of all the attention—the Queen, the Prince of Wales, or the Prime Minister. And this thought leads Clarissa back to the party she is hosting that very evening. As Clarissa reflects on the occupants of the car, its passing through Bond Street leads all the passersby, shop-owners, and drinkers in pubs to think of "the dead; of the flag; of Empire" (18). Just as fallen leaves might flutter as a car passes down a road in autumn, the narrative follows the motorcar and the reactions of people observing it from the street. Woolf offers the perspectives of Londoners of all classes as royalty passes, following the grey motorcar to the gates of Buckingham Palace, where a crowd of poor people has gathered to catch a glimpse of royalty (and to feel the gaze of royalty upon them). But, just as the bells strike 11 o'clock and the car finally passes through the palace gates, all eyes are intent upon a skywriting airplane that is tracing an advertisement for English toffee. Thus, commerce and "progress" intrude on the adoration of royalty in the modern scene.

Beginning a section that captures various points of view, Lucrezia Warren Smith attempts to follow the orders of Dr. Holmes and draw her husband out of his gloominess by pointing to the airplane writing in the sky above them as they sit on a bench in Regent's Park. Dr. Holmes has insisted that there is nothing wrong with Septimus. As if in direct contrast to Dr. Holmes's pompous assertions, the narrative reveals that Septimus, at that moment, is convinced that the trees are communicating with him and that the sounds of children and cars around him signal the birth of a new religion. Lucrezia moves away from her husband on the bench. Alone and isolated in a foreign country (she met and married Septimus in her home country of Italy), she feels helpless and unable to assist her mad husband. The narrative exchange of the Warren-Smiths is interrupted by Maisie Johnson asking for directions to the subway entrance. From here, Maisie carries the narrative along, fretting over the "queer" man and his "foreign-looking" wife, both of whom seemed to be in such distress. "Horror! horror! she wanted to cry" (27). From Maisie's reflection on the couple, the narrative point of view passes over to Mrs. Dempster, who sits feeding crusts of bread to the squirrels. Mrs. Dempster notes Maisie's youthful demeanor and reflects on her own life, her losses, achievements, and unfulfilled desires. She reflects on the airplane and the traveling she would have liked to do. From her, the narrative is swept on to other Londoners living their lives and noticing the sky-writing airplane.

At her doorstep, Clarissa wonders what is it that has everyone looking up. Thus, the airplane conveys the narrative back to the central character, Mrs. Dalloway, even as it connects her with the people in the London streets. Entering her home, Clarissa is absorbed in the "cool vault" of her house and feels like "a nun who has left the world and feels fold round her the familiar veils and the response to old devotions" (29). Greeted by the familiar features of her life as Mrs. Clarissa Dalloway, she receives with a subtle shock of abandonment the news that Richard will be lunching with Lady Bruton without her. She consoles herself with the lines from *Cymbeline* that she read in Hatchard's shop window: "'Fear no more,' said Clarissa. Fear no more the heat o' the sun" (30). Clarissa moves from a cheerful mood to feeling herself "suddenly shriveled" and nun-like. She retreats to her solitary attic bedroom to rest. Musing on the staid and solitary nature of her life as middle-aged Mrs. Dalloway, Clarissa again remembers her youth at Bourton and another central figure in that life, her friend Sally Seton. She had been in love with the reckless, daring Sally. It had been a love that she realizes one does not feel for a man; it is as if one is in league with and protective of the loved one. She remembers the "most exquisite moment of her whole life" when Sally had kissed her in the garden (35). Her reaction had been a revelation, a "religious feeling." They were interrupted by Peter Walsh, whom she felt was trying to separate them. This intrusion of Peter leads her back to thoughts of her own aging and her frailty after the bout of influenza she had been through after the war.

Later, as Clarissa sits in the drawing-room mending a tear in the dress she will wear that evening and reflecting again on the lines from *Cymbeline*, she has an unexpected visit from Peter Walsh. She had not read the letter announcing his trip to London from India to see his lawyers about marrying Daisy, a woman who is married and must first secure a divorce. As they visit, they assess each. Peter plays with his pocket knife and becomes agitated about Clarissa's idle life as a politician's wife. Beneath all of this is the memory they both share of her rejection of his marriage proposal so many years ago. Peter, emotional over their meeting and the feelings it has aroused, leaves abruptly when Clarissa's and Richard's daughter, Elizabeth, enters the room. Clarissa calls after him, "Remember my party," as Big Ben strikes 11:30.

The narrative point of view stays with Peter as he walks through London, chafing about Clarissa's rejection of him so long ago and noting the chiming of various clocks around him, reminding the reader of time's passage. Peter, too, reflects on his aging. He is passed by a group of soldiers marching toward Whitehall and finds he cannot keep pace with them anymore. He admires their discipline and vigor even as the narrator reminds us that it is this very uniformity of motion which has laid life to rest "under a pavement of monuments and wreaths," "drugged into a stiff and staring corpse of discipline" (51). Peter's admiration for the military training of these gawky young cadets is soured by this reminder of war and death, just as the passing of royalty in the car is tainted by memories of the war dead.

Peter Walsh crosses Trafalgar Square, feeling younger than he has felt in years, and notices a beautiful young girl who becomes in his mind "the very woman he had always had in mind" (52). He follows her as she passes through London and contemplates inviting her to have ice-cream with him. As she ultimately enters a flat red house of "vague impropriety," his fun is "smashed to atoms" and he recalls Clarissa's voice saying, "Remember my party" (54). Ending up in Regent's Park, Peter shares a reverie not unlike Clarissa's earlier thoughts about London and one's pride at belonging to it all. Peter dozes off to sleep on a bench in the park and has a curious dream about an Odysseus-like solitary traveler and an old woman who loses her sons in battle. He wakes with a start, saying to himself, "the death of the soul." This line returns him to a memory of an argument he had with Clarissa at Bourton, a disagreement that revealed to him the death of her soul at the hands of British or upper-class propriety (58). This brings him back to his early conviction that Clarissa would marry Richard Dalloway and his final argument with her, when he came up against her familiar hardness and rigidity.

Also in Regent's Park, Lucrezia and Septimus Smith are waiting until it is time to leave for their appointment with Sir William Bradshaw, a physician who might help Septimus with his madness, though Bradshaw prefers to call it "lack of proportion." The narrative point of view first rests with Lucrezia, who is struggling to make sense of her husband's queer shift from the man she met and married in Italy to the nervous man sitting on the bench holding an imaginary conversation with his erstwhile friend Evans, who was killed in the war. She argues with him in her mind, noting that she has left her home and country to be with him, that everyone has lost friends and loved ones in the war, and that one must push this sadness from one's mind. Septimus, meanwhile, is struggling with his belief that he is the "lord of men" who has been "called forth to hear the truth." This truth comes to him from the birds around him and from a vision of a dog that turns into a man before him. Talking to himself, he perceives the beauty of the world around him and the unity of all sounds; this, he realizes, is truth. His thoughts are interrupted by his wife, Lucrezia, asking him the time. He sees Peter Walsh walking toward them on the path; confusing Peter for his dead friend Evans coming toward him, he shouts, "For God's sake don't come" (70).

Passing the couple on the bench, Peter notices their unhappiness and wonders what trouble they might be in. Pulling back from this intimate scene, Peter carries the narrative point of view. In contrast to the Warren Smiths, his mood is uplifted by the scene around him, "Never had he seen London look so enchanting" (71). Peter reflects on how changed London has been by the past five years that he has been away, 1918–1923. He notes a new openness, in the press and in people's behaviors—particularly the behavior of women. And this thought leads him to Sally Seton and Clarissa. He had respected "the wild, the daring, the romantic Sally!"—although he was surprised to have received a letter from her announcing that she was going to marry and live in a large house near Manchester (72).

Peter drifts off to sleep and the narrative point of view shifts abruptly to Lucrezia Warren Smith waiting to cross the road as she and Septimus head to Dr. Bradshaw's office. From Lucrezia, the narrator takes us back into Septimus's past, revealing his love of literature and of Miss Isabel Pole, who lectured on Shakespeare. The narrative reveals a sensitive young man whose parents hoped to distinguish him with their gift of a name, a young man who went to fight in a war "to save an England which consisted almost entirely of Shakespeare's plays and Miss Isabel Pole" (86). He had distinguished himself as a soldier, was promoted, and developed a firm friendship with his commanding officer, Evans. We learn that when Evans died Septimus showed no sadness, but soldiered on and won promotion. He married Lucrezia with a growing panic that he could no longer feel "alive." This panic ultimately overtakes his life.

As Big Ben strikes twelve o'clock, the narrator links Clarissa Dalloway and the Septimus Smiths, noting that precisely at this hour Clarissa "laid her green dress on her bed, and the Warren Smiths walked down Harley Street" to keep their appointment with Sir William Bradshaw (94). The Warren Smiths meet with Dr. Bradshaw in his Harley Street office. Bradshaw tells Lucrezia that it is a matter of law; now that Septimus has mentioned suicide, he must go to a home in the country and "rest, rest, rest" (96). Lucrezia despairs, convinced that she has been abandoned by Bradshaw, whom she had believed would help them. After Bradshaw tells Lucrezia that her husband does not have a "sense of proportion," another pompous narrative voice offers a lengthy dissertation on Sir Bradshaw's goddess of "proportion" and how she has led him to prosper and succeed (99). But this goddess has a sister, we are told, and her name is "conversion." Conversion "feasts on the wills of the weakly." This goddess "offers help, but desires power" (100). And at once Lucrezia sees that Sir William Bradshaw is also devoted to the goddess of conversion. She knows that he "swooped" and "devoured" the weak and "she did not like the man" (102).

Following this scene, the punctilious Hugh Whitbread takes up the narrative point of view as he makes his way down Oxford Street to lunch with Richard Dalloway and Lady Bruton. In the course of their lunch and work, Lady Bruton mentions that Peter Walsh is back in London after a scandal with "some woman." The party moves awkwardly around the subject, reflecting on the ineffable flaw in Peter Walsh's character. On his way home, Richard buys Clarissa a bouquet of red and white roses and carries them home, intending to tell his wife that he loves her. Approaching his door, he hears Big Ben striking three o'clock, "first the warning, musical; then the hour, irrevocable" (117).

Richard finds Clarissa at her desk, agitated because she must invite a dull woman to her party and because her daughter Elizabeth is closeted upstairs in her room with Miss Doris Kilman, a religious zealot with whom Elizabeth has been spending a great deal of time lately. Richard gives Clarissa the flowers, talks of his luncheon, the return of Peter Walsh, and interprets Elizabeth's relationship with Miss Kilman as "a phase." He leaves for a committee at Parliament after insisting that Clarissa rest for an hour. And Clarissa reflects on his solicitousness and his unspoken love (for he did not tell his wife that he loves her). Clarissa notes to herself that there is a "dignity," a "solitude" in people that must be respected, even in marriage. Unlike Peter Walsh, Richard respects that solitude in Clarissa. As she tries to rest on the couch,

Clarissa discovers that she is agitated with both Peter and Richard because they do not appreciate that she gives parties. Peter mocks her, calling her the "perfect hostess." Richard, on the other hand, simply does not understand why she would excite herself when it is not good for her health. Clarissa concludes that she has no other talents and that she gives parties as an "offering" to life itself: Because she "loved life," she gave parties, "it was an offering; to combine, to create" (122).

Elizabeth enters the room quietly, leaving the door ajar with the listening Miss Kilman standing just outside. As if in rebuttal to Clarissa's dislike of her, Doris Kilman assumes the narrative point of view and protests that, yes, she stood on the landing, but she "had her reasons" (123). "She had been cheated" of happiness as a girl, she had lost her job during the war because she was not willing to condemn all Germans, and she was bitter and resentful toward all women of Clarissa's class and station. But she had found God two years ago. And now, when Clarissa comes out to bid them farewell as they set out to shop at the Army and Navy stores, she can look with a "steady and sinister serenity at Mrs. Dalloway" because God has helped her turn her envy into pity (125). As Miss Kilman and Elizabeth leave, Clarissa returns to the drawing room reflecting on "love and religion." She tries to remember if she had ever tried to "convert" anyone and concludes that "love and religion" destroy "the privacy of the soul" (127). Thinking about love, the privacy of the soul, and people who try to force others to convert to their expectations, Clarissa is interrupted by Big Ben striking the half hour, three thirty. And as the smaller clock, "which always struck two minutes after Big Ben," chimes in, Clarissa imagines the wave of its time spraying over Doris Kilman, a thought which delivers the narrative point of view back to Miss Kilman (128).

After their shopping, Miss Kilman and Elizabeth have tea together. Miss Kilman feels Elizabeth pulling away from her. Elizabeth longs to be out in the fresh air, away from the neediness of Miss Kilman and the pressure of shoppers. Upon their parting, Miss Kilman stumbles to the Abbey where she seeks rest through prayer from her envy and bitterness. Elizabeth takes a bus ride through London and ends up walking on the Strand, contemplating the career she might like and the pull of expectations from people like her mother and Doris Kilman. Aware of her duty to attend her mother's party, she boards an omnibus bound for Westminster.

With the Strand as the point of exchange, the narrative point of view shifts to Septimus, who is watching the light play on the objects in their flat and the Strand beyond. Septimus hears nature outside breathing the very lines from *Cymbeline* that Clarissa Dalloway has twice quoted in the course of the day: "Fear no more ... fear no more" (139). Then, as if released from his torments, all is normal again. He and Lucrezia joke about a hat she is making for Mrs. Peters, the landlady's married daughter. Septimus calls it an organ grinder's monkey's hat and they both laugh. Together, they fashion a more suitable hat and are happy with their mutual accomplishment. They settle into the pleasant routine of their evening. She reads the paper to him. Briefly, he is happy. Then he becomes anxious again and thinks of doctors Holmes and Bradshaw. Lucrezia insists that they shall not be separated. Hearing voices on the stairs, she goes to see who is there and finds Dr. Holmes. She insists that he cannot see her husband. Listening to their exchange, Septimus hears Holmes put her aside and proceed up the stairs. Septimus bolts. "But no; not Holmes; not Bradshaw," he tells himself (149). As Holmes enters the room Septimus flings "himself vigorously, violently down onto Mrs. Filmer's area railings" one floor below (226). Dr. Holmes gives Lucrezia a sedative and the narrative is taken up by Peter Walsh, who hears an ambulance, presumably the one that will retrieve Septimus's lifeless body.

Approaching his hotel, Peter Walsh considers the ambulance "one of the triumphs of civilization." To Peter, lately back from India, the ambulance signifies the "efficiency, the organization, the communal spirit of London" (151). Walking on toward his hotel, Peter contemplates a theory Clarissa had when she was young: She believed that all people are somehow connected so that once the seen part of us is gone, "the unseen might survive, be recovered somehow attached to this person or that" (153). This timely memory reiterates the connection between Septimus and Clarissa. When Peter arrives at the hotel at six o'clock, he finds a letter from Clarissa telling him how "heavenly" it was to see him. Peter has supper at the hotel and walks to the Dalloway's house for Clarissa's party.

Observing Clarissa as the "perfect hostess," as he once said she would be if she married Richard Dalloway, Peter Walsh regrets attending the party. He knows no one and is acutely critical of Clarissa as she greets each guest with, "How delightful to see you!" (167). Clarissa senses his judgment. She fears that the party will be a "complete failure." She berates herself for trying to pull it off. Then Clarissa spies a guest go right on talking as he "beat back" the curtain that had blown into the room, and with this gesture she is convinced: "So it wasn't a failure after all! It was going to be all right now—her party. It had begun. It had started" (170). As the party takes off, the Prime Minister arrives and makes the rounds with Clarissa and Richard. Meanwhile, the remaining characters from Clarissa's youth at Bourton arrive separately: Hugh Whitbread and Sally Seton (now called Lady Rosseter). Sally and Peter settle down together and talk of old times.

Sir William and Lady Bradshaw arrive late, offering as excuse the suicide of a young man who had been in the Army (Septimus Warren Smith). And Clarissa reflects "in the middle of my party, here's death" (183). She is unsettled by the news and feels a kinship with Septimus, though she has not heard his name. She intuits Septimus's distress at Bradshaw's "forcing the soul" and considers death an act of defiance. She concludes that, "She felt somehow very like him—the young man who had killed himself. She felt glad that he had done it; thrown it away. The clock was striking. The leaden circles dissolved in the air" (186). The novel concludes as Clarissa, finally no longer duty-bound to attend to all her guests, heads over to talk with Peter Walsh. He reflects: "What is this terror? what is this ecstasy? he thought to himself. What is it that fills me with extraordinary excitement? It is Clarissa, he said. For there she was" (194).

CHARACTER DEVELOPMENT

Mrs. Dalloway is a novel that explores the consciousness of key characters, most significantly Clarissa Dalloway and her double, Septimus Warren Smith. As a character, Clarissa Dalloway has come in for both praise and criticism; Woolf herself wrote in her diary that she feared that Clarissa would come off as "too stiff, too glittering and tinselly" (*Diary* Vol. II, 272). Indeed, Clarissa has been criticized as an upper-class snob, a mere socialite. Within the novel, both Doris Kilman and Peter Walsh voice this criticism, one convinced that she has trifled her "life away," the other calling her the "perfect hostess." Yet, Clarissa Dalloway is as much a victim of the social system that Woolf is interrogating as is Septimus. Though sane, Clarissa is struggling with doubt about the meaningfulness of her life. As a female member of the upper class, her options have been few. Now a woman of 52, she is described as nunlike and virginal. She fears her death and is sensitive to the criticism that she has nothing to offer the world, a criticism leveled by Doris Kilman (although never spoken directly to Clarissa Dalloway). The limited choices Clarissa had as an upper-class girl are brought home by her memories of her youth and her choice long ago to reject the marriage offer of Peter Walsh and accept that of Richard Dalloway. Having a choice only between whether to marry or whether not to marry is not liberating. Clarissa might marry Peter, a romantic who wanted her to embrace his idealism, sense of romance, and desire for social change. Peter was frustrated that Clarissa did not seem to want to move beyond the limitations then placed on her class and gender. Clarissa is frightened of his desire to trail blaze. Instead, she chooses the safe, steady, kind, and conservative Richard Dalloway. Marriage to Dalloway offers

Clarissa the clear and well-established role of the political wife. She reflects on her choice throughout the novel and twice concludes that Richard's respect for her privacy is what is preferable to a life with Peter, who was always prying into her thoughts.

Yet, although Woolf may have begun writing the novel as a reflection on a certain social set and "party consciousness," as Woolf called it in her diary, it became something quite different. As the work grew into a novel, Woolf wrote: "I want to give life and death, sanity and insanity; I want to criticize the social system, and to show it at work, at its most intense" (*Diary*, Vol. II, 248). At first, Woolf had intended to have Clarissa die in the novel. By creating a double for her in the character of Septimus Warren Smith, Woolf was able to achieve her goal of showing both "life and death, sanity and insanity." For, where Clarissa is sane, Septimus is insane and commits suicide by the end of the novel.

Woolf's intimate knowledge of the medical establishment that resulted from her own "madness" shaped her construction of both the character of Septimus and the doctors who attempt to treat him. Septimus Warren Smith is a young veteran of World War I. We learn that before the war he was a lover of literature and culture; he was especially a lover of the works of Shakespeare. A sensitive soul forced to play the role of a combatant, now, a few years after the war, Septimus is suffering from shell-shock (a concept first introduced to the medical establishment in 1922). Septimus has become convinced that his inability to feel at the time of his friend's death during the war has condemned him to criminal status. He imagines that the birds in the trees are speaking Greek and sending him messages. He sees his dead friend (Evans) approaching him across Regent's Park and sees him behind the walls of his flat. Septimus's perception of the world of postwar London is that of the insane. Yet, what is so striking about Septimus's point of view is the sanity it also contains: He sees the connectedness of all living things, the tragic nature of war for all human society, and the damage wrought by forcing souls to comply for the sake of theories and beliefs. In this way, Septimus is very like Clarissa. Clarissa is sensitive to the connections among people. She seeks to create connections with her party. Like Septimus, she rants against those who "force the soul," a line that both Clarissa and Septimus use several times in the novel to describe those whom they perceive to be tyrants or zealots, like Sir William Bradshaw.

Peter Walsh is the character who receives the most narrative attention after Clarissa and Septimus. Like them, he is an outsider: He does not fit into the smooth working of government like Richard Dalloway or Hugh Whitbread (whose very name reveals his milquetoast qualities). As the young man who proposed to Clarissa, Peter Walsh was a romantic who believed in social change, change, in fact, that Clarissa feared. Clarissa observes that he would have had her share everything of herself; he would not have respected privacy and distance between a man and a woman. Furthermore, he would have had her embrace his desire to forge social change, to throw off the stiff constraints of Victorian society.

Yet, for all his idealism, Peter does not realize his dreams of social change. He ends up in India as a colonial administrator perpetuating the empire, takes up with a married woman, and has come back to England to arrange for this woman to be divorced so that he can marry her. Peter's is a very conventional scandal. He is insecure and feels judged by Clarissa and her set, and spends the day trying to convince himself that he is still young. As he wanders through London, Peter's reflections on the cadets in training and the monuments to British military heroes suggest his own love of Empire and his inability to move beyond it. General Charles Gordon, who was a hero of Peter's childhood, is a symbol of British imperialism who has been reduced to a "marble stare" (51). This stare resonates with the "stiff and staring corpse" achieved by military discipline that Peter admires in the cadets who pass him in the park. Thus, Peter's latent infatuation with Empire and its methods of control and domination is revealed. Peter may think that he is a socialist and sensitive to the "death of the soul," but Clarissa's anxiety about his tendency to force others seems to have some justification.

Richard Dalloway and Lucrezia Warren Smith, the respective marriage partners of the two central characters, recognize the fragility of their spouses. Richard is attentive to Clarissa's needs and attempts to ensure a quiet and calm life for her. Clarissa appears to appreciate this; indeed she married Richard for his gentle respect for her privacy. But this seems to go too far. They no longer occupy the same bed or bedroom. Clarissa also resents Richard's solicitousness when he fails to recognize that her party-giving is the only creative gesture she can make, given her circumstances. Indeed, Richard appears to be rather obtuse when it comes to the subtleties of human relationships. Where Clarissa senses the subtlest of connections between people, Richard pragmatically goes about the business of working for a conservative government and writing letters for power-brokers like Lady Bruton, who would have all the superfluous people, perhaps even shell-shocked veterans from World War I, forced to emigrate.

Cut off from her country and her family, Lucrezia has no power to protect her husband from the Bradshaws and Holmeses of the world. Like Richard, she is solicitous toward her fragile spouse. She recognizes that he is going mad, and she attempts to help him by taking him to the park, engaging him in light conversation, and reminding him of the real world around them. She even attempts to protect him from the powerful forces that the doctors mount against her. But in the end, she is powerless to do anything. The final image we have of the suddenly and violently widowed Lucrezia is of her insensate on the couch from the drugs Dr. Holmes has administered. Her fate is suggestive of the fate of all those who are weak and without power or resources in this society.

In fact, the key characters in this novel that represent those who "force the soul," doctors Bradshaw and Holmes, are made to appear responsible for Lucrezia's and Septimus's fates. Dr. Holmes is an egotistical, self-important man who believes one can control one's mental health with the right attitude, hobby, or diet. Septimus recognizes him as a fool and refuses to see him. (Lucrezia only sees his true colors when it is too late.) But Holmes is persistent and Septimus begins to feel hunted. He reflects: "Human nature, in short, was on him—the repulsive brute, with the blood-red nostrils. Holmes was on him" (92). Where Holmes is brute force, the second specialist that Septimus sees is more insidious. Sir William Bradshaw, the "great doctor," is socially well-connected; he can and will call on these ties. Bradshaw can put Septimus away and sets about doing so. Speaking of "divine proportion" and "conversion," Bradshaw lets it be known that he has behind him the police and the good of society; for, to protect the good of society, he believes that he must control "unsocial impulses, bred more than anything, by the lack of good blood" (102). Bradshaw and Holmes use their power in society to subdue the disruption of illness and madness. As Woolf portrays them, they are the worst examples of arrogant, entitled male power.

Doris Kilman is a more nuanced portrait of the type who would "force the soul." Through Clarissa Dalloway's struggle with her, we discover that Doris Kilman is also a victim of the social structure and an outsider. Her limited options in life have been significantly reduced by the prejudices of the society around her. During the war, when she stands by her convictions and refuses to paint all Germans with the same brush, she loses her position teaching history at a school. Unable to secure another position, she is reduced to depend on the "charity" of men like Richard Dalloway, who employs her to teach his daughter history. As a result of her difficult life and extreme poverty, we learn, Doris Kilman has become a bitter and pious woman. As such, she attempts to force others to convert to her religion and her values. Clarissa is shocked by Miss Kilman's bitter force, but she recognizes that Miss Kilman has no real power in this society. In the face of the real forces that govern her world, Miss Kilman is just as weak and limited as Clarissa, Septimus, and Lucrezia.

THEMES

For a slim novel, Mrs. Dalloway engages in a remarkably comprehensive exploration of topics. Woolf addresses life, death, aging, war, tyranny, isolation, sanity, insanity, and much more. She manages to address so many topics by carefully controlling what she terms the design of her novel to reflect what she sees as an essential dualism in life. Thus, through the doubling of the central figures of Clarissa and Septimus, Woolf can convey not only the profound connections between these two apparently distant characters, but the opposites they embody. Throughout, the novel reflects the themes of isolation and connectedness, fear of death, and the roots of war in patriarchal society.

The connection between Clarissa and Septimus allows Woolf to explore the dualism of life. By weaving their stories together and suggesting their kindred vision of the world, Woolf invites readers to see the coexistence of apparent opposites, such as sanity and insanity. So, for example, we hear echoes of Septimus's mad claims that he receives messages from the birds and the trees in Clarissa's thoughts. Septimus reflects, "But they beckoned; leaves were alive; trees were alive. And the leaves being connected by millions of fibres with his own body" (22). Similarly, Clarissa reflects early in the novel on the connectedness she feels with the world: "she being part, she was positive, of the trees at home; of the house there, ugly, rambling all to bits and pieces as it was; part of the people she had never met" (9). Not only do Clarissa and Septimus both share this philosophy of the connectedness of all things (the essential truth that both perceive), but they both conceptualize this philosophy with a parallel metaphoric language in which trees, for example, become the objects that represent connectedness. Their shared vision is sane, but Septimus has been so wounded by his experience in the war that he cannot find joy in his insight, whereas Clarissa continually renews her love of life by returning to visions of the subtle, ineffable connection between all living things.

Yet Woolf does not let us lose sight of the isolation that is the opposite of that connection. Characters who are united by the narrative threads that Woolf weaves do not often connect with each other. The aging Mrs. Bentley envies young Maisie as she sees her walk past and reflects sadly on her own unrealized dreams. Maisie, for her part, is alone and frightened by the newness of the city with so many people bustling through their separate lives. No one comes to Lucrezia's aid, alone in a foreign city and struggling to cope with her husband's madness. Indeed, Clarissa, Septimus, and Peter are all isolated and lonely most of time. Though they may share perceptions, characters only actually come together in the most superficial and momentary ways in this novel, reinforcing Woolf's criticism of the isolating nature of the modern world.

A shared experience that unites all the characters in the novel, yet shatters and isolates them, is World War I. Virginia Woolf was not just a pacifist; by 1923 she was an increasingly outspoken critic of the way that patriarchal social structures led to armed conflict and war. Woolf would go on to address this topic unequivocally in her essays: A Room of One's Own (1929) and Three Guineas (1938). But in Mrs. Dalloway, Woolf demonstrates the impact of this society and the war through her characters. The war is repeatedly referred to throughout the novel, both directly and obliquely. Lady Bexborough, we learn, lost a son in the war; the people on the street think of the war dead while the car of some royal person, or perhaps the Prime Minister, passes. The character who most overtly demonstrates the impact of the war is Septimus Smith, who is shown to have gone mad not only because he witnessed the death of his friend Evans in the war but, more importantly, because he becomes aware that he fought for a naïve misunderstanding: "He went to France to save an England which consisted almost entirely of Shakespeare's plays" and romantic ideals (86). When he returns, his idealism destroyed, Septimus sees England composed of people who have "neither kindness, nor faith, nor charity beyond what serves to increase the pleasure of the moment" (89). Septimus realizes that he has been deluded; this insight is too much and he goes mad.

The forces that led to the war in the first place are embodied in the doctor who is supposed to "care" for Septimus when he returns to England with his spirit and mind broken. Sir William Bradshaw represents the worst of patriarchal culture: His lust for power and control, his inflated sense of his own authority, and the power that society grants him all lead to "the death of the soul" and to the physical death of Septimus Warren Smith. Thus, not only is Septimus destroyed emotionally by the war, but he returns to England to be destroyed physically by the same forces that led to war in the first place.

Woolf's repetition of the concept of "forcing the soul" throughout the novel conveys a complementary theme that echoes throughout the novel: the need to respect individual privacy. This is clear when Lucrezia recognizes that Sir William Bradshaw is devoted to the goddess of conversion who "offers help, but desires power" (100). By forcing Septimus's soul, Bradshaw seeks to aggrandize himself, not to help Septimus or respect his need for privacy. But other characters represent this force toward conversion: Clarissa voices the theme clearly when she repeats her argument that Peter would have robbed her of her privacy whereas Richard respects it. In addition, as she reflects on Miss Kilman, Clarissa thinks about conversion, implying that the "clumsy, hot, domineering, hypocritical" Miss Kilman wants to convert Elizabeth, Clarissa's daughter (126). Reflecting that "love and religion would destroy … the privacy of the soul" (126–27), Woolf emphasizes that any extreme, be it love or religion, can lead to tyranny. In this way, Woolf is ever sensitive to opposites that coexist, sensitive to the need for balance and not extremism. For extremism and the forcing of souls, as Woolf clarifies, leads to war and the oppression of others.

Woven into the themes of war and isolation is the theme of death. Clarissa's reflection on the "well of tears" in the world's late age implies a link between the subject of death in the novel with World War I. This is further conveyed through Septimus and his profound struggle with the death he witnessed in the war. But Clarissa also reflects on death and aging by remembering her youth at Bourton and the choices she made as a young woman that determined the path of her life. Clarissa regularly slips from a present-day awareness of her age, her physical limitations, or her stage of life to memories of her youth at Bourton and, particularly, that point at which she was trying to decide whether or not to marry Peter Walsh. As Clarissa goes about her day, it is as though she is weighing the choices she made years before. And this effort to weigh and assess leaves her doubting the value of her life and the choices she has made. This doubt and sense of death are connected to Clarissa's stage of life. Almost as though she recognizes herself as useless in the economy of reproduction, Clarissa refers to herself repeatedly as virginal and nunlike. She notes that she "had the oddest sense of being herself invisible; unseen; unknown; there being no more marrying, no more having children now" (11). Clarissa dimly perceives that her role in the social system has been completed. She has had a child and now, beyond child-bearing age, her value is considerably reduced.

Peter, too, is struggling to convince himself that he is not old and that there are still opportunities open to him. Yet many things combine in the text to suggest that Peter is old, that he has become something other than what his youthful idealism from the days at Bourton promised. He senses this himself, but the clearest assessment comes from those observing him. Clarissa is frustrated with his relationship with a much younger, married woman. Lady Bruton, Richard, and Hugh all gloss over Peter's return to London to procure a divorce for his lover, agreeing that he has some essential flaw. Still, Woolf is a generous writer who captures the complicated nature of her characters. She does not allow her readers to simply see Peter and Clarissa, or even Septimus Warren Smith, for that matter, as failures. Rather, she gently brings her readers to appreciate the complexity of life, the way it incorporates and makes room for apparently exclusive opposites.

MOTIFS AND SYMBOLS

Woolf is able to convey various themes through her skillful construction of motifs. Recurrent images, words, objects, or phrases that unify a work of literature, motifs accrue meaning that deepens the complexity of the novel. One of these motifs is evoked by the phrase from Shakespeare's play, *Cymbeline*, "Fear no more the heat o' the sun / Nor the furious winter's rages" (9). These lines are said as a eulogy over the body of Imogene in the play, as she is presumed to be dead. In fact, she is only drugged and will revive. When this line is first introduced in *Mrs. Dalloway*, as Clarissa stands at the window of Hatchard's shop, it is followed by the comment: "This late age of the world's experience had bred in them all, all men and women, a well of tears" (9). The sentence comments on the lines from Shakespeare and relates them to the modern moment of the story, the postwar world where survivors are still full of shock and sorrow, perhaps uncertain whether their lives and world are dead or merely numbed with pain. Clarissa repeats Shakespeare's lines when she learns that Lady Bruton had asked Richard to dine with her and had not included her in the invitation. Lady Bruton's snub leads Clarissa to fear "time itself." It makes her feel old, "shriveled, aged, breastless" and she retreats to her bedroom "like a nun withdrawing" (31). In this context again, the lines from Shakespeare are chanted almost as a way of warding off pain, alienation, and death. But also they suggest a eulogy for a past innocence and youthfulness that the war and the passing of time annihilated. Later Clarissa repeats them again, this time in a calmer, more accepting tone, as she sits sewing quietly. She acknowledges and tacitly accepts the inevitability of an end. The lines help her release the burden and sorrow of her heart. "Fear no more, says the heart," is the improvised version of the line she offers (39). Thus, Shakespeare's lines appear to gather around the theme of death and alienation, serving to calm Clarissa and relieve her of fear as she accepts these inevitable facts.

When Septimus repeats Shakespeare's lines later in the novel, they retain Clarissa's modifications with Septimus's additions: "Fear no more, says the heart in the body; fear no more" (139). The lines also retain the meaning they had when last repeated by Clarissa: Septimus asserts that he is "not afraid." Thus, uttered just before his last happy moments with his wife are intruded upon and shattered by the entrance of Doctor Holmes, the lines from Shakespeare seem to offer release from the burden of sorrows—"the well of tears"—that have tormented Septimus. Finally, the line is repeated one more time by Clarissa when she has heard of Septimus's death from the Bradshaws. Shocked that they would speak of death at her party, Clarissa retreats to a side room and reflects on Septimus's act, concluding that she admires his jump to death because he had preserved the "thing that mattered" in life. Clarissa intuits that Bradshaw had driven him to his death by "forcing the soul" (184). She repeats the lines from Shakespeare one last time, notes the chiming of the clock and reflects, "She felt somehow very like him—the young man who had killed himself. She felt glad that he had done it; thrown it away" (186). Uniting these two central characters, revealing them as doubles that represent two possible life paths, Shakespeare's lines—quoted, amended, and reflected upon—reveal the interconnectedness of all who have lived through "this late age of the world's experience" (9).

A related and opposite motif is the repetition of the phrase or idea of "forcing the soul," which Clarissa uses in her reflections on Septimus's suicide just as she does throughout the novel. Used with variation by Septimus, Lucrezia, and Peter, the motif of forcing the soul serves to reiterate the theme of death that is central to the story. It complicates the theme by suggesting, just as Clarissa does when she reflects on Septimus's suicide, that there are many ways to die and that there is the possibility of a kind of living death. This is precisely why Clarissa embraces Septimus's suicide: She sees it as an active choice against the forcing of the soul, a refusal to submit to the power and bullying of the patriarchal culture embodied in men like Bradshaw and Holmes.

Further symbols in the story serve to add complexity to the central themes. The chiming of London's clocks throughout the day does more than give structure to this novel; it conveys the passage of time on a much grander scale. The clocks bring us back to Clarissa's ongoing meditation on her life choices, her aging and her conviction that she is outside of the economy of reproductivity. She is a middle-aged woman defined by her husband's name, "this being Mrs. Dalloway; not even Clarissa anymore" (11). She moves from memories of her youth as the unrealized Clarissa to her present day self as a 52-year-old Mrs. Dalloway, the mother of a young woman and wife of a conservative politician. She has been defined by her roles and lost her name, her identity, in the process. The chiming of the clocks, then, marks the passage of time in Clarissa's life, as much as it marks the passages of the hours of one day in June 1923. One can also draw an analogy between the chiming of the clocks and the changing of British society. The novel calls our attention to this wider picture of time with Peter's comment on the postwar changes in London—the greater openness between the sexes and in the press. London and British society have changed since the war. The chiming of the clocks implies the march of time since the war and the profound changes in society that are occurring.

The novel is peppered with references to monuments throughout England, mostly military, that glorify the values of Britain as they have been passed on from the Victorians: heroism, self-sacrifice, and self-abnegation. Peter's meditation on the monuments to Gordon and other military heroes not only reveals his very British infatuation with empire, but subtly connects this empire with death and isolation. The Prime Minister, who attends Clarissa's party and perhaps passes by the crowds in a shuttered car, is a representative of empire that stirs nationalist pride that Woolf would have us see led to war. Septimus's choice to go into battle was based on this pride, trumped up by illusions of Empire and the duty of an English man to serve his country.

Trees and birds are symbolic of character throughout the novel. Both Clarissa and Septimus use the symbolism of trees to capture the unique imagery of their insights about life. Trees represent the connectedness of all life in the thoughts of each character, though, for the sane Clarissa, they do not preach that connection in a sermon; they remain symbolic. Birds are most commonly associated with Clarissa and Septimus, who are commonly evoked as birdlike in their manners and habits. Each, then, is revealed as delicate, flighty, and fragile. But the symbolism of birds is also associated with the most abhorrent characters in the novel: Holmes and Bradshaw. Both are described in language that evokes birds of prey: They swoop and devour. They are raptors. With this symbolism and imagery, Woolf works by suggestion and allusion, connecting characters through symbolic references.

LITERARY STYLE

Modernist writers broke the traditional structural and narrative modes for the novel. Like Joyce's *Ulysses*, *Mrs. Dalloway* challenges the structural scope of the novel form by focusing on a single day in the life of Clarissa Dalloway and her "double," Septimus Warren Smith. This doubling is achieved through shared reflections on objects, events, and hours in that single day. Doubling is also achieved by the way Woolf depicts both characters as sensitive and bird-like, each psychically wounded by the war and the bullying culture of patriarchy. But most importantly, the doubling is stylistically achieved by the degree to which the entire narrative is shared by the story of each character. As we witness Clarissa's day, so too do we observe Septimus as he travels through his fateful, final day. Even though Woolf's narrative allows for the point of view of even the most minor characters to emerge in the midst of the story, Clarissa and Septimus stand out as the central characters.

Also new to writers of Woolf's generation is their radical play with narrative point of view. The narrative point of view in Woolf's novel shifts suddenly between characters; it moves from direct discourse to free indirect discourse, blurring the narrative point of view. Like the language of a Shakespeare play, Woolf's style in this novel requires that her readers follow the rhythms and patterns that link the many characters and consciousnesses together through narrative. This style allows readers to experience the immediate perceptions and associations of the characters without the intrusion of an omniscient narrator. Free indirect discourse is a combination of two modes of discourse: direct discourse and indirect discourse. Using direct discourse, Woolf writes, "'I love walking in London,' said Clarissa Dalloway" (6). As is common with direct discourse in fiction, this is a clear statement attributed by quotation marks to the named character. Indirect discourse, in contrast, is not usually revealed by the character responsible for it; usually it is another character or the narrator paraphrasing what the speaker has said. For example, the preceding comment might be rendered in indirect discourse as "Mrs. Dalloway said she loved walking in London." Free indirect discourse, then, occurs when characters' thoughts are woven into the narrative fabric in such a way that it becomes difficult to tell whether the prose reflects the narrator's perspective, the thoughts of a character, or the thoughts of someone else about that character. In this case, "free" means that there is no clear attribution of text to speaker. For example, following the first line of the novel, which is "Mrs. Dalloway said she would buy the flowers herself," we encounter a statement that one might assume is Clarissa Dalloway's logic for this statement: "For Lucy had her work cut out for her. The doors would be taken off their hinges; Rumplemayer's men were coming" (3). Nothing directly attributes these sentences to Clarissa Dalloway. There is no omniscient narrator to tell us that this is what Mrs. Dalloway thought or said. Still, by reading carefully, one can usually deduce and attribute point of view in this work. The benefit of eliminating this omniscient narrator (or at least severely limiting its role) is that the reader can gain knowledge of the consciousness of the characters as they experience their world. We come to know Clarissa's consciousness and inner life because we enter into it, uninterrupted by commentary from an omniscient point of view.

A fascinating example of this technique occurs when Mrs. Dalloway bids farewell to Miss Kilman as she and Elizabeth Dalloway head off to the Army and Navy store. In the narrative, Miss Kilman is meditating on her desire to dominate Mrs. Dalloway. She wants to make Mrs. Dalloway "feel her mastery. If only she could make her weep; could ruin her; humiliate her; bring her to her knees crying" (125). Miss Kilman rationalizes that this is God's will too: "But this was God's will, not Miss Kilman's. It was to be a religious victory. So she glared; so she glowered." Immediately following this, we have the following narrative: "Clarissa was really shocked. This is a Christian—this woman!" (125). It is as if Clarissa Dalloway has been listening to Doris Kilman's thoughts. Using free indirect discourse in this way, Woolf is able to create a dialogue that cannot really occur between these two women, and thereby creates and enriches new layers of meaning.

Capturing the common ground between characters can also be seen when Septimus's love of Shakespeare presents him with the same lines from *Cymbeline* that Clarissa reads in the window of the bookstore and repeats to herself throughout the day: "Fear no more." With this shared point of reference, a eulogy said over the living body of Imogene in Shakespeare's play, we see in each character a literary mindedness, an artistic sensitivity that further connects them to each other, though they never meet.

The common ground between characters is also clear when one character takes over the narrative from another, as for example, when numerous minor characters respond to the sky-writing airplane. The shifting narrative point of view on this common object reveals details about each character. Thus, for example, whereas the plane reminds Mrs. Dempster of her lifelong desire to travel, Mr. Bentley sees the plane as a symbol of man's soul. A feature of each character emerges in the "present moment" by way of the shared point of reference, the airplane. Used throughout the novel, this narrative technique asks readers to be alert to shifts in point of view, alert to the nuanced perspectives of many characters, and open to the unique pattern of unconscious thought.

In addition to choosing indirect and free indirect discourse over an omniscient narrative voice that labels the thoughts and actions of each character, Woolf employs techniques that convey much of the narrative as the stream of consciousness of key characters. The term "stream of consciousness" was first introduced in the philosophical writing of William James, by which he meant the flow of human thought. Woolf uses various techniques that allow the thoughts of her characters to unfold, uninterrupted by an omniscient narrator. The key to following these characters' thoughts is to remember that Woolf, like many other Modernist writers, was intent upon conveying a direct representation of her characters' consciousnesses. Like James Joyce and D. H. Lawrence, Woolf attempted to use fiction to explore the interiority or psychic life of a character. Thus, for example, in the very opening of the novel we encounter Clarissa moving fluidly from thoughts of her party to memories of her youth at Bourton to memories of her quarrels with Peter Walsh.

Relevant to these opening lines, one observes another narrative feature of the novel: Virginia Woolf begins in medias res, in the middle of the action. This is consistent with the philosophical stance behind the modes of discourse she used in the novel, that is, Woolf resists omniscient authority. She does not offer us a traditional narrator and she does not assume the role herself by generating a grand narrative beginning. Rather, she uses indirect discourse to put us right into the thought-as-action that drives the entire novel. In the first two pages, we are allowed into the thoughts of two characters, given the names of several others, and never told who these people are. Instead, we learn the salient information about Woolf's characters from the characters themselves more often than we do from the narrator. The novel moves forward as though with the motion, mental and physical, of its characters; we are carried along with this motion, almost as though we are inside the minds of the characters.

Stylistically, then, the plot of this novel is made to progress by means of shifting perspective. It is also advanced by the way Woolf marks time in the novel, that is, by the striking of the clocks of London, most specifically Big Ben. In this way, we witness the passing of time as it is observed or marked by characters going about their days: At various points in the day, Clarissa notes the striking of the clock and reacts to it. Indeed, as the day grows old, Clarissa becomes increasingly conscious of her own aging and inevitable death. In a parallel way, Septimus's struggles intensify as the clocks of London "nibble" away the hours, ultimately concluding in his death as evening becomes night. The role of the London clocks, then, is not merely a forced structural apparatus provided by the author, but an echo of the reality of our own mortality. In this way, the one day in the life of Clarissa Dalloway expands to encompass the concept of an entire life.

HISTORICAL CONTEXT

Mrs. Dalloway was written between 1922 and 1924, when Woolf was struggling with her precarious emotional health. The numerous physicians she had seen are reflected in her descriptions of Holmes and Bradshaw and her descriptions of their treatment of Septimus Warren Smith. Her depictions of Septimus's mad scenes come out of her own very difficult experiences with mental illness. Woolf's acute sensitivity to the way that war had inflicted this madness on Septimus reflects her larger awareness of the powerfully disruptive and transformative impact of World War I on society as a whole. The postwar world that Woolf depicts in the novel was a world of change. British imperialism was waning and there were struggles for independence brewing in India and elsewhere in the Empire. The Labour Party had come into power in 1924 and transformed the conservative political scene of England. Indeed, the London that Woolf so intimately depicts in this novel was a changing city. So, as Peter Walsh notes, were the citizens of the city changing.

Woolf could not have known it at the time, but this was an interwar novel as well. It reflects both the radical change of consciousness that resulted from a "world war" and the optimism that managed to survive that war. It indicts tyranny and imperialism, yet sees the powerful pull such traditions and institutions continue to have on people. It is a novel that, in the end, rings hopeful even as it suggests a eulogy for an earlier and more innocent time.

Bibliography

Page numbers from the five novels and two poems discussed in this volume are from the following editions.

Conrad, Joseph. *Heart of Darkness*. New York: Penguin Putnam, Inc., 1999.
Eliot, Thomas Stearns. *Collected Poems 1909–1962*. New York: Harcourt Brace and Company, 1988.
Forster, Edward Morgan. *Howards End*. New York: Vintage Books, 1989.
Joyce, James. *A Portrait of the Artist as a Young Man*. New York: Penguin Books, 2003.
Lawrence, David Herbert. *Women in Love*. New York: Penguin Books, 1989.
Woolf, Virginia. *Mrs. Dalloway*. New York: Harcourt, Inc., 1981.

SELECTED NOVELS AND ESSAYS BY JOSEPH CONRAD

Almayer's Folly. London: Fisher Unwin, 1895.
Lord Jim: A Tale. Edinburgh and London: Blackwood, 1900.
The Nigger of the "Narcissus." London: Heinemann, 1897.
Nostromo. London: Harper, 1904.
The Secret Agent: A Simple Tale. London: Methuen, 1907
Typhoon and Other Stories. London: Heinemann, 1903.
Victory. London: Methuen, 1915.

SELECTED BIOGRAPHICAL AND CRITICAL WORKS ABOUT JOSEPH CONRAD

Achebe, Chinua. "An Image of Africa." *Massachusetts Review* 18 (1977): 782–94.
Brantlinger, Patrick. "*Heart of Darkness*: Anti-Imperialism, Racism, or Impressionism?" *Criticism* 27 (1985): 363–85.

Fleishman, Avrom. *Conrad's Politics*. Baltimore, MD: Johns Hopkins University Press, 1967.

Hawkins, Hunt. "Conrad's Critique of Imperialism in *Heart of Darkness*." *PMLA* 94 (1979): 286–99.

Morel, E. D. *King Leopold's Rule in Africa*. Westport, CT: Negro Universities Press, 1970.

Parry, Benita. *Conrad and Imperialism*. London: Macmillan, 1983.

Sherry, Norman, ed. *Conrad: The Critical Heritage*. London: Routledge, 1973.

Stampfl, Barry. "Marlow's Rhetoric of (Self-)Deception in *Heart of Darkness*." *Modern Fiction Studies* 37 (1991): 1873–96.

Watts, Cedric. "'A Bloody Racist': About Achebe's View of Conrad." *Yearbook of English Studies* 13 (1983): 196–209.

CONTEMPORARY REVIEWS OF *HEART OF DARKNESS*

Clifford, Hugh. "The Art of Mr. Joseph Conrad." *The Spectator* 89, November 29, 1902: 827–28.

"Five Novels." *The Nation* 76, June 11, 1903: 148–49.

Garnett, Edward. "Mr. Conrad's New Book." *The Academy and Literature* 63, December 6, 1902: 606–7.

Masefield, John, "Deep Sea Yarn." *The Speaker* 7, January 31, 1903: 442.

SELECTED POEMS, PLAYS, AND ESSAYS BY T. S. ELIOT

Ash-Wednesday. London: Faber & Faber; New York: Putnam's, 1930.

The Cocktail Party. London: Faber & Faber; New York: Harcourt, Brace, 1950.

Collected Poems, 1909–1962. New York: Harcourt Brace & Company, 1988.

To Criticize the Critic. London: Faber & Faber; New York: Farrar, Straus, 1965.

Four Quartets. London: Faber & Faber; New York: Harcourt, Brace, 1943.

The Letters of T. S. Eliot. Vol. 1 1898–1922. Ed. Valerie Eliot. New York: Harcourt Brace Jovanovich Publishers, 1988.

Prufrock and Other Observations. London: Egoist Press, 1917.

The Sacred Wood. London: Methuen, 1920.

Selected Essays, 1917–1932. London: Faber & Faber; New York: Harcourt, Brace, 1932.

Selected Prose of T. S. Eliot. New York: Harcourt Brace & Company, 1988.

The Use of Poetry and the Use of Criticism. London: Faber & Faber; Cambridge, MA: Harvard University Press, 1933.

The Waste Land. New York: Boni & Liveright, 1922.

The Waste Land: A Facsimile Transcript of the Original Drafts Including the Annotations of Ezra Pound. Ed. Valerie Eliot. London: Faber & Faber; New York: Harcourt Brace Jovanovich, 1971.

SELECTED BIOGRAPHICAL AND CRITICAL WORKS
ABOUT T. S. ELIOT

Ackroyd, Peter. *T. S. Eliot: A Life*. New York: Simon and Schuster, 1984.

Calder, Angus. *T. S. Eliot*. Atlantic Highlands, NJ: Humanities Press International, Inc., 1987.

Drew, Elizabeth. *T. S. Eliot: The Design of His Poetry*. New York: Charles Scribner's Sons, 1949.

Gordon, Lyndall. *T. S. Eliot: An Imperfect Life*. New York: Norton, 1998.

Kenner, Hugh, ed. *T. S. Eliot: A Collection of Critical Essays*. Englewood Cliffs, NJ: Prentice-Hall, Inc., 1962.

Martin, Jay, ed. *A Collection of Critical Essays on "The Waste Land."* Englewood Cliffs, NJ: Prentice-Hall, Inc., 1968.

Matthiessen, F. O. *The Achievement of T. S. Eliot: An Essay on the Nature of Poetry*. London: Oxford University Press, 1958.

Moody, A. David, ed. *The Cambridge Companion to T. S. Eliot*. Cambridge: Cambridge University Press, 2004.

North, Michael. *The Political Aesthetics of Yeats, Eliot, and Pound*. Cambridge: Cambridge University Press, 1991.

Ricks, Christopher. *T. S. Eliot and Prejudice*. London: Faber and Faber, 1988.

Selby, Nick, ed. *T. S. Eliot: The Waste Land*. New York: Columbia University Press, 1999.

Vendler, Helen. *Coming of Age as a Poet: Milton, Keats, Eliot, Plath*. Cambridge, MA: Harvard University Press, 2003.

CONTEMPORARY REVIEWS OF *THE LOVE SONG OF*
J. ALFRED PRUFROCK

Aldington, Richard. "The Poetry of T. S. Eliot." *Literary Studies and Reviews*. New York: The Dial Press, 1924. 181–91.

MacCarthy, Desmond. "New Poets." *The New Statesman* 16, 1921: 418–20.

Pound, Ezra. "T. S. Eliot." *Poetry: A Magazine of Verse* 10, 1917: 264–71.

Sinclair, May. "'Prufrock: and Other Observations': A Criticism." *The Little Review*, 1917: 8–14.

CONTEMPORARY REVIEWS OF *THE WASTE LAND*

Brooks, Cleanth, Jr. "The Waste Land: An Analysis." *Southern Review* 3, Summer 1937: 106–36.

Cowley, Malcolm. "The Dilemma of *The Waste Land*." *Exiles Return: A Literary Odyssey of the 1920's*. New York: Viking, 1951. 112–15.

Leavis, F. R. "The Significance of the Modern Waste Land." *New Beginnings in English Poetry*. London: Chatto and Windus, 1932. 90–113.

Ransom, John Crowe. "Waste Lands." *New York Evening Post Literary Review* 14 July 1923: 825–26.

Wilson, Edmund. "The Poetry of Drouth." *The Dial* 73, December 1922: 611–16.

SELECTED NOVELS, SHORT STORIES, AND ESSAYS BY E. M. FORSTER

Aspects of the Novel. London: Edward Arnold, Co., 1927.

The Celestial Omnibus and Other Stories. London: A. A. Knopf Vintage Books, 1911.

The Collected Tales of E. M. Forster. London: A. A. Knopf Vintage Books, 1947.

A Passage to India. London: Edward Arnold, Co., 1924.

A Room with a View. New York and London: G. P. Putnam's and Sons, 1911.

Two Cheers for Democracy. New York: Harcourt, Brace, and World, Inc., 1951.

Where Angels Fear to Tread. Edinburgh and London: Blackwood and Sons, 1905.

SELECTED BIOGRAPHICAL AND CRITICAL WORK ABOUT E. M. FORSTER

Beauman, Nicola. *E. M. Forster: A Biography*. New York: Alfred A. Knopf, 1994.

Bloom, Harold, ed. *E. M. Forster: Modern Critical Interpretations*. New York: Chelsea House, 1987.

Born, Daniel. "Private Gardens, Public Swamps: *Howards End* and the Revaluation of Liberal Guilt." *Novel* 25, 1992: 141–59.

Crews, Frederick C. *E. M. Forster: The Perils of Humanism*. Princeton, NJ: Princeton University Press, 1962.

Dowling, David. *Bloomsbury Aesthetics and the Novels of Forster and Woolf*. London: Macmillan, 1985.

Jameson, Fredric. "Modernism and Imperialism." *Nationalism, Colonialism, and Literature: Essays by Terry Eagleton, Fredric Jameson, Edward W. Said*. A Field Day Company Book. Minneapolis: University of Minnesota Press, 1990: 43–66.

Rosecrance, Barbara. *Forster's Narrative Vision*. Ithaca, NY: Cornell University Press, 1982.

Trilling, Lionel. *E. M. Forster*. Norfolk, CT: New Directions, 1943.

CONTEMPORARY REVIEWS OF *HOWARDS END*

Garnett, Edward. "Villadom." *Nation* 12, November 1910: 282–84.

Leavis, F. R. "E. M. Forster." In Leavis, *The Common Pursuit*. Harmondsworth: Penguin, 1962. 261–76.

Richards, I. A. "A Passage to Forster: Reflections on a Novelist." *The Forum*, 78 (6), December 1927: 914–20.

Woolf, Virginia. "The Novels of E. M. Forster." *The Death of the Moth and Other Essays*. New York: Harcourt, Brace, 1967: 342–50.

SELECTED NOVELS AND SHORT STORIES BY JAMES JOYCE

Chamber Music. London: Elkin Matthews, 1907.
Collected Poems. New York: The Viking Press, 1937.
Dubliners. New York: The Modern Library, 1926.
Exiles. London: Grant Richards Ltd., 1918.
Finnegan's Wake. London: Faber and Faber; New York: The Viking Press, 1939.
James Joyce: Poems and Shorter Writings. Eds. Richard Ellmann, A. Walton Litz, and John Whittier Ferguson. London: Faber and Faber, 1991.
Ulysses. Paris: Shakespeare and Company; London: The Egoist Press, 1922.

SELECTED BIOGRAPHICAL AND CRITICAL WORK ABOUT JAMES JOYCE

Beebe, Maurice. "The *Portrait* as Portrait: Joyce and Impressionism." *Irish Renaissance Annual* 1. Ed. Zack Bowen. Newark, DE: University of Delaware Press, 1980.
Beja, Morris, ed. *"Dubliners" and "A Portrait of the Artists as a Young Man": A Casebook*. London: Macmillan, 1973.
Booth, Wayne C. "The Problem of Distance in *A Portrait of the Artist*." *The Rhetoric of Fiction*. Ed. Wayne C. Booth. Chicago: University of Chicago Press, 1961.
Deane, Seamus, ed. *A Portrait of the Artist as a Young Man*. New York: Penguin, 1992.
Deming, Robert H., ed. *James Joyce: The Critical Heritage*. Two volumes. London: Routledge, 1970.
Ellmann, Richard. *James Joyce*. New York: Oxford University Press, 1982.
Fargnoli, A. Nicholas and Michael P. Gillespie. *James Joyce A–Z: The Essential Reference to His Life and Writings*. New York: Oxford University Press, 1995.
Kenner, Hugh. "The *Portrait* in Perspective." *James Joyce: Two Decades of Criticism*. Ed. Seon Givens. New York: Vanguard Press, 1963.
Kershner, R. B., Jr. "Time and Language in Joyce's *Portrait*." *ELH* 43, 1976: 604–19.
Scholes, Robert. "Joyce and Epiphany: The Key to the Labyrinth." *Sewanee Review* 72 (Winter 1964): 65–77.
Wollaeger, Mark A. *James Joyce's* A Portrait of the Artist as a Young Man: A Casebook. Oxford: Oxford University Press, 2003.

CONTEMPORARY REVIEWS OF *A PORTRAIT OF THE ARTIST AS A YOUNG MAN*

Anonymous. *New Age* 12, July 1917. *James Joyce: The Critical Heritage*. Ed. Robert H. Deming. London: Routledge and Kegan Paul, 1970.

Pound, Ezra. "At Last the Novel Appears." *Egoist* 4 (2, February 1917): 21–22. *James Joyce: The Critical Heritage*. Vol. 1. Ed. Robert H. Deming. London: Routledge and Kegan Paul, 1970: 85.

Lewis, Wyndham. "An Analysis of the Mind of James Joyce." *Time and Western Man.* Ed. Wyndham Lewis. London: Chatto and Windus, 1927: 91–130.

Wells, H. G. "Review of *A Portrait of the Artist.*" *James Joyce: The Critical Heritage*. Vol. 1. Ed. Robert H. Deming. London: Routledge and Kegan Paul, 1970.

SELECTED NOVELS, SHORT STORIES, AND ESSAYS BY D. H. LAWRENCE

Aaron's Rod. New York: T. Seltzer, 1922.

The Complete Poems of D. H. Lawrence. Ed. Vivian De Sola Pinto and F. Warren Roberts. New York: Viking, 1964.

The Complete Short Stories of D. H. Lawrence. 3 vols. Harmondsworth, Middlesex: Penguin, 1976.

Kangaroo. New York: T. Seltzer, 1923.

Lady Chatterley's Lover. New York: Dial Press, 1944.

Mornings in Mexico. New York: A. A. Knopf, 1927.

The Plumed Serpent, Quetzalcoatl. New York: A. A. Knopf, 1951.

The Prussian Officer and Other Stories. Ed. John Worthen. Cambridge: Cambridge University Press, 1983.

The Rainbow. Ed. Mark Kinkead-Weeks. Cambridge: Cambridge University Press, 1989.

Selected Literary Criticism. Ed. Anthony Beal. New York: Viking Press, 1956.

Sons and Lovers. New York: M. Kennerly, 1913.

Studies in Classic American Literature. New York: T. Seltzer, 1923.

The White Peacock. London: Heinemann, 1911.

Women in Love. New York: Penguin, 1995.

SELECTED BIOGRAPHICAL AND CRITICAL WORKS ABOUT D. H. LAWRENCE

Adamowski, T. H. "Being Perfect: Lawrence, Sartre, and *Women in Love.*" *Critical Inquiry* 2 (1975): 345–68.

Beal, Anthony. *D. H. Lawrence*. Edinburgh and London: Oliver and Boyd, 1964.

Bloom, Harold, ed. *D. H. Lawrence's Women in Love*. New York: Chelsea House, 1988.

Draper, R. P. *D. H. Lawrence: The Critical Heritage*. New York: Barnes and Noble, 1970.

Kermode, Frank. "The Novels of D.H. Lawrence." *D. H. Lawrence: Novelist, Poet, Prophet*. Ed. Stephen Spender. London: George Weidenfeld and Nicolson Ltd., 1973.

———. *D. H. Lawrence*. New York: The Viking Press, 1973.

Leavis, F. R. *D. H. Lawrence: Novelist*. New York: Penguin, 1964.

Ross, Charles L. "Introduction" to *Women in Love*. New York: Penguin, 1989.

———."Homoerotic Feeling in *Women in Love:* Lawrence's 'Struggle for Conscious Being' in the Manuscripts." *D. H. Lawrence: The Man Who Lived*. Ed. Partlow and Moore. Carbondale: Southern Illinois University Press, 1980.

Sagar, Keith. *The Life of D. H. Lawrence*. London: Eyre Methuen, 1980.

Sanders, Scott. *D. H. Lawrence: The World of the Five Major Novels*. New York: The Viking Press, 1973.

Spender, Stephen, ed. *D. H. Lawrence: Novelist, Poet, Prophet*. London: George Weidenfeld and Nicolson Ltd., 1973.

Spilka, Mark. *The Love Ethic of D. H. Lawrence*. Bloomington: Indiana University Press, 1955.

CONTEMPORARY REVIEWS OF WOMEN IN LOVE

Anonymous Review of *Women in Love*. From *Saturday Westminster Gazette*. R. P. Draper's *D. H. Lawrence: The Critical Heritage*. New York: Barnes and Noble, 1970: 167.

Evelyn Scott. "Review of *Women in Love*." *The Dial*. R. P. Draper's *D. H. Lawrence: The Critical Heritage*. New York: Barnes and Noble, 1970: 162.

Middleton Murry, John. "Review of *Women in Love*." From *The Nation and Athenaeum*. R. P. Draper's *D. H. Lawrence: The Critical Heritage*. New York: Barnes and Noble, 1970: 172.

SELECTED NOVELS AND ESSAYS BY VIRGINIA WOOLF

Between the Acts. San Diego: Harvest/Harcourt Brace Jovanovich, 1969 (1941).

The Captain's Death Bed and Other Essays. New York: Harvest/Harcourt Brace Jovanovich, 1950.

The Collected Essays of Virginia Woolf, 4 vols. New York: Harcourt, Brace & World, 1967.

The Common Reader. London: Hogarth Press, 1925.

The Death of the Moth and Other Essays. New York: Harvest/Harcourt Brace Jovanovich, 1942.

Jacob's Room. San Diego: Harvest/Harcourt Brace Jovanovich, 1922.

Moments of Being. Ed. Jeanne Schulkind. 2d ed. San Diego: Harvest/Harcourt Brace Jovanovich, 1985.

Night and Day. San Diego: Harvest/Harcourt Brace Jovanovich, 1920.

Orlando: A Biography. Harvest/Harcourt Brace Jovanovich, 1928.

Three Guineas. New York: Harbinger/Harcourt Brace & World, 1938.

The Waves. San Diego: Harvest/Harcourt Brace Jovanovich, 1931.

SELECTED BIOGRAPHICAL AND CRITICAL WORKS
ABOUT VIRGINIA WOOLF

Abel, Elizabeth. *Virginia Woolf and the Fictions of Psychoanalysis*. Chicago: Chicago University Press, 1989.

Bowlby, Rachel. *Virginia Woolf: Feminist Destinations*. London: Basil Blackwell, 1988.

DiBattista, Maria. *Virginia Woolf's Major Novels: The Fables of Anon*. New Haven, CT: Yale University Press, 1980.

Fleishman, Avrom. *Virginia Woolf: A Critical Reading*. Baltimore: Johns Hopkins University Press, 1975.

Holtby, Winifred. *Virginia Woolf: A Critical Memoir*. London: Wishart, 1932.

Hussey, Mark. *Virginia Woolf A–Z: The Essential Reference to Her Life and Writings*. New York: Oxford University Press, 1995.

Leaska, Mitchell. *The Novels of Virginia Woolf: From Beginning to End*. New York: John Jay Press, 1977.

Lee, Hermione. *Virginia Woolf*. New York: Alfred A. Knopf, 1997.

Marcus, Jane. *Art and Anger: Reading like a Woman*. Columbus: Ohio State University Press, 1988.

———. *Virginia Woolf and the Languages of Patriarchy*. Bloomington: Indiana University Press, 1987.

Poole, Roger. *The Unknown Virginia Woolf*. 3d ed. Atlantic Highlands, NJ: Humanities Press International, 1990.

Prose, Francine, ed. *The Mrs. Dalloway Reader*. Orlando, FL: Harcourt, Inc., 2003.

Rosenthal, Michael. *Virginia Woolf*. New York: Columbia University Press, 1979.

Spilka, Mark. *Virginia Woolf's Quarrel with Grieving*. Lincoln: University of Nebraska Press, 1980.

Zwerdling, Alex. *Virginia Woolf and the Real World*. Berkeley: University of California Press, 1986.

CONTEMPORARY REVIEWS OF MRS. DALLOWAY

Bullet, Gerald. "A Review." *Saturday Review*. May 30, 1925: 558.

Forster, E. M. "The Novels of Virginia Woolf." *New Criterion*. April 1926: 277–86.

Hawkins, E. W. "The Stream of Consciousness Novel." *Atlantic Monthly*. September 1926: 357–60.

Hughes, Richard. "A Day in London Life." *Saturday Review of Literature*. May 16, 1925: 755.

Kennedy, P. C. "A Review." *New Statesman*. June 6, 1925: 229.

RELATED SECONDARY SOURCES

Ayers, David. *Modernism: A Short Introduction*. Malden, MA: Blackwell Publishing, 2004.

Baldik, Chris. *The Oxford English Literary History, Volume 10: 1910–1940: The Modern Movement*. Oxford: Oxford University Press, 2004.

Bloom, Harold, ed. *British Modernist Fiction 1920 to 1945*. New York: Chelsea House Publishers, 1987.

Campbell, Joseph. *Hero with a Thousand Faces*. Princeton, NJ: Princeton University Press, 1972.

Gilbert, Sandra, and Susan Gubar. *No Man's Land Volume 1: The War of the Words*. New Haven, CT: Yale University Press, 1988.

Kenner, Hugh. *A Sinking Island: The Modern English Writers*. New York: Alfred A. Knopf, 1988

Kershner, R. B. *The Twentieth-Century Novel: An Introduction*. Boston: Bedford Books, 1997.

Levenson, Michael, ed. *The Cambridge Companion to Modernism*. Cambridge: Cambridge University Press, 1999.

Nichols, Peter. *Modernism: A Literary Guide*. Berkeley and Los Angeles: University of California Press, 1995.

Roberts, Adam, ed. *The Oxford Authors: Alfred Tennyson*. Oxford: Oxford University Press, 2000.

Scott, Bonnie Kime, ed. *The Gender of Modernism: A Critical Anthology*. Bloomington: University of Indiana Press, 1990.

Sherry, Vincent. *The Great War and the Language of Modernism*. Oxford: Oxford University Press, 2003.

Stansky, Peter. *On or about December 1910: Early Bloomsbury and its Intimate World*. Cambridge, MA: Harvard University Press, 1996.

Symons, Julian. *Makers of the New: The Revolution in Literature, 1912–1939*. New York: Random House, 1987.

Index

Abyss, the, 43, 45, 53, 54, 141
Accountant, the (*The Heart of Darkness*), 11, 14, 20
African Mistress (*The Heart of Darkness*), 18–19, 23–24
Anglican Church, 114, 132
Aquinas, Thomas, 73, 78
Arnall, Father (*A Portrait of the Artist as a Young Man*), 66, 70
Augustine, Saint, 134–36, 142, 144
Aunt Juley (*Howards End*), 38, 40, 41, 47, 51

Bast, Jacky (*Howards End*), 40, 42–43, 46, 48, 50, 53
Bast, Leonard (*Howards End*), 40, 42–50, 52–54, 56, 58
Belgian imperialism in the Congo, 10, 21, 31
Bell, Clive, 5, 152
Bell, Vanessa (née Stephen), 5, 152
Belvedere College, Dublin, 62, 67
Bennett, Arnold, 5, 153
Berlin Treaty, the, 23, 32–33
Birkin, Rupert (*Women in Love*), 89–111
Blast, 6, 114
Bloomsbury Group, 4–5, 8, 36, 152, 153

Bradshaw, Sir William (*Mrs. Dalloway*), 159, 160, 162–66, 168, 170–72, 175
Brangwen, Gudrun (*Women in Love*), 89–111
Brangwen, Ursula (*Women in Love*), 89–111
Brickmaker, the (*Heart of Darkness*), 21, 27
British Empire, 2, 172, 175; imperialism of, 6, 29, 36, 53, 62, 165, 175
British society, 1, 4, 59, 89, 154, 171
Brussels, Belgium, 12, 19, 23, 25, 28, 33
Bruton, Lady (*Mrs. Dalloway*), 157, 160, 165, 169–70
Buddha, 19, 134–36, 142; Buddhist, 143

Cambridge University, England, 152
Campbell, Joseph, *The Hero With a Thousand Faces*, 138–39, 141
Capitalism, 3, 51, 53
Casey, Mr. John (*A Portrait of the Artist as a Young Man*), 65
Catholic Church, 62, 65, 73, 84
Chaucer, Geoffrey, 154; *The Canterbury Tales*, 140–41
Chief Accountant (*Heart of Darkness*), 14, 22, 24

Clongowes College, Dublin, 62, 64–67,
   69–70
Congo, the, 10, 17, 18, 20–29, 32–33
Congo Free State, the, 32
"Congo Reform Association, the," 32
Congo River, 10, 13, 15, 20, 25, 27,
   29, 30
Connee, Father (A Portrait of the Artist
   as a Young Man), 66–67
Conrad, Joseph (née Josef Konrad
   Nalecz Korzeniowski), 9–34; bio-
   graphical context, 9–11; experience
   in Congo, 10–11; Almayer's Folly, 9
Count of Monte Cristo, The (Alexandre
   Dumas), 67, 69
Cranly (A Portrait of the Artist as a
   Young Man), 74, 78, 82
Crich, Diana (Women in Love), 94,
   106–7
Crich, Gerald (Women in Love),
   89–111
Crich, Laura (Women in Love), 90
Crich, Thomas (Women in Love), 90, 98
Crich, Winifred (Women in Love),
   94–96
Cubism, 4, 84, 143
Cyprus, 46, 50

Daedalus, 69, 72, 81–82
Dalloway, Clarissa, 154–76
Dalloway, Elizabeth (Mrs. Dalloway),
   158, 160–61, 169, 173
Dalloway, Richard (Mrs. Dalloway),
   157–58, 160, 162–66, 169, 170
Dante Alighieri, 116, 120, 124, 136,
   140, 142, 144–45; The Divine
   Comedy, 120, 127, 140, 145, 146
Dante Riordan (A Portrait of the Artist
   as a Young Man), 63, 69, 79, 84
Davin (A Portrait of the Artist as a
   Young Man), 73–74, 77, 81
Davitt, Michael, 64, 76
Dedalus, Simon (A Portrait of the Artist
   as a Young Man), 65, 68–69, 74–76
Dedalus, Stephen (A Portrait of the
   Artist as a Young Man), 20, 36, 61,
   63–84

Dempster, Mrs. (Mrs. Dalloway),
   157, 174
Director of Companies, The (Heart of
   Darkness), 11, 20
Dolan, Father (A Portrait of the Artist
   as a Young Man), 66, 80
Doolittle, Hilda (H. D.), 4, 7
Dramatic monologue, 118, 120, 129, 143
Dublin, Ireland, 61, 66–67, 69, 72

Edward VII, King of England, 1, 2, 148
Edwardian, 2, 3, 5, 58–59; literature,
   5, 20, 29, 80; writers, 5, 30, 153
Egoist, The, 63, 114
Eliot, Thomas Stearns, 3–7, 20,
   113–49; biographical context,
   113–18; Four Quartets, 114; "The
   Function of Criticism," 114;
   "Hamlet and His Problems,"
   127; "The Love Song of J. Alfred
   Prufrock," 21, 26, 113–15, 118–31;
   Murder in the Cathedral, 114; "Notes
   on The Waste Land," 138; "The
   Perfect Critic," 114; Preludes, 114;
   Prufrock and Other Observations, 114,
   148; Rhapsody on a Windy Night, 114;
   The Sacred Wood, 114; "Tradition
   and the Individual Talent," 114,
   116–17; "Ulysses, Order, and Myth,"
   114, 137; The Waste Land, 2, 114,
   115–17, 131–49; "What Dante
   Means to Me," 116
Eliot, Vivien (née Vivienne Haigh-
   Wood), 113, 114–16
Emma (A Portrait of the Artist as a
   Young Man), 67, 70, 73–74, 78–79
England: arts in, 2–6; changes in early
   20th century, 2–3, 51–53, 149, 175;
   growth and industrialization of, 2–3,
   53; post-war, 153, 164, 170–71, 175;
   suffrage in, 7–8, 112
English Review, The, 88
Epic hero, 120, 126, 130, 146
Epiphany, 72, 81–84
European Imperialism, 20, 22–23, 31–33,
   36, 53, 176; in Africa, 12, 22–24, 32
Evans (Mrs. Dalloway), 159, 164, 168

Fascism, 85, 149
Faustus, 21–22
Fisher King, the, 132–34, 137, 146
Ford, Ford Madox (née Hueffer), 6,
    31, 58
Forster, Edward Morgan, 5, 29, 50–53,
    55–59, 107; *Aspects of the Novel*,
    37; biographical context, 35–37;
    The Longest Journey, 36; *Maurice*, 8;
    A Passage to India, 37; *A Room with
    a View*, 36; *Where Angels Fear to
    Tread*, 36
Free indirect discourse, 57, 83, 173
French Symbolists, 3, 116, 127, 131,
    144, 146–47
Freud, Sigmund, 3, 110
Fry, Roger, 1, 5
Futurism, 4; "Futurist Manifesto,"
    84–85

Gaudier-Brzeska, Henri, 6
Georgians, the, 153
Gordon, General Charles, 165, 172
Grail Legend, the, 134, 137–38, 146
Greek mythology, 138, 154

Hamlet, 124, 126
Harrison, Benjamin (United States
    president), 33
Harvard University, 113, 115, 148
Hawthorne, Nathaniel, 151
Heart of Darkness (Conrad): character
    development, 19–24; historical
    context, 31–33; narrative style,
    29–31; plot summary, 11–19;
    symbols and motifs, 26–29; themes
    in, 24–26
Helmsman, the (*Heart of Darkness*),
    16, 25
Hero-adventurer, 139, 140–41
Hogarth Press, the, 153
Holmes, Dr. (*Mrs. Dalloway*), 156–57,
    162, 165–66, 170–72, 175
Holy Grail, the, 132, 137
Howards End (Forster), 2, 35–59, 107;
    character development, 49–51;
    historical context, 58–59; plot

summary, 37–48; style, 55–58;
    themes, symbols, and motifs, 51–55
Huebsch, B. W., publisher, 63

Icarus, 69, 71–72, 81–82
India, 158, 162, 165, 175
Intended, the (*Heart of Darkness*),
    18–19, 22, 23
Ireland, 62, 72–74, 80–81
Irish Home Rule, 64–65, 77
Irish Nationalism, 62, 65, 77, 81
Italy, 156, 159; Italian literature, 146;
    Italian sonnet, 130

John the Baptist, 124, 130
Joyce, James, 4, 6, 20, 57, 110–11,
    154, 174; "Araby," 79; biographical
    context, 61–63; *Chamber Music*,
    63; *Dubliners*, 63; and experimen-
    tal modernism, 61–62; *Finnegan's
    Wake*, 7, 82–83; *A Portrait of the
    Artist as a Young Man*, 3, 7, 36, 61;
    Stephen Hero, 61; *Ulysses*, 7, 78,
    154, 172

Kilman, Doris (*Mrs. Dalloway*),
    160–61, 163, 166, 168, 173
King's College, London, 36, 151
Kurtz (*Heart of Darkness*), 14–19,
    21–23, 25, 27, 30–31

Labour Party, the, 1, 175
Laforgue Jules, 3, 116
Lawrence, David Herbert Richard, 4, 6,
    20, 87, 174; biographical context,
    87–89; *The Rainbow*, 88, 105; *The
    Sisters*, 89; *Sons and Lovers*, 85, 88;
    The White Peacock, 88
Lawrence, Frieda (aka Frieda
    Weekley), 88, 105
Lawyer, the (*Heart of Darkness*),
    11, 20
Leopold, King of Belgium, 10, 28,
    32–33
Lewis, Wyndham, 3–6, 114
Liberalism, 36, 49, 51, 56
Literary Review, The, 153

Loerke (*Women in Love*), 100–101, 104, 109

London, England: in 1910, 1; in *Heart of Darkness*, 26; in *Howards End*, 37–39, 41, 46–48, 53, 55, 59; in *The Love Song of J. Alfred Prufrock* and *The Waste Land*, 115, 116–17, 133–35, 140, 145, 148–49; in *Mrs. Dalloway*, 155–60, 162, 164–65, 169, 171, 173, 175–76; in *A Portrait of the Artist as a Young Man*, 63; in *Women in Love*, 89, 91, 112, 114

Love Song of J. Alfred Prufrock, The, 21, 26; analysis of, 119–27; poetic style and technique in, 129–31; symbols in, 127–28; summary of, 118–19

Lynch, Vincent (*A Portrait of the Artist as a Young Man*), 73–74, 78

Mansfield, Katherine, 4, 7
Marinetti, Fillipo, 3, 6, 84
Marlow, Charles (*Heart of Darkness*), 11–31
Marvel, Andrew, 119, 131; "To His Coy Mistress," 131
Matadi, in Congo, 10, 32
Metaphysical poets, 119, 131
Methuen Publishers, 88
Mock heroic style, 130
Modernism, 1, 3, 6, 56; British, 4–5, 117–18, 153; European, 5; experimental, 61
Modernist period, 2, 8, 56, 84; hero and anti-hero, 20–21, 26, 29–31, 147; literature, 6–7, 10, 31, 111, 148–49, 153; style, 29–30, 143, 146; writers, 3–4, 29, 56, 59, 84–85, 109–10, 114, 116, 146, 154, 172
Modernity, 7, 56
Montefeltro, Guido Da (Dante's *Inferno*), 120, 126
Moore, G. E., 4, 36, 52; *Principia Ethica*, 36
Mrs. Dalloway (Woolf), 2, 3, 8, 151–76; character development, 163–67; historical context, 175–76; literary

style, 172–75; plot summary, 154–63; themes, 167–72

Nellie, the (*Heart of Darkness*), 11, 16, 19–20
New Critical Theory, 117
New Imperialism, the, 23, 33

Objective Correlative (T. S. Eliot), 6, 116–17, 127, 147
Odysseus, 141, 158

Paris, France, 61, 74, 78, 84, 115–16
Parnell, Charles Stewart, 64–65, 69, 76–77
Pater, Walter, 4, 152
Patriarchy, 50–51, 172
Petronius: *Satyricon*, 132; Sybil, 144
Philomel, 133–34
Poetry (literary journal), 114
Portrait of the Artist as a Young Man, A, (Joyce), 3, 7, 21, 36, 61–85; character development, 74–79; historical context, 84–85; narrative style, 82–84; themes, symbols, and motifs, 79–82
Pound, Ezra, 4–6, 63, 88, 113–16, 131, 139; "make it new," 7–8, 131, 154

Quest literature, 132, 137–38, 140, 145–47

Regents Park, London, 156, 158–59, 164
Roddice, Hermione (*Women in Love*), 91–94, 97–98, 102, 105, 109
Roman: references in *Heart of Darkness*, 11–12, 24; references in *A Portrait of the Artist as a Young Man*, 66; references in *The Waste Land*, 132
Ruskin John, 40, 58
Russian, the (aka the harlequin in *Heart of Darkness*), 17–18, 21, 23, 31

Saint Augustine, 134–36, 142, 144
Sanskrit, 135, 142
Schlegel, Helen (*Howards End*), 36–38, 41–50, 52–56, 58

Schlegel, Margaret (*Howards End*),
    36–37, 40–59
Schlegel, Tibby (*Howards End*), 38,
    46–47, 51
Scott, Sir Walter, 151, 154
Seton, Sally (*Mrs. Dalloway*), 157,
    159, 162
Shakespeare, William, 131, 144, 154,
    159, 168, 171, 173; *Cymbeline*, 155,
    157–58, 161–62, 170, 174; sonnet, 119
Smith, Lucrezia Warren (*Mrs.
    Dalloway*), 156, 159–60, 162,
    165–68, 171
Smith, Septimus Warren (*Mrs.
    Dalloway*), 154, 156–57, 159–64,
    166–72, 175
Spenser, Edmund, 134, 146;
    "Prothalamion," 134, 145
Stanley Falls, Congo (aka Malebo),
    10, 32
Station Manager, the (*Heart of
    Darkness*), 14–15, 17–19, 21–22, 27
Stephen, Thoby, 151–52
Strachey, Lytton, 5, 36
Stream of Consciousness style, 83, 174

Times Literary Supplement, 114
Tiresias (*The Waste Land*), 134–36,
    138, 142
Thackery, W. M., 151, 154
Thames river: in *Heart of* Darkness,
    11–12, 15–16, 19–20, 26, 29; in
    The Waste Land, 134–35
Trilling, Lionel, 51–52, 57

University College, Dublin, 61, 77

Verdenal, Jean, 115–16
Victoria, Queen of England, 1, 2
Victorian period, 1, 4, 6, 102, 148,
    151–52, 165, 172; literature of, 5, 20,
    56–57, 80; writers, 2, 3, 30, 59, 118,
    129
Vorticism, 4, 6

Walsh, Peter (*Mrs. Dalloway*), 155,
    157–60, 163–65, 169, 171, 174

Waste Land, The, (Eliot), historical
    context, 148–49; poetic style,
    146–48; structural analysis, 137–43;
    summary, 131–37; themes and
    symbols, 143–46
Weston, Jessie L., *From Ritual to
    Romance*, 132–33, 137–38
Whitbread, Hugh (*Mrs. Dalloway*),
    155, 160, 162, 164, 169
"Whited Sepulchre" (*Heart of
    Darkness*), 19, 28
Wilcox, Charles (*Howards End*), 38,
    41–42, 44, 47, 51–52, 58
Wilcox, Dolly (*Howards End*), 48, 51, 58
Wilcox, Evie (*Howards End*), 37,
    42–45, 48, 51
Wilcox, Henry (*Howards End*), 37,
    42–50, 52–54, 56
Wilcox, Paul (*Howards End*), 38–39,
    41, 48–49, 51, 58
Wilcox, Ruth (*Howards End*), 38,
    41–42, 48–49, 51, 55
Women in Love (Lawrence), 88–91;
    character development, 101–5;
    historical context, 112; plot
    summary, 89–101; symbols, 108–9;
    themes, 105–8
Woolf, Leonard, 5, 36, 152–53
Woolf, Virginia (née Adeline
    Virginia Stephen), 56–57, 85,
    110–11, 151–76; *Between the Acts*,
    153; biographical context, 151–54;
    The Common Reader, 153; "How It
    Strikes a Contemporary," 2, 153;
    "Mr. Bennett and Mrs. Brown,"
    1, 153; "Modern Fiction," 153;
    "Notes on an Elizabethan Play,"
    153; "On Not Knowing Greek,"
    153; *Orlando*, 153; *A Room of
    One's Own*, 168; *Three Guineas*,
    168; *To the Lighthouse*, 153; *The
    Waves*, 153
World War I, 7–8, 85, 88, 89, 105, 112,
    115, 131, 133, 144, 148, 155–57,
    164–65, 168–69, 175

Yeats, William Butler, 6, 88

About the Author

MARLOWE A. MILLER is Associate Professor of English at the University of Massachusetts, Lowell.